THE POLITICS OF INTERSECTIONAL PRACTICE

Representation, Coalition and Solidarity in UK NGOs

Ashlee Christoffersen

First published in Great Britain in 2025 by

Bristol University Press
University of Bristol
1-9 Old Park Hill
Bristol
BS2 8BB
UK
t: +44 (0)117 374 6645
e: bup-info@bristol.ac.uk

Details of international sales and distribution partners are available at bristoluniversitypress.co.uk

© Bristol University Press 2025

British Library Cataloguing in Publication Data
A catalogue record for this book is available from the British Library

ISBN 978-1-5292-3609-5 hardcover
ISBN 978-1-5292-3610-1 paperback
ISBN 978-1-5292-3611-8 ePub
ISBN 978-1-5292-3612-5 ePdf

The right of Ashlee Christoffersen to be identified as author of this work has been asserted by her in accordance with the Copyright, Designs and Patents Act 1988.

All rights reserved: no part of this publication may be reproduced, stored in a retrieval system, or transmitted in any form or by any means, electronic, mechanical, photocopying, recording, or otherwise without the prior permission of Bristol University Press.

Every reasonable effort has been made to obtain permission to reproduce copyrighted material. If, however, anyone knows of an oversight, please contact the publisher.

The statements and opinions contained within this publication are solely those of the author and not of the University of Bristol or Bristol University Press. The University of Bristol and Bristol University Press disclaim responsibility for any injury to persons or property resulting from any material published in this publication.

Bristol University Press works to counter discrimination on grounds of gender, race, disability, age and sexuality.

Cover design: Andrew Corbett
Front cover image: Mary Martins www.marymartins.com

This book is dedicated to all those who work in the equality NGO sector over the long haul

Contents

List of Tables		vi
About the Author		vii
Acknowledgements		viii
1	Introduction: Equality Policy, the NGO Sector and Intersectionality	1

PART I

2	Assessing Intersectionality's Operationalization: Fields and Issues of Practice	23

PART II

3	Contextualizing Intersectionality: Equality Policy, Austerity and Relations with the State	57
4	Perceptions and Practices: The Spectrum of 'Intersectionality'	79

PART III

5	Representation: The Politics of Intersectionality in Practice	113
6	Coalition: Solidarity and Intersectional Practice	146
7	Conclusion: Intersectional Practice – Ideas, Politics and Policy	177

Appendix 1: Participants	211
Appendix 2: Selection and Methods	217
Notes	222
References	226
Index	247

List of Tables

4.1	Applied concepts of intersectionality	82
5.1	Representation and applied concepts of intersectionality	144
7.1	The politics of intersectional practice: representation, coalition and competing concepts of intersectionality	206
A1.1	Research participants	211
A1.2	Research participant equality characteristics	213
A1.3	Research participant job role	215
A1.4	NGO characteristics	215

About the Author

Ashlee Christoffersen (she/her) is Banting Postdoctoral Researcher at York University, Canada and Honorary Fellow at the University of Edinburgh, UK. Her research is about the operationalization of the Black feminist theory of intersectionality in policy and practice: its influence and possibilities, as well as the discursive and material resistance it faces. She also has a particular interest in intersectional research methodology. Her publications include 'The politics of intersectional practice: competing concepts of intersectionality', *Policy & Politics* (2021a); with Akwugo Emejulu, '"Diversity within": the problems with "intersectional" white feminism in practice', *Social Politics: International Studies in Gender, State & Society* (2023); 'Is intersectional racial justice organizing possible? Confronting generic intersectionality', *Ethnic and Racial Studies* (2022); co-edited with Aerin Lai and Nasar Meer, *Advancing Racial Equality in Higher Education* (2023); and 'The whiteness of "sex discrimination": theorising white feminist ideology in politics', *European Journal of Politics and Gender* (2024). Prior to re-entering academia, Ashlee worked in the trade union movement and NGOs, and remains involved in grassroots activism.

Acknowledgements

First, I am incredibly grateful to my research participants, in particular to the staff of the equality networks that I was privileged to work with, for your warmth and generosity, and for all the work that you do. Second, to Emily Ross and Anna Richardson at Bristol University Press, who have been fantastic to work with on this project, and to Mary Martins for providing the cover art. Third, I am greatly indebted to my extraordinary PhD supervisory team: Richard Freeman, Nasar Meer and Akwugo Emejulu. Thank you also to my former supervisor Anuj Kapilashrami and to my studentship supervisor at the University of Victoria, Rita Kaur Dhamoon. Fourth, I wish to thank many colleagues for the sustenance and support that I have received while working with/knowing you these past few years, including: Nasar, Akwugo, Louise Jackson, Fiona Mackay and other wonderful colleagues on the Gender Equalities at Work project, Orly Siow, Leah McCabe, Ethel Tungohan, Aerin Lai, Leah Bassel, Olena Hankivsky, Gemma Hunting, Marie Storrar, Khursheed Wadia, Kevin Guyan, Tim Aldcroft, Kat Smith, Talat Yaqoob, Emilia Yasamin Belknap, Putri Viona Sari, Cristina Asenjo Palma, Tatiana Cary, Rachel Barry, Cat Wayland, Fernando Tormos-Aponte, Ania Ostrowska, and those in the networks that I have been privileged to be part of including the University of Edinburgh's RACE.ED and GENDER. ED networks, the European Consortium for Political Research Standing Group on Gender and Politics, the Feminist Gender Equality Network Third Sector Trans Justice Group, and to numerous others who have provided valuable feedback on early paper drafts and presentations. To my many other close friends smart enough to stay well away from working in academia/ policy, in London, Edinburgh, Vancouver and beyond.

I am also grateful to the European Consortium for Political Research and University of Edinburgh School of Social and Political Science for the recognitions of the thesis from which this book draws upon (Joni Lovenduski PhD Prize in Gender and Politics, Outstanding Thesis Award), and for recognitions from the Scottish Graduate School of Social Science and Southern Political Science Association. I am also grateful for funding from the UK Economic and Social Research Council, University of Edinburgh College of Arts, Humanities and Social Sciences, and the Government of Canada.

I owe many other colleagues, comrades, scholars and friends along the way to ending up immersed in research about intersectional justice, from Vancouver to London to Edinburgh, and back to Vancouver, from SFPIRG, the Vancouver Area Anticapitalist Convergence, and the Vancouver Bus Riders Union, to SOAS, the Trades Union Congress, Kairos in Soho/centred and the Equality Challenge Unit and beyond.

As a 'first generation' academic, my family has not always necessarily understood *why* I'm doing what I'm doing but you (Mom (Pat), Dad (Bjarne), Tristan, Abbie, Auntie Sue, and all) have always been incredibly supportive of my education and this project nonetheless, and that means everything. I could not have done this without the loving support of my beautiful wife Lorna: I am so grateful for you. Last, to Lola: my former (sadly, passed) beautiful, loving/angry cat, and to Alma, my current, beautiful, loving/angry kitten, both of whom sat with me while I wrote this.

Copyright notice

Parts of this book are adapted with permission from portions of:

Christoffersen, Ashlee. 2019. 'Are we all "baskets of characteristics?" Intersectional slippages and the displacement of race in English and Scottish equality policy'. In *The Palgrave Handbook of Intersectionality in Public Policy*, edited by Olena Hankivsky and Julia S. Jordan-Zachery, 705–32. Basingstoke: Palgrave [reproduced with permission of the Licensor through PLSclear].

Christoffersen, Ashlee. 2020. 'Barriers to operationalizing intersectionality in equality third sector community development practice: power, austerity, and in/equality', *Community Development Journal* 55(1): 139–58 [by permission of Oxford University Press].

Christoffersen, Ashlee. 2021a. 'The politics of intersectional practice: competing concepts of intersectionality', *Policy & Politics* 49(4): 573–93.

Christoffersen, Ashlee. 2022. 'Is intersectional racial justice organizing possible? Confronting generic intersectionality', *Ethnic and Racial Studies* 45(3): 407–30. https://doi.org/10.1080/01419870.2021.1928254 [available under Creative Commons Attribution License CC BY 4.0].

Christoffersen, Ashlee and Akwugo Emejulu. 2023. '"Diversity within": the problems with "intersectional" white feminism in practice', *Social Politics: International Studies in Gender, State & Society* 30(2): 630–53 [by permission of Oxford University Press].

1

Introduction: Equality Policy, the NGO Sector and Intersectionality

Race, class, gender and gender identity, disability status, ethnicity, sexual orientation, nationality, migration status and faith remain salient markers of inequality in the UK, as they do elsewhere, and in many ways increasingly so (Equality and Human Rights Commission 2018b; Government Equalities Office 2018; Byrne et al 2020; TransActual 2021; Refugee Action 2023; Resolution Foundation 2023). Yet these inequalities have predominantly been addressed separately. Since little progress has been made by the separate single-issue approach in terms of achieving equality for the most marginalized (Bassel and Emejulu 2017; Women's Budget Group et al 2017), there is growing recognition that pursuing social justice requires policy makers and organizations to engage with intersectionality.

The idea of intersectionality is to focus on the ways that inequalities are simultaneous and mutually constituting. I define intersectionality fully in Chapter 2; for the purposes of this introduction, by intersectionality I mean the understanding that structures of inequality are mutually constituting and thus cannot be addressed separately (Crenshaw 1989, 1991; Collins 1990). Intersectionality names Black women's theorizing of the social world's foundational organizing logics of white supremacy, gendered racism and racialized sexism. This theory has long been articulated by Black women not only in the US, but also in the UK (Amos et al 1984; Anthias 1993; Mirza 1997) and by Indigenous women and women of colour elsewhere (for example, Meyer 2014 as cited in Hancock 2016).

Yet while interest in it grows, intersectionality continues to be widely thought of as a challenging theory to *apply*. Existing literature aiming to fill this gap between theory and practice has usually focused on how to operationalize intersectionality in *research* or *social movements*, while this book fills a key gap in knowledge in focusing on *policy* and *non-governmental organization (NGO) sector practice*.

While several authors have now noted intersectionality's fluidity of meaning (for example, Nash 2019), up to now there has not been an empirical study exploring how both policy makers and practitioners *themselves* understand intersectionality, and how these understandings relate to policy and practice. This book represents the first in-depth exploration of intersectionality's applications in the UK, specifically how equality NGOs (which have been predominantly focused around single issues/identities) in England and Scotland conceptualize and operationalize the politically transformative frame of 'intersectionality'. The UK is a particularly important case to study intersectionality's operationalization, since its internationally unique unification of equality legislation and architecture creates opportunities to consider the interactions of equalities (Squires 2009; Hankivsky and Christoffersen 2011; Hankivsky and Cormier 2011; Hankivsky et al 2019).

To contextualize this book, I conducted this research and write from a particular social position, experience and identity. Namely, from the perspective of a white, cisgender woman, married to a transgender woman, and who is non-disabled, queer, bi, a settler and migrant from the global North (Canada) turned Londoner for ten years and a 'New Scot' for seven, a 'first generation' academic from a working-class background, and former practitioner in my sector of interest (I explore aspects of this positionality and how they relate to the research further in Christoffersen (2018b)). The latter means that I am complicit with and implicated in much of the analysis to follow.

As background to what led me to undertake this research, I will open with an anecdote from my time in 'practice' (a term I use primarily to contrast to academia/'theory'); for my purposes, 'practice' is the work of NGO sector practitioners in social action and interaction (Freeman 2019), with one another, with their constituents, and with policy makers and those delivering services in the public sector. Specifically, this practice involves, variously, delivering services, community development and policy and campaigning work.

Back in 2013, I worked full-time at a Black-led[1] LGBTQ[2] community development and infrastructure[3] organization that worked across London (one of many victims of austerity, the organization has now dissolved). That year, I led on the organization and delivery of an event for the London LGBTQ Learning Network (a loose network of staff, volunteers, activists, campaigners, trustees and members of diverse London LGBTQ organizations) about 'inclusion' and 'access' issues. The theme of the event was motivated by evidence, including my own research at the time (Kairos in Soho 2011, 2012), that the LGBTQ sector was generally excluding and inaccessible to disabled LGBTQ people (among others), yet for a variety of reasons disabled people are disproportionately represented among LGBTQ people. The event was developed in close consultation with disabled LGBTQ organizations[4] and activists, and included speakers both sharing knowledge/evidence, as well as personally testifying to the violence of policy; workshops; food; and entertainment, and aimed to create dialogue ultimately leading to changes in organizational practice to be more inclusive, as well as the collective development of policy 'asks'.

As an organization, under respected leadership we were well regarded within the equality NGO sector (a sector I explain further below), and by funders, for producing 'diverse', inclusive, and accessible events, and we had the resources to do so. This event (composed of around 50 LGBTQ people) was particularly diverse across the spectrum of race (around half white and half people of colour[5], mostly Black[6] but including some from a variety of other racial and ethnic backgrounds) and socially constructed disability, namely physical, sensory and learning impairment, and D/deafness;[7] and the intersection of the two (with minoritized sexuality and/or gender identity).

The event created encounters across differences and power relations that many had not experienced before. It was fraught with tension (in truth, it was more or less a disaster). Amid our attempted implementation of our commendably *written* safer spaces policy, ableist uncomfortability (even, disgust) with the presence of particular impairments was palpable, as was white fragility and struggles to reassert white hegemony in a space where some white people felt minoritized. Racism and antiBlackness that remained mostly unspoken but which was evident in looks, gesture and tone, abounded. In one session, non-disabled participants (as well as some disabled ones) struggled with or objected to the mobilization of the reclaimed word 'crip' by disabled activists and facilitators, while in this context a highly problematic and regrettable comparison was made by a participant on the mic to other 'reclaimed' language (wherein a supposedly reclaimed word was spoken aloud in an act of violence to the many Black participants). This happened near the end of the event, and suffice to say that few people left feeling good; some less than others.

One result of the event was a severing of relationships carefully built over years between my (non-disabled[8]) organization and key disabled LGBTQ campaigners. Without doubt, there are things that I/we[9] should have done differently, and I/we did not manage what ultimately transpired well (to say the least). Yet we had created similar spaces of community building across these differences before fairly successfully, so the outcomes of this particular event were unexpected at the time. I share this story then, partly as an act of humility to foreground my critiques of equality work to follow, as well as to give a sense of what is at times the messiness, the complexity, the *sheer difficulty*, of trying imperfectly to do the work of intersectionality in microlevel, everyday equality 'practice'. Perhaps one reason that most in the LGBTQ sector, at least speaking for London at that time, did not really bother (Kairos in Soho 2011, 2012; centred 2014): indeed, today in 2024, *much equality work remains hugely siloed, predominantly focused around single issues/ identities, and serving relatively homogeneous and intersectionally privileged groups.*

In relation to intersectionality and practice in the equality NGO sector, this role left me wondering: is this it? What else would applying intersectionality involve, beyond creating spaces for people's 'whole selves'? When representing the organization in equality sector infrastructure (bringing together different equality sub-sectors, including racial justice, disability, feminist, LGBT(Q)I,[10] refugee and intersectional combinations), I wondered, at a more collective level working with other equality organizations, what else could it involve, beyond awareness raising and creating those relationships? In those networks, I observed colleagues struggling for new concepts and new ways of working that would be better aligned to raised awareness of multiple inequalities, brought on largely by the then-new equality policy context: the Equality Act 2010 brought together disparate anti-discrimination legislation on separate issues (the equality policy context is explored further below).

While colleagues struggled for new concepts and ways of working, I felt that intersectionality was the answer, one that challenged fundamentally the status quo of equality work, and one that was often met with resistance. At the same time, in the NGO sector as well as (especially) in a subsequent role supporting equality and diversity practitioners in the public sector, I observed the term 'intersectionality' being used in ways that were far removed from how I had understood it, back as an undergraduate Women's Studies student and activist in early 2000s Vancouver (unceded, stolen territories of the xʷməθkʷəy̓əm (Musqueam), Sḵwx̱wú7mesh (Squamish), and səlilwətaɬ (Tsleil-Waututh) peoples). As I have continued work in equalities, and scholarship on meanings given to intersectionality in multiple country contexts, this observation, unfortunately, grows stronger by the day.

In 2016, based on my involvement in intersectionality research (Hankivsky and Christoffersen 2008, 2011; Christoffersen and Behrens 2014) and my own reading of the literature, I saw that there was little research on how intersectionality was operationalized, particularly by NGOs, and especially in the UK. Coalitions were often called for, but what exactly would happen in them? Moreover, the research on intersectionality's application that did exist lacked attention to how it was understood – when practitioners use this term 'on the ground', what do they mean? I felt that was a useful starting place to contextualize how it was then operationalized.

In the remainder of this chapter, I outline the context – equality policy, which has been an important driver engendering current policy and NGO sector interest in intersectionality – and describe the equality NGO sector. Then, I discuss the book: I provide an overview of my core arguments, explain the research underpinning it, and outline the chapters.

The context

UK equality policy

Beginning in the late 1990s, under Tony Blair's Labour government, equality law and policy in the UK began to move from a purely anti-discrimination approach to a more proactive one placing positive duties on government to promote equality of opportunity. This move was heavily influenced by recognition of institutional racism in the public sector following the Macpherson inquiry (Macpherson 1999) into the murder of Stephen Lawrence, and by European Union directives (themselves influenced by UK law, notably in the field of race equality (Meer 2017)).

The Equality Act 2010 was developed following a period of comprehensive review of equality legislation instituted by the then Labour government (explored thoroughly in Hankivsky and Christoffersen 2011). The Act covers England, Scotland and Wales (that is, Great Britain), and brings together disparate anti-discrimination legislation on separate issues, covering nine 'protected characteristics': race; disability; sex; age; religion or belief; sexual orientation; gender reassignment (that is, transgender status); pregnancy and maternity; and marriage or civil partnership. In spite of lobbying from NGOs, some groups (notably refugees) are not specifically recognized in the Act. It replaced separate legislation on race, gender and disability, and regulations on age, sexual orientation, and religion and belief (I explore the Act's relationship to intersectionality in detail in Chapter 3). The Equality and Human Rights Commission (EHRC), established in 2007, similarly replaced separate commissions on race, disability and gender. The EHRC links equality agendas with human rights: its mandate is to challenge discrimination, and to protect and promote human rights. It holds some enforcement power for the Equality Act.

The Act places proactive obligations to eliminate discrimination and harassment, advance equality of opportunity and promote good relations for people with 'protected characteristics' on more than 40,000 public bodies (including central government departments, local governments, and health, education, policing and transport bodies) through the public sector equality duty (PSED). The PSED replaced earlier separate positive duties for race, disability and gender that were in effect from 2001, 2006 and 2007, respectively.

In Westminster, the Government Equalities Office (GEO) has overall responsibility for the Act. However, responsibility for 'equality strands'[11] remains siloed across government departments: the GEO is an agency that leads on gender equality, sexual orientation and gender reassignment. The recently renamed Department for Levelling Up, Housing and Communities leads on race and faith, and the Department for Work and Pensions leads on disability and age.

Regulations that accompany the Act and support the PSED (known as the 'specific duties') differ in the nations of the UK. The duties on public bodies are weakest in England and Westminster, and strongest in Scotland.

In England, the PSED came into force on 5 April 2011. Public bodies are required to publish information to demonstrate their compliance with the equality duty annually, and one or more equality objectives every four years. The duty to carry out equality impact assessment (EIA) on policy, and to engage with the protected groups, is notably absent from requirements in England. Public bodies are not required to specify how progress will be measured against their equality objectives, nor to report on progress.

Evaluations of implementation of the Equality Act, and in particular the PSED, have indicated relatively poor and uneven compliance across regions and sectors in England (Equality and Human Rights Commission 2012c, 2013, 2018c; Northamptonshire Rights and Equality Council 2012).

The Equality Act 2010 was the product of a Labour government. It did not receive the same support from the subsequent Conservative minority and majority governments led by David Cameron from 2010, which removed or chose not to enact some of the provisions and regulations to support the Act in England and at Westminster. More recently, the UK leaving the European Union in 2021 has engendered further uncertainty, since the Act and its predecessors were designed in large part to implement EU directives concerning equality.

Although the legislation remains in place, the context of Westminster equality policy has changed considerably since 2019, and particularly since 2022 – a topic which could form a book of its own. The present Conservative government displays increasingly open hostility towards pursuit of equality along identity-based lines (with some exception given to a whitened and neoliberal version of gender equality (Christoffersen 2024)). Indeed, the government has officially denied that identity-based inequalities exist, particularly along the lines of race (Meer 2022) and transgender status, while mountains of empirical evidence to the contrary, amplified by COVID-19, have been ignored in the context of the so-called culture wars. At the same time, the government has increasingly sought to implement progressively racist and inhumane immigration and nationality policies (Siddique 2023), and has near spearheaded a backlash against trans rights (O'Thomson 2023). This backlash is one arguably instrumentalized to draw attention away from rapidly falling living standards disproportionately impacting intersectionally marginalized people, including those whom the government seeks to scapegoat. The EHRC has gone from being a reasonably respected, if severely under-resourced, source of evidence on inequalities, to being widely discredited in equality circles due to government appointments of commissioners hostile to equalities, and blatant transphobia (O'Thomson 2023). Yet the hostility to equalities of recently appointed commissioners to the EHRC is rivalled by that of parliamentarians with responsibility for the equalities portfolio, including the current Minister for Women and Equalities. In this context, equality NGOs are increasingly in contention with government bodies of various kinds.

Scottish equality policy

In Scotland, as in the other devolved nations, devolution has influenced the development of a distinctive equality agenda and architecture (Chaney 2012b). In contrast to England, the most powerful political parties in the Scottish parliament since its inception, the Scottish National Party and the Scottish Labour Party, have shown a greater political commitment to equality, which is reflected in a stronger and growing regulatory framework surrounding the Equality Act 2010. In contrast to Westminster where equality strands are siloed across departments, the Equality Unit, now part of the Equality, Inclusion and Human Rights Directorate, leads on this work. Another important distinction is that owing to it being a smaller country, and its employment of a 'participative democratic' model (Hankivsky and Christoffersen 2011; Chaney 2012a), equality NGOs have much greater access to equality policy makers, including both elected politicians and civil servants, in Scotland than at Westminster.

The Scottish specific duties came into force on 27 May 2012 and include: a duty to report progress on mainstreaming; to publish equality *outcomes* (stronger than 'objectives' in England), and to report on progress towards these; to equality impact assess and review policies and practices; and a duty of the Scottish Ministers to publish proposals to enable better performance of the Act. The mainstreaming duty, which applies to Scotland and not England, can be understood as an evolution of 'gender mainstreaming' to all equality strands (Hankivsky and Christoffersen 2011; Hankivsky et al 2019). The objective of mainstreaming is that equality be considered as a core part of all policy and public sector decision-making.

Greater compliance with the PSED has been found in Scotland than in England in most areas (Equality and Human Rights Commission Scotland 2013; Equality and Human Rights Commission 2017; 2018c), though notably not the requirements on occupational segregation reporting in relation to race and disability (Equality and Human Rights Commission 2017). Yet, there is limited evidence of *impact* for those with protected characteristics (Equality and Human Rights Commission 2018a).

The way that the Equality Act brings together disparate equality areas creates both opportunities and challenges for intersectionality's operationalization, which I explore in detail in Chapters 2 and 3 (Parken and Young 2008; Squires 2009; Bassel and Emejulu 2010; Parken 2010; Hankivsky and Christoffersen 2011; Hankivsky and Cormier 2011; Solanke 2011; Hermanin and Squires 2012; Walby et al 2012a; Gedalof 2013; Christoffersen 2019; Hankivsky et al 2019).

The Equality Act 2010 and its predecessor legislation across race, disability and gender, can largely be understood as the products of contentious claims-making, for rights and from refusals of exclusion from the welfare state, by a range of actors from intersecting marginalized groups. Among these actors sits the equality NGO sector, which plays a key, and at times overlooked, role in equality policy making.

The equality NGO sector in England and Scotland

I define the NGO sector as comprising voluntary and community organizations as well as social enterprise organizations.[12] While they are often problematically conflated,[13] I distinguish the *NGO sector* from the *grassroots* (grassroots organizations, social movements, individual activists and campaigners); for my purposes, NGOs are either formally constituted or funded, and usually both. If they are not currently funded, they are seeking funding (formal constitution as, for example, a charity, among other forms is usually a requirement of funding). Given that most are funded, NGOs tend to have paid members of staff. Grassroots organizations in contrast are not necessarily formally constituted, and are not funded in the same way; they do not have paid members of staff. In other words, there are differences of composition, experience and interests between these sectors. Equality NGOs are not necessarily on the front lines of creating social change toward social justice; indeed, depending on readers' ideological perspective, they may be interpreted as functioning more to prevent than to further needed social change. In other words, I do not argue that this sector is necessarily where the most radical and interesting interpretations and applications of intersectionality are likely to be found. Nevertheless, the work of this sector has important material effects and implications for intersectionally marginalized groups (I explore this term below) and intersectional justice (a concept I elaborate further in Chapters 2 and 7).

Equality NGOs have been tirelessly campaigning for policy change, as well as delivering activity and, increasingly, services aimed at creating greater equality for decades, at local, national and UK-wide levels. They currently do so within severe constraints of austerity (this context is explored further in Chapter 3). By 'equality NGOs' I mean specifically NGOs that have emerged because of inequality related to markers of identity, and which aim to increase equality, including racial justice, feminist, disability rights, LGBTI rights, and migrants rights' organizations, among others; in other words, '[organizations] run by and for one or more equalities groups, including Black and minority ethnic people, disabled people, faith groups, lesbians, gay men and bisexuals, migrant workers, older people, refugees and asylum seekers, transgender people, women, young people, and other marginalised groups' (National Equality Partnership 2008, 4).[14] Equality practice in this sector includes attempts to influence equality policy as well as its implementation, as well as other work to increase equality: equality practitioners in the NGO sector have a degree of autonomy from equality policy in how they practise equality and apply intersectionality. They may have 'other ways of knowing and seeing, that resist the lens of law' (Cowan 2016, 116). I do not offer a hard and fast definition of 'equality' in the context of the sector, nor does much of the literature *of* the sector. Within it, equality can be understood as fluid and dynamic (Cowan and Calder 2013), accorded different meanings by context and by actor, and targeting different bodies. It is undoubtedly true that some organizations and practitioners in the UK equality sector were 'doing' intersectionality long before it became a buzzword among policy makers (for example, among organizations that are intersectional in constitution, for instance the Black women's sector), though this may not always have been named or considered as such. These organizations have been instrumental to the limited recognition of intersectionality that does exist in equality policy (explained in detail in Chapter 3).

The NGO sector is hugely diverse, with very large and relatively powerful charities at one end of the spectrum, and smaller, more community-based organizations at the other. Equality organizations tend toward the latter part of this spectrum, with a few larger charities and a plethora of smaller voluntary and community organizations, many of them 'cross-strand' or 'intersectional' (working at the intersection of one or more 'equality strands', for example, Black women's organizations).

The term 'equality sector' is found mainly within publications *of* the sector (for example, National Equality Partnership 2008; Inclusion Scotland et al 2017). Within this broader sector, practitioners identify with sub-sectors (LGBTI, racial justice, and so on) (themselves not easily defined (Kairos in Mayblin and Soteri-Proctor 2011; Soho 2011, 2012; centred 2014); within which the extent to which individual organizations and practitioners identify with a broader 'equality' sector varies.

These sub-sectors have distinct histories and complexities, and are by no means cohesive in the sense that there is necessarily agreement or unity within them; in fact, there has often been conflict around political choices, particularly the extent of independence vs. co-option vis-à-vis the state. While there has been a range of research on the NGO sector, equality sub-sectors have been relatively neglected, with some exceptions (Sudbury 1998; McCabe et al 2010; Craig 2011; Kairos in Soho 2011, 2012; centred 2014; Colgan et al 2014; Vacchelli et al 2015), and there is little that covers the equality sector as a whole.

This literature shows that the equality sector is distinguishable from much of the rest of the NGO sector by several features:[15] self-organization; activist/ 'new social movement' histories of organizing around shared experiences of discrimination (racial justice, LGBTI rights, disability rights, feminist, migrants rights) (Craig 2011); marginality to the rest of the NGO sector, including underfunding (Small 1994; Kairos in Soho 2012); being particularly stretched in capacity, given under-resourcing coupled with high needs of marginalized communities (Craig 2011; Kairos in Soho 2012); and finally, sharing *specialist knowledge* of identity-based social inequalities, and how they manifest. Equality organizations are mainly led by and for equality groups, and experience intersecting inequalities of racism, sexism, homophobia, and so on when trying to carry out their work. Though many claim activist histories, in this moment they have varied and complex relationships to contemporary grassroots and activist organizations working around the same or similar issues (Glasius and Ishkanian 2015; Bassel and Emejulu 2017; Ishkanian and Ali 2018). While the equality sector is predominantly composed of single-identity/strand organizations (working on one equality area), there are also many that have long been advancing intersectional justice claims, with the Black women's sector a key example. Organizations focused around multiple identity axes (in this book, referred to as 'intersectional' organizations) are marginal to, and under-resourced compared with, the (already marginal) equality sub-sectors (Sudbury 1998; Kairos in Soho 2011, 2012; centred 2014). Recent years, characterized by austerity, have seen the closure of many such organizations, while many others are entirely voluntary (and not by design).

The practice of equality organizations varies across three main functions: community development/engagement; campaigning and policy engagement; and service delivery. While these are distinct organizational functions, equality organizations, perhaps more than other types of NGOs, tend to engage in multiple functions. They arose to provide peer support, self-help solutions and community services due to exclusion from mainstream services, as well as to effect policy change to further the rights of discriminated against groups. As predominantly self-organized groups with activist traditions, equality organizations differ from top-down understandings of community development as state intervention (Hoggett 2008), wherein practitioners may not have any prior personal connection with communities, and are there to 'create' political agency (Emejulu 2011). Many equality organizations are funded by the state, but not all. For those that are, gaining state funding, in itself, was often the product of years of struggle. I explore equality organizations' relationships with the state in greater detail in Chapter 3.

In both equality policy and in the equality sector, the term intersectionality has been growing in popularity, driven by both public discourse as well as the still relatively new multi-strand equality policy context (Christoffersen 2019; Hankivsky et al 2019), as I explore further in Chapter 3. Some more recent sector publications about intersectionality alone include Equality Network (2016); Women's Budget Group et al (2017); Drill (2020); Close the Gap (n.d.). Yet, intersectionality presents a huge challenge to the equality sector, since it remains largely siloed into single-identity/issue sub-sectors structured from the understanding that equality groups are homogeneously and singularly marginalized.

Overview of the book

Given the increasing interest in intersectionality arising from the equality policy context, and its growing popularity in both policy and the equality sector, this book is based on research that had the following objectives:

- to explore, describe and understand the development, meaning and use of intersectionality within the equality sector;
- to explore the relationship between equality policy and NGO sector equality practice (particularly how equality policy enables/inhibits intersectionality's operationalization in the NGO sector);
- to assess what some of the implications of identified practice in using intersectionality might be for intersectionally marginalized groups.

In other words, I was interested in exploring the interrelationships between three fields: equality policy, the equality sector and intersectionality. I expand upon the research design further below.

This book is entitled *The Politics of Intersectional Practice*. By *politics*, I mean relations of power in which the applied meaning of *intersectionality* is contested; relations characterized by competing interests and conflict among a range of differentially socially located actors, namely between actors within the equality sector, and between actors from the sector and those of the state.

I explore and compare the development and use of intersectionality: what it means, how these meanings are used in practice, and how this relates to equality policy; and theorize approaches to operationalization of intersectionality based on results, with reference to intersectionality theory and research.

I develop a typology of five competing applied concepts of intersectionality circulating in UK NGO equality organizing and policy, each with different implications for intersectionally marginalized groups and intersectional justice. I argue that in the current context, operationalizing intersectionality is fundamentally about: (i) representation (not only who is represented, but also whether and how to represent) and (ii) coalition and solidarity, and conflicts around each are driven by these competing concepts of intersectionality; in other words, competing concepts are at the heart of the politics of who does intersectionality, and how.

I argue that intersectionality's operationalization necessitates a twin focus on common issues and intersectionally marginalized identities, including emergent ones. Equality organizations can build greater unity through ensuring shared understandings of intersectionality, and work to balance acting in solidarity while prioritizing the agency of those who are intersectionally marginalized.

Research design

Researching how people, organizations and networks of them conceptualize a contested theory/idea, and how they perceive themselves to operationalize it as well as what they actually do, is inevitably complex. This particular project lent itself to a qualitative approach interested in perceptions, experiences, practices,[16] interactions and accompanying texts (that is, documents). To explore how equality organizations understand and operationalize intersectionality, I therefore used a mixed qualitative method design to study intersectionality's conceptualization and use within three networks of equality organizations in three cities in England and Scotland. These networks bring together racial justice, feminist, disability rights, LGBTI rights, migrants' rights organizations, and intersectional combinations of these. Networks of organizations, rather than simply organizations, were selected because coalition is a consistent theme in intersectionality literature on social movement organizations and the NGO sector, as explored further in Chapter 2 (Cole 2008; Bilge 2016; Collins and Bilge 2016; Rodriguez et al 2016; Broad-Wright 2017).

Equality networks represent a site of dialogue and joint working where there is not necessarily a significant tradition of, or space for, this within the equality NGO sector and movements, in a context where equality seeking has predominantly been conducted in 'single-strand' or 'siloed' ways; and in a context where solidarity and coalition are undermined by austerity politics. As I noted in an earlier co-authored paper, 'In the United Kingdom, the model of the Equality and Diversity Forum (EDF) [now named Equally Ours] is perhaps unique internationally in providing a formalized space for equality-seeking and human rights groups to come together across the "strands" and having a focus on multiple discrimination' (Hankivsky and Christoffersen 2011, 45). Equally Ours was described as 'a well-funded, independent civil society discussion forum that is explicitly cross-strand and involved in consultations on equalities issues' (Walby et al 2012a, 464). In addition to this UK-wide network, this model also exists at city and region levels in England and Scotland.

Similar to those who argue that a joined-up equality infrastructure creates opportunities for intersectionality in policy (Krizsan et al 2012c), I selected networks based on the premise that networks of equality organizations, representing a joining up of single-issue equality areas, create opportunities for dialogue and solidarity building that might engender or further intersectional meaning and practice. Networks are spaces where equality meets intersectionality, where practitioners have cause to problematize the relationships between different inequalities (that is, to seek to understand and operationalize intersectionality). Participants in scoping research that I conducted between November 2016 and February 2017 verified that thinking through and applying intersectionality, and preventing a 'siloed' approach, were intended outcomes of the coming together of representatives of different equality areas in networks. They felt that generally networks are a site of knowledge development/reflection/difference/challenge in the NGO sector.

The networks

The selected networks aim broadly at cooperation to address identity-based inequality and advance equality, and work predominantly at local level. They are policy intermediaries and tend, at decision-making levels, to be composed of relatively powerful organizations in their respective sub-sectors. These organizations are predominantly 'single-strand' and have been established for some time.

1. The first network is composed of NGOs, public sector organizations, and individual practitioners and community members, and was established relatively recently (later than 2010/post Equality Act). It describes itself as a member-led network that seeks to advance equality, promote human rights and address poverty in the city. The network explicitly takes an intersectional approach to equality. This network is less independent from the public sector than the others in its structure.
2. The second network is composed of equality single-strand NGO forums and other equality organizations, established after 2010. It describes itself as a policy network to enable cross-sector cooperation on equality. The network states that it aims to work intersectionally.
3. The third network is composed of primarily equality and human rights NGOs, and is the most established – it formed several years before the Equality Act (between 2000 and 2005). It describes itself as a network of organizations and community groups working to advance equality, respond to discrimination and aim for social justice. This network is the largest of the three. It works explicitly around intersectionality.

Networks were all funded to varying degrees by either the public sector and/or independent grant-making bodies, had dedicated staff members and were hosted within other NGOs.

While networks themselves were all explicitly committed to operationalizing intersectionality, of course, commitments varied among participants and the organizations that they worked for. Yet, most participants identified intersectionality as being important to their work and few were openly resistant to it. Implicit resistance will, however, be discussed throughout the book.

In order to ensure the anonymity of individual participants, I anonymize at four levels: individuals, organizations, networks and cities. Throughout the book, participants are identified by their broad job role; the equality sub-sector in which they work; whether their organization is funded or unfunded; size of the organization; and where possible the country in which the organization is based. Where insider knowledge of the sector may identify individuals by these characteristics, or where data are particularly sensitive, they are omitted. Greater detail about research participants is included at Appendix 1. For the purposes of the book which is predominantly concerned with practice in organizations, in terms of individual positionality the equality sub-sector that the participant represents is the most important characteristic to contextualize them. This is usually synonymous with an aspect or aspects of the identity of the participant (given that equality organizations are mainly led and staffed by their target communities). As general rules, the sector is predominantly composed of women (hence there are few quotes from white men in what follows), all other marginalized characteristics tend to be underrepresented in specific sector organizations, and all sectors but the racial justice and migrants rights sectors or intersectional organizations including work on race and/or ethnicity and/or migration status are white-led and predominantly white.

I suggest that the complexity of both intersectionality and the social world of the equality sector means that one methodological approach or method on its own was insufficient to research the relationship between them, and to do so 'intersectionally'. Intersectional research demands attention to context, experience, iteration between data and theory, multiplicity, positionality and power relations between researcher and participants (May 2015; Hancock 2016; Christoffersen 2017). To address this multidimensionality, my methodology drew on a diversity of methodological approaches: principally, participatory research and ethnography. I also used multiple methods: I conducted interviews, focus groups, participant observation and documentary analysis. These methods are detailed in Appendix 2.

Participation

My use of participatory methodological approaches was key to the overall ethical orientation of the project, because intersectionality calls for attention to power relations between researchers and research participants. However, given the complexity of intersectional positionality (Christoffersen 2018b), use of participation was not thought to straight-forwardly 'equalize power' between myself and participants. Perhaps more significantly than attempting to equalize power, participation was viewed as key to knowledge production, wherein knowledge is considered to have more value should it resonate with a number of partial, situated (and shifting and contingent) perspectives (rather than from merely mine as a researcher).

While equality networks were engaged at an early stage and were involved in both research design and data collection, the key arena of participation was meaning-making and knowledge production. To this end, through the latter stages of fieldwork and afterwards, I held several sessions to share and co-construct findings with participants, focused in particular on my proposed typology of intersectional practice set out in Chapter 4, employed thereafter as an analytic framework in the book. Overall, participants validated that they recognized these concepts, that is, they resonated; in other words these knowledge claims were assessed through dialogue (Collins 2014). Our collective thinking in these sessions informed my analysis to follow.

Ethnography

My methodology was ethnographic, albeit differing from traditional ethnography in terms of time spent geographically immersed in the field. My time spent with participants depended on the opportunities for participation and observation offered by each network's structure. For about 1.5 years (May 2017 to December 2018[17]), I participated in the daily lives of the networks: which for most members means, primarily, attending semi-regular meetings and events, and participation in network email lists. The research, therefore, has particular ethnographic characteristics: at times my role as a researcher was (partially) obscured either to myself and/or to participants; and I occasionally influenced the social worlds that I participated in and thus the research narratives. In relation to intersectionality, conducting ethnography allowed me to build relationships with participants over time, which can be important to establish trust when conducting qualitative research across difference (Edwards 1990).

Based on my research with three equality networks, interviews with policy makers and other key equality sector actors, together with my analysis of equality policy documents, as well as drawing on background knowledge gained from my own previous research in the areas of UK equality policy and equality organizing (Hankivsky and Christoffersen 2011; Kairos in Soho 2011, 2012; centred 2014; Christoffersen and Behrens 2014; Christoffersen 2018a; Hankivsky et al 2019), I offer a theory of competing applied concepts of intersectionality (within which sit a large range of ungeneralizable more specific practices). In other words, the interpretations in this book are offered from the context of both a pre-existing 'insider' status in relation to the sector, as well as in-depth ethnographic and participatory research using multiple methods. When I generalize to a network in the following chapters, I am usually speaking of the paid staff of the network and their points of view as inscribed in documents (unless otherwise stated). There were competing perspectives within the networks (since indeed these are subject to power dynamics of race, disability, sexuality, age, faith, and trans and migration status).

Chapter summaries

In Chapter 2, 'Assessing Intersectionality's Operationalization: Fields and Issues of Practice', I situate the book within existing knowledge of intersectionality, and more specifically within knowledge of intersectionality's operationalization. I discuss the latter in distinct and yet related fields of practice (public policy, social movements and the NGO sector), as well as key 'issues in practice' which are particularly relevant to the study of intersectionality in the NGO sector: representation, and coalition and solidarity. I provide a rationale for my research, one motivation for which is the fact that there is debate about what intersectionality *is* and *means* among scholars, suggesting that there is no one agreed meaning among practitioners either. I identify gaps in knowledge including intersectionality's operationalization in the *NGO sector*, in the *UK context*, and how practitioners *themselves* understand intersectionality. I draw on key debates within intersectionality studies to establish the parameters of how I employ intersectionality as a framework throughout the book.

In Chapter 3, 'Contextualizing Intersectionality: Equality Policy, Austerity and Relations with the State', I analyse the context in which equality NGOs conceptualize and operationalize intersectionality, namely: (i) equality policy and discourse; (ii) austerity; and (iii) the sector's relationships to the state. I situate equality organizations' work within public discourses arising from UK and Scottish equality policy, and analyse the implications of equality policy for intersectionality. I introduce equality work and discourse as being distinct from the discourse of social 'inequality'; analyse intersectionality's take-up, uses and meanings in equality policy documents; and analyse the external barriers that equality organizations face when seeking to operationalize intersectionality. These include challenges relating to neoliberal austerity, and power relations between equality organizations and state actors. I find that *in equality policy, there are a range of definitions of intersectionality* which thus leaves it underdetermined. *Its deployment is largely individualized; merely descriptive; additive; and superficial.* Moreover, *meaningful engagement with race as a central category of intersectionality theory is lacking in policy*. The meanings and uses of intersectionality in equality policy are both influenced by and influence understandings of intersectionality among NGOs. Finally, *equality organizations are significantly hampered in their attempts to operationalize intersectionality by the low status they occupy vis-à-vis the state and by neoliberal austerity contexts*.

INTRODUCTION

In Chapter 4, 'Perceptions and Practices: The Spectrum of "Intersectionality"', I outline a typology of five competing 'applied concepts' of intersectionality derived from my data. Competing concepts are important because each has different implications for intersectionally marginalized groups and intersectional justice. These concepts are: 'generic intersectionality' (little focus on any equality strand or strands in particular, similar work delivered to benefit 'all'); 'pan equality intersectionality' (addressing issues that affect all, or most, marginalized equality groups); 'multi-strand intersectionality' (addressing equality strands in parallel, equivalently, separately and simultaneously); 'diversity-within' (addressing intersections within an equality strand); and finally, 'intersections of equality strands' (work of and with specific groups sharing intersecting identities). I employ this typology as an analytic framework in the remaining chapters. For each of the five concepts, I: explain what it is and provide examples of how it works in practice; analyse who holds the understanding, and what they identify as their sources of knowledge about intersectionality; analyse how the concept gained prominence, including salient differences between England and Scotland; and analyse what the implications of this concept are for intersectionally marginalized groups. I argue that *the term 'intersectionality' is understood and used in multiple, contradicting ways, some of which are likely to be more effective than others at furthering equality for intersectionally marginalized communities, while others further entrench inequalities, at times in insidious ways*. Participants consistently defined intersectionality at an individual level, to the exclusion of other levels, so the detail of practice is often related to inclusion and access. However, there are important differences related to these concepts concerning this attention to representation.

In Chapter 5, 'Representation: The Politics of Intersectionality in Practice', I explore issues of representation (who is represented, and whether and how to represent) in efforts to operationalize intersectionality. This chapter asks, in what ways does it matter *who* uses intersectionality, and *for* whom? How can practitioners go about representation to advance intersectional justice? I analyse self-organization, and the extent to which single-strand equality organizations, and networks of them, represent equality 'communities' and those who are intersectionally marginalized within them; explore the relationship between representation and intersectionality in equality organizing; and explore conflicting perspectives on representation. Many participants perceive that intersectional practice is fundamentally about: (i) representation of those who are intersectionally marginalized, and previously excluded, and (ii) the question of representation, namely, whether, and how, to represent. I argue that *competing concepts of intersectionality create conflicting views on and approaches to representation*. Issues of representation also influence which concepts *of* intersectionality are employed by participants, in a cyclical relationship. Given that equality organizations are not often representative of (all) intersectionally marginalized sub-groups, there is a plurality of organizations focused on multiple identity axes; yet social change in the interests of intersectional justice demands a higher level of organization, which the sector approximates through networks and coalitions.

In Chapter 6, 'Coalition: Solidarity and Intersectional Practice', I examine a second key issue to understanding and using intersectionality: coalition, within which I also consider relationship building and solidarity. In this chapter, I ask, when applying intersectionality together, what do equality networks do, and how? How do competing concepts of intersectionality circulate, and with what effects for intersectional solidarity and intersectional justice? I discuss barriers *to* coalition and solidarity, particularly engrained siloed thinking and attitudes; examine coalitions at work, through analysis of network engagement on local equality strategies; and analyse challenges and conflicts that emerge. Finally, I share lessons in terms of how intersectional political solidarity can be built, and the concepts of intersectionality that it requires; and what some of the limits to this are. I argue that while coalition is a core part of intersectional practice, *which concept of intersectionality is employed by both coalitions themselves and participants in them determines how successful they are at building relationships of solidarity to further intersectional justice.*

Finally, in Chapter 7, 'Intersectional Practice: Ideas, Politics and Policy', I explore the implications and contributions of my findings. Competing concepts of intersectionality serve distinct interests and are thus championed by particular actors; this politics is evident in conflicts about, and in the arenas of, representation and coalition. I reflect on recommendations arising for policy and practice. While there are few ideal solutions to the problems of intersectionality's conceptualization and operationalization in siloed policy and practice, from the perspective of thinking through the implications for intersectionally marginalized groups, some compromises and imperfections may be deemed more acceptable than others. Ultimately, I argue that the way in which 'intersectionality' is mobilized in competing and contradicting ways in policy and practice suggests that in this context, new, more specific and more transformative concepts are required, and offer some thoughts arising from my findings on what intersectional practice for *intersectional justice* might involve.

Conclusion

As intersectionality is growing in popularity in academic, public and policy discourse internationally, this book fills a key gap in knowledge of how it is understood and used 'on the ground' by practitioners in equality organizations. Scholarship concerned with equality, gender, race, intersectionality and social justice will be enriched by research about intersectionality's conceptualization and operationalization among equality practitioners and policy makers. The book will also be of wider interest to those concerned with the politics of knowledge and the role of ideas in policy and organizations. It additionally has significant practical appeal, in disseminating knowledge/practice across equality practitioners, as well as policy relevance in informing intersectionality's growing interpretation and application by policy makers in countries such as Scotland and Canada.

I will end this introduction by returning to my own complicity in the ways that intersectionality is conceptualized and operationalized in the equality NGO sector. In naming the five applied concepts that I have found to be identified with intersectionality *as* intersectionality, I aim *not* to further the association of problematic practices *with* intersectionality, though I fully acknowledge that this is one possible outcome (and valid criticism) of my work. It is important to note that all of these approaches to intersectionality were meaningfully held by some participants, while for others, perhaps, some act as strategic misunderstandings. For clarity, I would ideally argue that three of these concepts be *disassociated* from 'intersectionality' (which of these I mean will become clear in Chapters 3 to 7); in the meantime, I stress the importance of careful examination of the specific meanings given to intersectionality in equality policy and practice.

PART I

2

Assessing Intersectionality's Operationalization: Fields and Issues of Practice

In this chapter, I will establish a platform for the following chapters as to existing knowledge, and gaps in knowledge, concerning operationalization of intersectionality. I will begin by setting out some key debates within intersectionality studies which form the parameters of how I assess meanings given to intersectionality in equality policy and practice: specifically, the extent to which intersectionality is additive or constitutive; intersectionality and levels of analysis; privilege, relationality and focus on those who are most disadvantaged; and intersectionality's relationship with race and the social locations of Black women and women of colour. Next, I focus in particular on existing knowledge concerning intersectionality's application in distinct and yet related fields of practice, as well as on key 'issues in practice' which are particularly relevant to the study of intersectionality's operationalization in the NGO sector: representation, and coalition and solidarity.

The term 'intersectionality' is increasingly ubiquitous: As Kimberlé Crenshaw already noted some years ago, 'today, nearly three decades after I first put a name to the concept, the term seems to be everywhere' (Crenshaw 2015). The term was named by Kimberlé Crenshaw (Crenshaw 1989; 1991), but as Crenshaw and many others have noted, the theory to which it refers has a much longer history. Vivian M. May (2015), Crenshaw herself and others (for example, Smith 1998; Collins and Bilge 2016; Hancock 2016) have demonstrated that intersectionality has important origins, histories (and ongoing development) within wider Black, women of colour's and Indigenous women's activism, thought and writing. Intersectional analyses can be found, for example, in the work of anti-slavery and women's rights activist Sojourner Truth in 1851, educator/philosopher Anna Julia Cooper in 1892 and activist/journalist Ida B. Wells in the 1890s (Truth 1851; Cooper

1892; Wells 1892). In the 1960s through the 1980s in North America, ideas of intersectionality were further elaborated by women of colour in the broader social contexts of civil rights, Black Power, Native American/Indigenous, Chicana and Asian American movements (for example, Combahee River Collective 1977), as well as in collaborations between these (for example, Moraga and Anzaldúa 1983; Collins and Bilge 2016). In the UK, this theory was elaborated in a British context by Black feminists and within coalitional movements of Black women and women of colour mobilizing under a political 'Black' identity (Amos et al 1984; Anthias 1993; Mirza 1997). These works, among others, articulate diverse Black and Asian women's experiences, organizing and activism; the role of race as a central organizing logic of the UK and its imperialist projects; as well as issues of racism and imperialism within white feminist movements.

There is debate among intersectionality scholars on what precisely intersectionality *is*: a theory (Collins 2019b), a heuristic device (Lutz 2015), a paradigm (Hancock 2007, 2013), a 'liberation/political framework' (Jordan-Zachery 2007); '*a theory of knowledge* that strives to elucidate and interpret multiple and intersecting systems of oppression and privilege' (Hankivsky and Christoffersen 2008, 275, emphasis added). For others, it is a 'form of social action' (May 2015, 19). Crenshaw views it as a 'frame' (Equal Rights Trust 2016).

The fact that there is debate around both what intersectionality *is*, as well as what it *means*, is a central motivation for this book. If there is robust debate about this among intersectionality theorists and scholars, what is it, and what does it mean, to those working for equality 'on the ground'? How do definitions among the latter relate to academic debates? How does what it is understood to mean relate to how it is practised/applied?

Crenshaw employed the term to describe the ways that Black women's experiences and identities are marginalized by tendencies to treat race and gender as mutually exclusive categories in antidiscrimination law, feminism and antiracist movements, with all focusing on the most powerful/privileged members of groups (white women, Black men) and taking them as representatives of the group as a whole. Crenshaw shared examples of legal cases wherein Black women were forced to choose between bringing a claim of discrimination on the basis of either race or gender, and could not say that they had been discriminated against because of the combination of both (Crenshaw 1989), and explored how race and gender intersect to construct violence against women of colour, and to marginalize it as an issue within feminism and antiracist movements (Crenshaw 1991).

Concurrently, intersectionality theory was elaborated in Patricia Hill Collins' seminal text *Black Feminist Thought: Knowledge, Consciousness and the Politics of Empowerment*, which drew on a rich history of Black women writers and scholars to focus attention on the ways in which systems of oppression are interlocking and interdependent within a 'matrix of domination' (Collins 1990).

The value of intersectionality as a theory of knowledge for social justice has been recognized by scholars, practitioners and activists across disciplines and sectors. As Crenshaw wrote:

> If ... efforts ... began with addressing the needs and problems of those who are most disadvantaged and with restructuring and remaking the world where necessary, then others who are singularly disadvantaged would also benefit ... placing those who currently are marginalized in the center is the most effective way to resist efforts to compartmentalize experiences and undermine potential collective action. (Crenshaw 1989, 167)

Interest in intersectionality is in part driven by the extent to which it enables more accurate and sophisticated understandings of the multidimensional reality of social life.

There are now several published thorough explorations of the origins and parameters of intersectionality (Carastathis 2016; Collins and Bilge 2016; Hancock 2016; Nash 2019; see also Nash and Pinto 2023). A full exploration of the history of intersectionality is beyond the scope of this chapter, and I do not wish to try to duplicate what others have done well. I also do not discuss critiques of intersectionality in detail, but see Puar (2013), Menon (2015), Curry (2017) and Nash (2019).

Defining and conceptualizing intersectionality

Intersectionality is a contested term. Defining, characterizing and historicizing intersectionality have been the subject of several books (May 2015; Collins and Bilge 2016; Hancock 2016), and authors have suggested conceiving it as a field of study rather than as simply a theory (Cho et al 2013; Collins 2015; Hancock 2016). Drawing on the work of Patricia Hill Collins, I define it as the understanding that social inequalities are interdependent and indivisible from one another: 'race, class, gender, sexuality, ethnicity, nation, ability, and age operate not as unitary, mutually exclusive entities, but rather as reciprocally constructing phenomena' (Collins 2015, 2). Systems of inequality including capitalism/class, sexism, racism, antiBlackness and white supremacy, heterosexism, cisgenderism, ableism, and borders therefore constitute one another, meaning that they construct one another and interact to create institutions and social positions (Crenshaw 1989, 1991; Collins 1990; Yuval-Davis 2006; Hankivsky and Christoffersen 2008; May 2015). Social institutions and positions are, therefore, shaped by multiple, mutually constituting, factors or divisions operating simultaneously. These factors include, among others, race, sexuality, gender and gender identity, Indigeneity, D/deafness, disability status, age, class, nationality and faith.

Factors or social divisions are not separable from one another, because they constitute one another: at an individual level a person is not a lesbian on one hand and Black on the other; rather they are the combination of these at the same time. These different elements form and inform each other and cannot be separated, because they are not lived or experienced as separate. Social divisions are mutually constituting, so that for example there is little analytical value in discussing 'women' generically, but only particular categories of women, wherein gender is constituted by other elements, resulting in a specific inhabiting and experience of gender which is qualitatively different from others. Intersectionality 'strives to understand what is created and experienced at the intersection of two or more axes of oppression (e.g. race/ethnicity, class, and gender) on the basis that it is precisely at the intersection that a completely new status, that is more than simply the sum of its individual parts, is formed' (Hankivsky and Christoffersen 2008, 275). Yet intersectionality emerges from a context where 'woman' is always-already constructed as white (Lewis 2017), one where the figure of the Black woman has been discursively and materially degendered through slavery and its afterlife, and in its wake (Spillers 1987; Hartman 2008; Sharpe 2014, 2016).

While social divisions are indivisible from and bound up in each other, they are also not reducible to one another. At the same time, they are also not the same as one another, though they may share features in common, and should not be conflated together (Yuval-Davis 2006). The point of intersectional analysis is 'to analyse the differential ways in which different social divisions are concretely enmeshed and constructed by each other and how they relate to political and subjective constructions of identities' (Yuval-Davis 2006, 205). Factors structuring social positions consist of categories whose boundaries are not fixed, are contested, and meanings that are historically contingent (Yuval-Davis 2006).

Debates: additive vs constitutive

While I have laid out a constitutive definition of intersectionality as integral to it, in fact a key debate in the literature centres on the additive vs constitutive nature of intersectionality, and indeed of identity and inequality. Among the multiple definitions and typologies of intersectionality (for example, McCall 2005; Hancock 2007; Collins 2015; Walby, Armstrong, and Strid 2012b), a strand of white feminist academic thought employs particular definitions of intersectionality suggesting that inequalities can be separated from one another, exemplified by Walby et al (2012b, 2012a) (see also, Christoffersen and Emejulu 2023). Theorists historically mainly concerned with gender, they argue for a conception of the relationship between inequalities as 'mutually shaping' rather than mutually constitutive, 'which suggests that while the effects of one inequality on other inequalities may be discerned, the separate systems of inequality remain' (Walby et al 2012a, 453), because 'the recognition of the differences between the ontologies of inequalities is necessary in order to [analyse] and assess current and previous practices that have been important in developing appropriate measures to tackle inequalities' (Walby et al 2012a, 474). However, other theorists have not seen recognition of differing ontologies and a conceptualization of inequalities as mutually constitutive as being contradictory from one another: 'although discourses of race, gender, class, etc. have their own ontological bases which cannot be reduced to each other, there is no separate concrete meaning of any facet of these social categories, as they are mutually constitutive in any concrete historical moment' (Yuval-Davis 2013, 7). It may be questioned whether 'mutual shaping' should be considered as intersectionality at all, forgoing as it does what is considered a key tenet by many of its theorists, that is, mutual constitution/construction (for example, Collins 1990). A 'mutual shaping' approach would seem to justify a continued focus on gender alone, without attention to other factors which construct it. For Walby et al, mutual shaping 'acknowledges the way that systems of social relations change each other at the point of intersection, but do not become something totally different' (Walby et al 2012b, 235). This is in contradiction to what many Black feminists have argued are systems of social relations that together produce social institutions and positions that *are* qualitatively different from those produced by one system of social relations alone (Crenshaw 1991). The 'mutual shaping' model offered represents an additive approach to intersectionality, in that it suggests that inequalities can be separated from one another; the idea that they change one another only at the 'point of intersection' (Walby et al 2012b, 235) suggests the existence of a point at which there is no intersection. While few authors are explicit in their employment of a 'mutually shaping' rather than 'mutually constitutive' approach, it is apparent in many white feminist treatments of intersectionality which discuss it as 'gender plus' and only in relation to gender, women, women's studies and feminism (Christoffersen and Emejulu 2023).

Debates: levels of analysis

The key debate as to the additive vs constitutive nature of intersectionality is, in turn, closely related to debates about levels of analysis: 'the question of whether to interpret the intersectionality of social divisions as an additive or as a constitutive process is still central … what is at the heart of the debate is conflation or separation of the different analytic levels in which intersectionality is located' (Yuval-Davis 2006, 195). While some seek to critique individualized uses of intersectionality and reinsert structural analyses, for Collins' earlier work, 'intersectionality' was precisely the individual counterpart to the matrix of domination (Dhamoon 2011).

Others posit that while an additive view of intersectionality tends to restrict itself to consideration of identity and experience (Yuval-Davis 2006), intersectionality can be analysed at different levels (institutions/structures, intersubjective/community/cultural relations, representation, and individual identity and experience), which should not be conflated (Yuval-Davis 2006). For Collins and Sirma Bilge, intersectional inquiry involves analysing power relations both via the intersections of social inequalities, and across domains of power (structural, disciplinary, cultural, interpersonal) (Collins and Bilge 2016). Crenshaw distinguished between structural intersectionality (the ways that intersections of inequalities structure social locations to produce qualitatively different experiences); political intersectionality (the ways that identity-based movements marginalize those experiences); and representational intersectionality (cultural constructions of intersectionally marginalized social groups, for example Black women) (Crenshaw 1991).

Some intersectionality theorists have warned against a disproportionate focus on the level of identity characteristic of additive models of intersectionality, advocating instead analysis and action on processes and systems (for example, Dhamoon 2011). Rita Dhamoon (2011) outlines risks associated with focusing solely on identity categories: the reification of these categories, 'whereby the boundedness of identity becomes overconflated and rigid *even when multiple axes of identity are considered*' (Dhamoon 2011, 233, emphasis in original); and, reinforcement of the inequalities that intersectional analysis aims to challenge, by leaving categories of privilege invisible in problematizing marginalized groups (Dhamoon 2011). Restricting analysis of intersectionality to identity categories obscures understanding of it as the 'fusion of social structures that creates specific social positions' (Bassel and Emejulu 2010, 538), evidencing and reinforcing an additive view that these structures can be separated from one another.

In light of these debates, this book takes a broader view of intersectionality as a multilevel concept, and I analyse empirical understandings of intersectionality in relation to whether these are at an individual or a more structural level of analysis.

Debates: privilege, relationality and focus on those who are most disadvantaged

A core conceptual component of intersectionality is relationality (Collins and Bilge 2016; Collins 2019b), a move from 'either/or' binaristic, essentialist thinking, to a 'both/and' frame (May 2015; Collins and Bilge 2016) centred on relationships and connections. Key to this are power relations of privilege and oppression. The idea of mutual constitution of elements of identity is equally applicable to privileged identities, not just marginalized ones, though for the former these elements of identity function as 'transparent/invisible' or 'unmarked' because they are those that are privileged or that hold power in relation to those that do not (Carbado 2013). There are debates around the extent to which privileged categories receive attention in the name of intersectionality. On one hand, the theory is inclusive of, and indeed describes how, we are all subject to intersecting axes of oppression/privilege. On the other hand, some are clearly more oppressed/privileged than others in particular contexts. Is it a priority to use intersectionality to study the privileged? Is this privilege always acknowledged when intersectionality is thus employed (for example, in the study of differences among white women)? Or, is it an injustice to use intersectionality in this way? Should intersectionality be reserved for the study of those who are intersectionally marginalized, and along particular lines (for example, of race and gender)? These choices bear some relation to the identity and interests of the researcher (Mügge et al 2018). Yet, if there is no focus on dominant identities along with marginalized ones, then dominant identities 'operate as the natural and unmarked ... social position rather than as a particular and 'different' representation of them' (Carbado 2013, 823).

Nevertheless, concepts emerging from intersectionality scholarship and praxis, including: intersectional justice, which 'focuses on the mutual workings of structural privilege and disadvantage, i.e. that someone's disadvantage is someone else's privilege ... actions tend to be centered on people and groups of people who face the highest structural barriers in society – premised on the idea that if we reach the people at the greatest structural disadvantage, then we can reach everybody' (Center for Intersectional Justice 2018); intersectional solidarity (Tormos 2017); and affirmative advocacy (Strolovitch 2007) (discussed later) explicitly link intersectionality to concern for those who are (most) intersectionally marginalized, following Crenshaw (Crenshaw 1989, 1991).

Appropriations and co-optations

As the term 'intersectionality' becomes more popular and is used more widely, its meaning is a ground of contestation in several sites, within and outwith academia. As engagement with intersectionality increases, the body of feminist/critical race literature that is critical of the way that intersectionality is being applied, theoretically and in practice, is correspondingly growing (for example, Alexander-Floyd 2012; Bilge 2013; Jordan-Zachery 2013; Lewis 2013; Tomlinson 2013a, 2013b; May 2015). In short, several authors argue that, in Vivian M. May's words, 'though intersectionality is widely known, acclaimed, and applied, it is often construed in ways that depoliticise, undercut, or even violate its most basic premises' (May 2015, i).

From this perspective, literature on intersectionality can be considered as falling into several broad categories. First, there is literature which may be interpreted as co-opting intersectionality for neoliberal and/or white supremacist ends, emptying it of meaning (as in the previous example of Walby et al). Second, there is literature naming and critiquing these uses of intersectionality, within which some warn of risks and seek to retrieve intersectionality (for example, May 2015; Case 2017), and reclaim it (Alexander-Floyd 2012) while others find fault with it and employ alternative concepts (for example, Puar 2013). Third, there is literature which employs intersectionality in a way that more or less ignores co-opted uses, and in so doing avoids giving these further representation and legitimation (Bassel and Emejulu 2010, 2014, 2017). Finally, there is literature that employs intersectionality in new fields and ways (for example, Kelliher 2018).

Within feminist studies, Bilge argues that 'intersectionality ... has been systematically depoliticized' (Bilge 2013, 405): 'originally focused on transformative and counter-hegemonic knowledge production and radical politics of social justice, [it] has been commodified and colonized for neoliberal regimes' (2013, 407).

In wider academia, intersectionality has demanded engagement from academics in a variety of disciplines. Often, it is resisted/discarded, which May has termed 'intersectionality backlash' (May 2015, 1). At other times, it is enthusiastically taken up, but its meaning subverted. For example a tendency has been observed, and named, among some European thinkers 'to find valuable a "purified" intersectionality, quarantined from its exposure to race' (Tomlinson 2013a, 266; Lewis 2013), a process Bilge calls 'whitening' and observes within feminist studies and elsewhere (Bilge 2013). Indeed, focus on race within intersectionality canons has been found to be less prevalent in Europe than in the US (Mügge et al 2018).

In policy and practice, in part due to the relative novelty of attempts to operationalize it, and also to the workings of gendered racism, it is potentially vulnerable to co-optation, including attempts to distance it from its radical origins in Black and women of colour's activism, and its fundamental orientation toward social justice. On the first point, while Black women can be viewed as the key subjects of intersectionality (Jordan-Zachery 2013), it is being controversially operationalized in pursuit of a more generalized 'equality' and applied to an array of marginalized social groups by academics, policy makers and practitioners alike. Intersectionality theorist Ange-Marie Hancock has argued for the inseparability of intersectionality's analytic/ontological project from its 'project to render visible and remediable previously invisible, unaddressed material effects of the sociopolitical location of Black women or women of color' (Hancock

2016, 33), while her UK-based collaborator Nira Yuval-Davis responded that this risks presuming an (essentialized) particular space of marginalization across historical and geographic context (Yuval-Davis 2015). In different sites of practice, depending on whether race, 'a central analytic element that cannot be jettisoned without inflicting fatal violence on the integrity of intersectionality's intellectual project' (Hancock 2016, 13) continues to be a central focus, intersectionality's contemporary uses may variously be found to be an expanded application of intersectionality, or an elision of Black women/women of colour and the particular intersection of race and gender. Yet, Jennifer Nash, whose work has developed and highlighted Black feminist theory apart from and irreducible to intersectionality, has argued that Black feminist critique of intersectionality's appropriation can fall into proprietary narratives negative for both Black feminism and Black feminists because they engender a defensiveness which serves to stall Black feminist theorizing. Nash argues for a 'letting go' (Nash 2019). For Nash, 'letting go' can be partly accomplished through re-examining the concept and position of 'transnationalism' in Women's Studies/academic feminism, and its relationship to intersectionality, each attaching to differently racialized bodies; so letting go involves 'surrendering' the attachment of intersectionality to Black women and embracing its intimacy with wider 'women of colour' theory/theorizing (Nash 2019). The book, written to and about US academic feminism, arguably leaves open questions of the politics of intersectionality's mobilization by cross-racial and actors racialized as white in policy and practice: namely, whether this surrender can conceivably extend to the mobilization of intersectionality by these actors, with what conditions and under what circumstances.

Nash's argument is compelling, and yet it remains important to carefully examine dynamics of appropriation in a European context similarly characterized by antiBlackness, and which disavows and displaces race (Lewis 2013; Mügge et al 2018). Attention to race/gender also relates closely to definitions of intersectional justice, namely prioritization of those who are most disadvantaged. In this book, I do not methodically normatively assess practitioner concepts of intersectionality against whether they are specifically about race/gender, nor do I, as a white woman, take a firm position in these debates. However, I employ an antiracist feminist frame throughout, in which white supremacy is considered a central structure of social life (intersected with others) including the contexts in which I research (Mills 2017b). This is an important framework to identify, since it does not necessarily follow from uses of 'intersectional feminist'. Moreover, I am cognisant of Black feminist theorizing of the ways in which Black women, 'as both representation and embodied, sentient being[s]' (Lewis 2017, 117) are effaced, discursively and materially made absent. I therefore note the potential for meanings and uses of intersectionality in policy and practice to be both a site of this epistemological and material erasure of Black women, as both knowledge producers and actors in these social worlds, as well as a site of their resistance to it (in other words, perhaps, their 'presencing') (Lewis 2017).

Critique of the ways in which intersectionality may have been appropriated and co-opted is closely related to the question of what intersectionality is, and is *for*. Is it (merely), an understanding or analytic? Or is a praxis-oriented social justice orientation an integral part (Collins and Bilge 2016; Mügge et al 2018)? In fact, research by Mügge et al found that most intersectionality scholars in their sample agreed that there was a political project to intersectionality; but there is not necessarily agreement on what the project *is* (Mügge et al 2018). Although there may be some agreement on intersectionality's political nature among academics, how this travels into policy is another matter (Christoffersen 2019), as I explore in Chapter 3.

Intersectionality's operationalization

I have explicated my own understanding of intersectionality through exploration of key literature, and highlighted some major points of debate that inform my analysis to follow. I turn now to examining intersectionality's operationalization. I have divided the section to follow into public policy; social movements; and the NGO sector. At times I use the terminology of 'policy *and* practice', to distinguish policy makers from public sector practitioners and the NGO sector. However, policy makers are also practitioners of a particular kind (Freeman et al 2011; Freeman 2019). Moreover, the boundary between policy/public sector and the NGO sector is often not clear cut, as will be explored further in Chapter 3; nor is that between the NGO sector and social movements. While boundaries between the NGO sector and grassroots organizations are contestable, I contend that there remain important, though not totalizing or completely generalizable, distinctions in terms of composition, experience and interests which warrant separate explorations.

Fields of practice
Public policy
Though concerns about appropriations and co-optations of intersectionality have been raised, application of intersectionality to research (Bowleg 2008; Choo and Ferree 2010; Christoffersen 2017), policy and practice has been identified as a priority by many (Hankivsky and Cormier 2011; Hankivsky and Jordan-Zachery 2019a). The bulk of literature on intersectionality's operationalization has focused on this in relation to empirical research (McCall 2005; Hancock 2007), while literature on intersectionality and policy is now also relatively established (Manuel 2006; Hankivsky 2012;

Jordan-Zachery 2017; Hankivsky and Jordan-Zachery 2019b; Williams 2021). Within this, intersectionality is often considered in the context of equality mainstreaming (Hankivsky 2005; Parken and Young 2008; Hankivsky and Cormier 2011). There has been particular attention to intersectionality as it relates to health policy, largely emerging from scholars concerned with gender, social inequalities and the social determinants of health (Hankivsky and Christoffersen 2008; Sen et al 2009; Hankivsky 2011; Hankivsky et al 2014; Kapilashrami et al 2015), as well as those concerned with race/ethnicity and health (Weber and Fore 2007). This attention has been heightened since the context of COVID-19 (Bowleg 2020; 2021, Hankivsky and Kapilashrami 2020a, 2020b; Christoffersen 2020b, 2021b).

In both research and policy, 'the knowledge gap between the theoretical construct of intersectionality and its practical application has been identified as a priority area of concern' (Hankivsky and Cormier 2011, 225), and while relatively recently it was argued that 'methods for integrating intersectionality into policy development, implementation, and evaluation are in their very early stages of development' (Hankivsky and Cormier 2011, 217), it is increasingly being taken up internationally (May 2015), at least in name; and there are several tools available for policy makers (see, for example, Hankivsky 2012; Opportunity Agenda 2017). Yet notwithstanding available methodologies of application, operationalizing intersectionality in public policy also requires political will and adequate resources (Hankivsky and Cormier 2011). It further demands new knowledge and new approaches to knowledge, which will be explored further in the final section of this chapter.

An intersectional approach to policy making would be one that takes into account the complexity of people's social positions described earlier, incorporating an understanding of these as being mutually constituted rather than added together; as well as one that considers social divisions in operation at a structural level, beyond shaping individual social position and experience. An intersectional approach would differ from those that start from one social division (for example, gender) and then add on others. In contrast, 'the field of gender mainstreaming ... has focused on the differential effects of policy on the lives of men and women, without properly recognizing the diversity among men and women' (Hankivsky and Cormier 2011, 218). Even as intersectionality is taken up, at least nominally, 'some decision makers continue to espouse one-dimensional approaches ... which a number of scholars and activists ... have argued elsewhere, cannot be adapted to address multiple inequalities' (Hankivsky and Cormier 2011, 220). In other words, 'there is some agreement that [policy makers] have been much more successful at authoring and implementing variations on additively organized diversity policies than creating robustly intersectional ones' (Townsend-Bell 2019, 735).

Applying intersectionality in policy would undoubtedly require an approach accounting for greater complexity than those usually evidenced in equality policy: 'the need to focus on numerous differences and complex realities using a multilevel analysis to uncover exclusions and vulnerabilities can be considered both a strength and a challenge for those seeking to work within an intersectionality paradigm' (Hankivsky and Cormier 2011, 218). From an intersectionality viewpoint, even 'targeted policies are often as ineffective as general policies in that both fail to address multiple identities and within-group diversity' (Hankivsky and Cormier 2011, 218).

Some models have been proposed to apply intersectionality to policy making or to specific policy areas, particularly health policy. Bishwakarma, Hunt and Zajicek (2008), set out an early framework to systematically integrate intersectionality in the policy making process using a typical policy cycle. Hankivsky et al (2014) present an intersectionality-based policy analysis framework (IBPA) in the particular context of health policy. Its 'aim as a policy tool is to better illuminate how policy constructs individuals' and groups' relative power and privileges vis-à-vis their socio-economic-political status, health and well-being' (Hankivsky et al 2014, 1–2), and it includes guiding principles and a set of descriptive and transformative key questions and sub-questions to shape policy analysis. Applying these to seven policy issues within health in order to demonstrate IBPA's potential, they identify characteristics of the IBPA framework: the interrogation of the implicit assumptions underpinning policies; the attention to historic and contemporary framings of social issues and policy problems; the self-reflexive method for capturing complex multidimensional power dynamics that shape everyday lived experiences; and ability to generate new perspectives and insights about policy issues and affected populations and directions for renewed advocacy efforts aimed at social justice (Hankivsky et al 2014).

A particularly challenging recommendation for policy analysis from this literature is that 'when analysing social problems, the importance of any category or structure (e.g. socioeconomic status, race, or gender) cannot be predetermined; the categories and their importance must be discovered in the process of investigation' (Hankivsky and Jordan-Zachery 2019a, 7). This is challenging to siloed thinking that dominates policy and practice; as well as to contentions among intersectionality scholars that the importance of the intersection of race and gender is constant. It also raises significant questions about how this approach can be operationalized in a way that avoids a genericism that may reproduce inequalities. Yet there are clear examples where the importance of this insight is apparent. For instance, when (binary) gender is predetermined as the only or the most important category structuring the social problem of domestic violence and abuse, (gendered) domestic abuse experienced by LGBTI people from family members is conceptually elided, as well as being materially elided when policy responsibility for this sits in women's/gender policy units, and resourcing is limited to criminal justice and services for heterosexual and cisgender women (Christoffersen and McCabe, forthcoming).

To date, the extent to which an intersectional approach has been taken up by policy makers is limited. Across Europe empirical research published in 2012 found that 'there is scope for the implementation of new intersectional practices, but ... this will require a more embedded intersectional thinking among equality professions than is apparent to date' (Krizsan et al 2012a, 239). Today, examinations of intersectionality's applications in policy are growing, though this growth is dependent upon growth of policy applications themselves. For example, MariaCaterina La Barbera, Julia Espinosa-Fajardo and Paloma Caravantes studied intersectionality's attempted implementation in the city of Madrid, Spain. They identified important obstacles to successful implementation, including the absence of an enabling legal framework and guidelines; limiting interpretations of intersectionality; lack of training; siloed structures and cultures; and lack, and misuse of, data. These are also, conversely, potential enabling factors for intersectionality's implementation when present (La Barbera et al 2022). This case study underlines the importance of political will to operationalizing intersectionality in policy (Hankivsky and Cormier 2011), since the subsequent local government did not continue an explicit commitment to intersectionality (La Barbera et al 2022).

The different levels at which intersectional analysis can be undertaken discussed earlier, particularly more macro and structural levels, are underexplored in policy contexts, where discussion of intersectionality occurs primarily at the level of identity; in other words, the dominant approach to intersectionality in policy is to consider it at the personal identity level, as an attribute of individuals (Parken 2010; May 2015; Christoffersen 2019). As has also been the case with systems of inequality conceptualized singularly, it is simply less challenging to established structures and ways of thinking for policy makers to locate the 'problem' of intersectionality within marginalized individuals rather than institutions. Locating it in this way is also consistent with neoliberalism and the 'diversity' turn in equality work (Mohanty 2003, 2013; Squires 2008a; Ahmed 2012). Finally, 'although it is being taken up in many policy applications, it is often applied in ways that reduce it to an anodyne notion of diversity or that downplay race and racism' (May 2015, 150).

The detail of some policy applications of intersectionality described in literature (Parken and Young 2008; Parken 2010; Walby et al 2012a) have emphasized looking for commonality across different equality areas, in other words issues that are common to groups still ultimately in some way separately conceived. There are potential problems with intersectionality's application being limited in this way. First, there is the potential that the specific ways in which these identified common issues are related to specific intersectionally marginalized groups (for example, women of colour) get lost in this process of seeking what might be described as the 'lowest common denominator'; proposed solutions could potentially then inadequately be 'one size fits all' if specificity is not taken into account. Second, seeking commonality leaves unclear what happens when difference is just too different for this to work. If issues are not common, it is unclear where they fit. Third, this approach fails to adequately consider the relationality of oppression and privilege, a characteristic theme of intersectionality theory (Collins and Bilge 2016). Rather than there simply being a range of common issues with common solutions to benefit all, there may be cases where 'solutions' for one equality group may lead to more unequal outcomes for another (in which cases, consideration of effects at the intersections of these would be instructive).

Though the extent to which an intersectional approach has been taken up by policy makers internationally is limited, the literature has identified countries in the UK as attempting to apply intersectionality to policy (Squires 2009; Hankivsky and Christoffersen 2011; Hankivsky and Cormier 2011; Christoffersen 2019, 2021a; Hankivsky et al 2019), as will be described in full in Chapter 3. This is largely because legislation on different inequalities has been amalgamated into the Equality Act 2010, as has the equality architecture into the EHRC. Yet, as is the case elsewhere, there is a profound contradiction between the way that identity and equality are conceptualized in UK equality law and a consistent intersectional approach to antidiscrimination and social justice (Bassel and Emejulu 2010; Solanke 2011; Gedalof 2013). Little progress has been made in terms of the 'institutionalization of intersectionality' (Hermanin et al 2012). At the time the Equality Act 2010 was being debated and the EHRC was being established, it was thought by some that a joined-up equality infrastructure could lead naturally to greater intersectional thinking (Squires 2009; Hankivsky and Christoffersen 2011; Walby et al 2012a). For some, this was not a desirable outcome: 'the inclusion of multiple inequalities within the same equality institutions adds to the potential of the diversity project undermining the equality project' (Walby et al 2012a, 469). It may be reasonable to assume that 'institutional and legislative changes – from single and unitary equality approaches to multiple, integrated approaches – create policy arenas for interaction between inequalities, and thus potential for intersectional practices' (Krizsan et al 2012a, 233).

A 'multi-strand mainstreaming model' trialled in Wales (Parken and Young 2008; Parken 2010) was called 'arguably ... the most fully developed and promising method' to applying intersectionality in public policy (Hankivsky and Cormier 2011, 220–21). Described as 'midway between a single strand and intersectional approach' (Parken 2010, 95), this model, while innovative in the context of policy making, is limited by reliance on actors with 'single-strand' expertise and experience; does not consider the inclusion of intersectional organizations (working at the intersection of more than one equality area); and draws on the NGO sector only as a replacement where public sector representatives deemed appropriate do not exist. Indeed:

> while being inclusive in terms of all equality strands is commendable, this process does not allow for a decision-making process that would allow for choosing particular intersections to focus on nor the possibility of recognizing what social locations may be the most 'significant explanatory through-lines'... in any given context or situation ... the approach could arguably be improved if in addition to 'strand' experts the process would allow for the crosssectoral participation of those who have insights and expertise in how to conceptualize and work across interactive strands. (Hankivsky and Cormier 2011, 226)

In summary, policy applications of intersectionality tend to remain additive ones in which equality areas are singularly conceived, and the relation of these to policy issues is predetermined; and consideration of intersectionality is largely limited to the level of individual identity and experience. This singular conceptualization as well as the pursuit of commonalities continue to efface specific intersectional marginalities, including those experienced by women of colour. The UK has been identified as a site for the potential expansion of intersectional approaches.

Mieke Verloo (2013) has argued that the literature suggests four political and policy approaches to address intersectionality: reactive ones which highlight stigmatizing effects (of, for example, existing policy); pragmatic ones interested in how intersectionality can be applied with existing policy tools; substantial ones that call for more transformative change; and procedural ones that focus on the inclusion of underrepresented political actors. In Verloo's terms, I am interested in procedural approaches, namely relations between civil society actors, and between these actors and the state. Verloo calls for further research on the decision-making of cross-movement actors on multiple inequalities.

Social movements

Beyond studies of policy, much available research on intersectionality's operationalization has taken grassroots, campaigning social movement organizations as its focus (Chun et al 2013; Cruells and García 2014; Tungohan 2015; Terriquez et al 2018; Irvine et al 2019a; Beaman and Brown 2019; Ishkanian and Peña Saavedra 2019). Such research variously investigates, respectively, intersectional movements, constituted at the intersection of multiple inequalities, intersectional praxis (Townsend-Bell

2011) within wider social justice movements (Irvine et al 2019b), or inclusion of intersectional concerns within single-issue equity-seeking movements.

An important early study looking at how intersectionality is employed in the context of a social movement organization is 'Intersectionality as a social movement strategy: Asian Immigrant Women Advocates' (Chun et al 2013). In terms of focusing on a particular intersectionally marginalized group, they argue that

> organizing and activism among women of color have long recognized the importance of using the particular grievances of one group as a point of entry into a larger struggle … AIWA [Asian Immigrant Women Advocates] uses its privileged composite identity as a starting point for critique and contestation and as a unique and generative space from which power can be challenged in multiple sites and on multiple scales—from the body and the household to the workplace and the broader life of the community. (Chun et al 2013, 921)

Their case study finds that in the context of the US organization Asian Immigrant Women Advocates (AIWA),

> intersectionality is deployed in three key ways: as a framework for analyzing the interlocking arenas of gender, family, work, and nation; as a reflexive approach for linking social movement theory and practice; and as a guiding structure for promoting new identities and new forms of democratic activity among immigrant women workers. (Chun et al 2013, 920)

More concretely, this is manifested by variation of sites of work: 'AIWA's work takes place in no single physical locus because the problems that AIWA's constituency faces are not confined to the shop floor, the neighborhood, the family, or the offices of governments' (2013, 917). They write:

> This approach [of promoting new identities] rejects the subordination of one oppression to another. It does not focus solely on gender, class, race, or language, nor does it organize along single-axis identities such as Chinese or Korean or Vietnamese immigrants, Asian Americans, women, or workers. Rather, it offers participants many different points of entry and engagement at the intersections of their diverse and plural identities. In doing so, AIWA promotes an approach to identities as tools to be used in complicated, flexible, and strategic ways. (Chun et al 2013, 918)

In contrast to uses of intersectionality in public policy which reduce it to identity, 'the intersectionality that guides AIWA primarily focuses on power rather than personal identities; it neither evades nor embraces social identities in the abstract but promotes thinking strategically and situationally about which differences matter and why' (Chun et al 2013, 925).

Based on an exploration of two migrants' rights organizations in Canada, Ethel Tungohan has argued that 'intersectionality provides activist organizations with a normative framework and guidelines for action and is best advanced through the use of a multi-pronged advocacy approach that engages multiple stakeholders, promotes strategically shifting portrayals of its members, and takes place in multiple scales' (Tungohan 2015, 1).

Though intersectionality as a contemporary social movement strategy has been less common in the UK (Bassel and Emejulu 2017), one project examined how social movements define and translate intersectionality into practice, drawing on the case of feminist organization Sisters Uncut (Ishkanian and Peña Saavedra 2019). The authors find that for movements to be able to enact 'intersectional prefiguration', they need to have a collective identity; a commitment to organize in an intersectional way; and adopt particular methods. These include creating safer spaces, and means of confronting and acknowledging harms and tensions with a commitment to addressing and transforming these as a group. Challenges in enacting intersectionality included issues of voice, participation and representation, particularly in relation to class as it intersects with other aspects of identity, and in working through specific tensions that emerge. Moreover, 'specific tools and continuous, iterative action are necessary to translate intersectionality into practice' (Ishkanian and Peña Saavedra 2019, 13).

Further literature on intersectionality and social movements is discussed in my subsequent section on 'issues in practice'.

NGO sector

As demonstrated above, there is a growing literature on intersectionality and public policy, including its application in UK equality policy. There is also a growing literature on intersectionality in social movements. In contrast to taking 'social movements' as subject (for example, Irvine et al 2019a), this book specifically examines NGOs, which I distinguish from the grassroots. Namely, I explore the far less documented conceptualization and operationalization of intersectionality by organizations and practitioners in the equality NGO sector. There has been little research on intersectionality in established equality NGOs or coalitions/networks of organizations, particularly in the UK context. Moreover, there is a lack of literature specifically exploring *how* intersectionality is understood.

This gap in knowledge about the NGO sector is important since it plays a key role in equality policy making. As Hankivsky and Cormier note, 'the role that equality seeking groups and advocates can play in such processes [of applying intersectionality in public policy making] are critical' (Hankivsky and Cormier 2011, 227). A key text exploring the extent to which intersectionality has been taken up by policy makers in the EU is 'Institutionalising intersectionality: the changing nature of European equality regimes' (Krizsan et al 2012c). However, in focusing only on policy makers, this book leaves an important gap in analysis of the NGO sector, and its influence on policy:

> By focusing exclusively on institutional changes, the authors have, in my view, inadvertently excluded an important part of the story of the shift to intersectional approaches to equality – namely the contentious and competing claims-making of civil society actors, particularly feminist, anti-racist, disability rights and gay rights movements and groups ... if intersectionality can be operationalized in such a way as to minimize the contributions of key civil society actors with a vested interest in equality policy processes, I wonder what intersectionality means ... and whose experiences, analyses and interests are privileged and/or silenced in our discussions about equality policy. (Emejulu 2014, 1922–23)

Literature on intersectionality and equality policy in the UK has largely been similarly state-centric (see, for example, Walby et al 2012a), while the NGO sector influenced and continues to influence the policy take-up of intersectionality, and in complex and contextual ways in the different countries of the UK (for influence on the Equality Act, see for example, Trades Union Congress 2012); and the impact of the equality policy context on practice in the NGO sector is underexplored.

Research on the NGO sector is also of interest in its own right, beyond its relationship with public policy. Intersectionality itself may be considered to be co-constituted, with critical inquiry, by 'critical praxis' (Collins and Bilge 2016), highlighting the importance of documenting how equality practitioners in the NGO sector are operationalizing or 'doing' intersectionality:

> practitioners and activists are often frontline actors for solving social problems that come with complex social inequalities, a social location that predisposes them to engage intersectionality as critical praxis ... for practitioners and activists, intersectionality is not simply a heuristic for intellectual inquiry but is also an important analytical strategy for *doing* social justice work. (Collins and Bilge 2016, 42)

Crenshaw wrote 'my own take on how to know intersectionality has been to do intersectionality ... I've consistently learned more from what scholars and activists have done with intersectionality than from what others have speculated about its appeal' (Crenshaw 2011, 222).

Literature on intersectionality's application in the UK NGO sector is relatively undeveloped, with some exceptions (Sudbury 1998; Bassel and Emejulu 2014, 2017; Christoffersen and Behrens 2014; Christoffersen 2020a, 2021a, 2022; Christoffersen and Emejulu 2023), while in the sector, engagement with intersectionality is growing.

The available literature provides evidence of a lack of capacity and political will to understand and involve those with marginalized intersecting identities in the NGO and public sectors. A literature review found that much available literature from the equality NGO sector on intersectionality was focused on establishing this 'intersectional need', evidence built in part to use to fund intersectionally focused work (Christoffersen and Behrens 2014). While here the institutional and funding environment is identified as a barrier to operationalizing intersectionality, conversely, NGO sector organizations at times use intersectionality to their advantage: based on ethnographic research in US LGBT organizations, Jane Ward (2008) identified institutionalization as a barrier to intersectional practice, namely the use of intersectionality by non-profit organizations to further their own financial interests.

Some US research (Strolovitch 2006, 2007; Marchetti 2014; English 2019) has sought to assess the extent to which civil society equality organizations engaged in lobbying and advocacy address issues affecting intersectionally marginalized groups. This research tends to consider intersections of just two axes of oppression (for example, the extent to which women's organizations address issues concerning low-income/working-class women). For 'intersectional organizations', organized around multiple crossing inequalities at their core, the above approach would be far less relevant. Nevertheless, this research is instructive in its findings that organizations disproportionately represent the interests of advantaged sub-groups (Strolovitch 2006, 2007; English 2019), and use stronger tactics to do so than for issues deemed to affect intersectionally disadvantaged sub-groups (Strolovitch 2006, 2007). In fact, 'issues affecting advantaged subgroups receive more attention than majority issues' (Strolovitch 2007, 8). When women's organizations specifically do discuss intersectionally marginalized women, this representation is uneven, disproportionately focused on sexual orientation and gender identity to the exclusion of other characteristics including race (English 2019). In her initial formulation of intersectionality, Crenshaw (1991) was partially driven by the tendency of single-issue organizations to prioritize the issues and experiences of the advantaged/privileged within them, rather than those affecting intersectionally marginalized people (that is, Black women). In my own research on which this book is based, I have specifically sought to include intersectional organizations in the knowledge that interests of intersectionally marginalized people are marginal in single-strand organizations, as this literature shows (albeit in the US context).

The approach of deductively measuring the extent to which organizations represent the interests of 'disadvantaged sub-groups' was not one that I adopted, for several reasons. First, it is difficult to quantify what the issues of concern to particular groups are, particularly in an intersectional framework in which social groups are conceived as heterogeneously intersected by both privilege and oppression. I did not wish to predefine what issues were most relevant to different groups, nor to limit these to what was on the 'political agenda'; there is no agreement on priority issues even within groups. Second, those identifying within the equality sector in the UK, and those organizations that the equality networks that I researched are composed of, include not only policy engagement/advocacy organizations, but also service providers and community development organizations. UK equality organizations increasingly cross these boundaries as they move to follow funding in an austerity context; and networks of equality organizations are inclusive of all of these. Third, and most importantly, my project began from a point which can be conceptualized as ontologically prior to assessing whether single-strand organizations address issues pertinent to intersectionally marginalized sub-groups, where it was not assumed that addressing issues deemed to affect intersectionally marginalized sub-groups would necessarily be the sole or primary ways that organizations perceive themselves as operationalizing intersectionality. As such, it has identified other means of operationalizing intersectionality. In other words, consideration of whether organizations' identified priority issues affect their overall constituencies or subsets of intersectionally marginalized people within them (Strolovitch 2006, 2007; Marchetti 2014; English 2019) forecloses consideration of other models of intersectional practice, which I will present in Chapter 4. This book seeks to understand how organizations understand the term (which in some cases does and in others does not signify to them this idea of reorienting agendas to the issues affecting the intersectionally marginalized), and how they are using what they understand as ideas of intersectionality in their work. This issue of agenda-setting is important as one way that organizations perceive themselves to be operationalizing intersectionality, but some participants do not include this in their narratives of operationalizing intersectionality. Importantly also, my research was interested in the practicalities of how agendas would change. Extant literature has focused on *whether* advocacy organizations represent intersectionally marginalized groups within groups (Strolovitch 2006, 2007), or the factors that make this more likely (Marchetti 2015; English 2019; Dwidar 2022). In operationalizing intersectionality in particular ways (the extent to which single-issue organizations address issues deemed relevant to a (singly) intersecting sub-group (Strolovitch 2006, 2007), and the extent to which they mention intersectional identities in particular policy processes (English 2019; Dwidar 2022)), this research leaves a gap in understanding of how practitioners and organizations *understand themselves* to operationalize intersectionality.

In addition to quantifying whether organizations focus on issues affecting intersectionally disadvantaged sub-groups, Dara Strolovitch develops a concept of 'affirmative advocacy' to explain how organizations that do so, do this, by:

> creating decision rules that elevate issues affecting disadvantaged minorities on organizational agendas; using internal processes and practices to improve the status of intersectionally disadvantaged groups within the organization; forging stronger ties to state and local advocacy groups; promoting 'descriptive representation' by making sure that staff and boards include members of intersectionally marginalized subgroups of their constituencies; resisting the silencing effects of public and constituent opinion that are biased against disadvantaged subgroups; and cultivating among advantaged subgroups of their constituencies the understanding that their interests are inextricably linked to the well-being of intersectionally disadvantaged constituents. (Strolovitch 2007, 10)

The concept of affirmative advocacy has subsequently been further developed as 'intersectional advocacy' (for example, Dwidar 2022). More recently this analysis has extended to consideration of the role of descriptive representation of intersectionally marginalized people in leadership roles in NGOs in determining whether or not they do intersectional advocacy (Dwidar, Marchetti and Strolovitch in progress).

I turn now to examining key issues in practice relevant to the study of intersectionality's conceptualization and operationalization in the NGO sector: representation, and coalition and solidarity. These issues form the themes of Chapters 5 and 6.

NGO sector: issues in practice
Representation

Representation (who is represented) is normatively, politically and epistemologically (Collins 1990; Mügge et al 2018) important to intersectionality. Intersectionality presents a challenge to ideas that the equality NGO sector is representative, which I discuss in detail in Chapter 5.

Much of the available literature on intersectionality and representation adapts concepts from literature on women's political representation/gender and political representation, which draw on key concepts in political theory: descriptive, substantive and symbolic representation, formulated to consider elected representatives (Pitkin 1967). Descriptive representation is representation via demographic similarity. Substantive representation is the extent to which representatives represent the *actual interests* of those they represent. More recently, representation has been theorized as a practice of claims-making (Saward 2006; see also Siow 2023 on the relationship between the latter and substantive representation). Representation also remains a central concern of poststructuralist and postcolonial theory.

Descriptive representation has been argued to be, if nothing else, symbolically important to marginalized groups (Phillips 1995): in order to achieve recognition, 'including those previously excluded matters *even if* it proves to have no discernible consequences for the policies that may be adopted' (Phillips 1995, 39). However, descriptive representation becomes difficult both to conceptualize and to measure when considered from an intersectional perspective that factors in a multitude of social divisions (age, disability, minority faith, migrant status, sexual orientation, trans[1] identity, and so on), and conceiving of all of these as overlapping: the combinations become almost infinite. For example, among my research participants, I collected equality monitoring data across seven categories, identified in law as markers of discrimination and exclusion. Each category has between three and 24 answer choices or sub-categories. Together this represents more than 245 septillion possible combinations. My monitoring data also do not include several representational categories which emerged as important in my research. In other words, intersectionality's ontological project (Hancock 2016) reveals the near impossibility, and inherent imperfection of ideas of descriptive representation (Mendez 2018). Suzanne Dovi thus argues that preferred descriptive representatives should have 'strong mutual relationships with dispossessed subgroups of historically disadvantaged groups' (Dovi 2002, 729).

In a similar vein, intersectionality also complicates Iris Marion Young's concept of group representation (Young 1990). This aims to avoid the essentialism of an assumed relationship between descriptive and substantive representation, in arguing that previously excluded groups should have spaces and resources in which they might agree priorities and interests. In recognition of how intersectionality complicates the concept of descriptive representation and ideas of a 'group', within intersectionality literature, marginalized groups have themselves been conceived as *coalitions* (Crenshaw 1991; Chun et al 2013; Carastathis 2016) rather than reified identity groups. Although intersectionality's ontological project complicates descriptive representation, much intersectionality literature highlights the epistemological and political importance of representation of perspectives of intersectionally marginalized people (Collins 1990; Mügge et al 2018).

Assuming a relationship between descriptive and substantive representation would seem to rely on essentialism. For this reason, a range of research has sought to measure the extent to which these two forms of representation are related empirically (for example, Childs 2004). In particular, the literature on the substantive representation of women is concerned with the extent to which female representatives articulate 'women's interests' (Phillips 1995; Lovenduski 2005; Childs 2008). This literature on representation tends to reproduce problems that intersectionality responds to, that is, thinking of women homogeneously, and as having similar gender-related interests. Therefore, it reproduces privileging of the advantaged within groups (affluent white women of particular social positions), and erasure of others. Feminists writing from an intersectional perspective have pointed to the importance of intersectional approaches to otherwise homogenizing accounts of interests (for example, Smooth 2006; Hancock 2014) in substantive representation.

Indeed, intersectionality, and particularly the idea of the simultaneity of privilege and oppression, substantially complicates the concept of substantive representation. From this perspective, within marginalized groups, there are *opposing* interests. Moreover, sometimes pursuing equality is about removing privileges, unearned advantages that people have. Therefore, certain actions which would benefit intersectionally marginalized groups are not necessarily in the (at least short-term) interests of those with whom they share other aspects of identity, on which bases their interests may be aligned (or would be perceived as such). In other words, from an intersectional perspective, it is not possible to be representative of the substantive interests of, for example, all LGBTI people, because this social group is composed of competing interests along lines of privilege and oppression constructed by other axes of inequality. Thus, there is disagreement within groups as to what common interests are (Tungohan 2015; Irvine et al 2019b).

An influential interjection into literature on representation has been Michael Saward's theorization of representation as a social practice of claims-making, which constitutes the represented (Saward 2006). Yet from an intersectional perspective, a similar problem may emerge as in consideration of both descriptive and substantive representation: 'the represented' may be singular in its constitution. However, this concept of representation is useful in that it allows for interrogation of which subjects and which understandings of social relations are constituted in the process of representation (Squires 2008b; Siow 2023). Yet, it urges focus away from who representatives are, in favour of interrogation of claims themselves, which is a departure from the feminist political science literature on descriptive and substantive representation.

Although a comprehensive exploration is beyond the scope of this chapter, representation is also a central consideration of postcolonial, poststructuralist theory which informs contemporary intersectionality studies. This literature problematizes the extent to which intersectionally marginalized people, in dominant, violent discourses, can be represented, in the sense of being heard, at all (Spivak 2003). In the absence of participation, Linda Alcoff highlights the violence of 'speaking for', or representation itself (Alcoff 1992).

The literature broadly concludes that: (i) representation of marginalized groups is important symbolically for recognition (Phillips 1995); (ii) though substantive representation does not necessarily follow from descriptive representation, there is some relationship between the two (Phillips 1995); (iii) determining 'substantive interests' is challenging and risks essentialism; (iv) the process of representation is constitutive of who and what is being represented (Saward 2006); and (v) there is a need to be critical of the possibilities, normative desirability and unintended consequences of representation (Alcoff 1992; Spivak 2003). I have shown that intersectionality complicates existing concepts of representation.

The literature raises a more normative question of whether we can, or should expect equality organizations to, represent the substantive interests of intersectionally marginalized people, with some positing that 'without knowing the demographic composition of groups' supporters, it is difficult to assess whether they are under or over-representing particular groups' (Marchetti 2014, 107) – that substantive representation need be dependent on, and expected only where there is, descriptive representation. More normatively, intersectional justice arguably demands that (for example) white-dominated women's organizations claiming to represent 'women's interests', regardless of whether their members are all white women, either reorient their agendas or cease these claims. Perceptions of whether or not equality organizations represent all members of their target group are closely related to perceptions of organizational legitimacy; yet these standards are not applied equally across race and minority faith (Jones et al 2015). Equality organizations, and especially those of particular kinds, experience an extra burden of representation.

Since intersectional representation is not an issue related solely to either descriptive or substantive representation of whole equality groups or subgroups (both the descriptive and substantive representation of whole groups being impossible given the multitude of social divisions, and conflicting interests), arguably it is related to the normative content of what is being represented, and whether it is in the interests of intersectional justice and those who are intersectionally marginalized. The question of how to measure this raises several methodological and conceptual issues, some of which I have already mentioned. Who determines who the priority intersectionally marginalized groups are and what their interests are, and how? What is the role of specialist knowledge (the knowledge that equality practitioners and organizations develop that is not merely a product of their identities) in determining this? Which social positions represent intersectionally marginalized positions is contingent in several respects. This means that it changes, with changing conditions of social life, demographics and development of critical intersectional thinking. Needless to say, there is also no agreement on this. Perhaps responsiveness to these changes would be a more telling measure of how 'intersectional' organizations are than identifying whether they focus on issues pertaining to intersectionally disadvantaged sub-groups statically conceived. Another possible measure would be whether organizations seek to remove advantages of advantaged sub-groups, which may or may not be the precise same processes as acting on issues pertinent to those who are intersectionally marginalized. There is little evidence of organizations seeking to adapt their issues explicitly to 'those of the most intersectionally marginalized' and working out what these are. This is one reason that self-organization is critical. I have specifically sought to include self-organized organizations in my research, as I explore further in Chapter 5.

Coalition and intersectional solidarity
Coalition

Coalition has been consistently identified as important to intersectional practice, particularly in literature concerning intersectionality, social movement organizations and the NGO sector (Strolovitch 2007; Cole 2008; Bassel and Emejulu 2014; Collins and Bilge 2016; Broad-Wright 2017; Irvine et al 2019b; Dwidar 2022; Dursun 2022). Specifically, coalitions are identified as a way that intersectionality can be practised, as a means to mitigate political intersectionality issues including movement 'silos' (Crenshaw 1991): 'intersectional coalitions can be a useful alternative to categorical and single identity-based projects' (Rodriguez et al 2016, 208) because they facilitate thinking 'about social categories in terms of stratification brought about through practices of individuals, institutions and cultures rather than only as characteristics of individuals' (Cole 2008, 443).

In their summary of three empirical studies of intersectional praxis, Collins and Bilge write: 'these examples show different dimensions of how groups recognize the significance of coalitions and alliances, both within their own organization and across organizations ... [they] place difference and multiplicity at the core of their social justice praxis' (Collins and Bilge 2016, 42). Studies by Cole and Roberts and Jesudason positively highlight the complementarities of intersectionality and coalition (Cole 2008; Roberts and Jesudason 2013). The latter is a case study of a planned use of intersectionality as a tool in cross-movement coalition building, which involves specifically acknowledging intersecting identities of participants; honesty and trust building; and articulating common values and developing a shared advocacy agenda (Roberts and Jesudason 2013). Recent research finds that NGOs are significantly more likely to pursue intersectional advocacy in coalitions than when acting alone (Dwidar 2022).

Yet, as Sirma Bilge cautions, '[intersectionality's] relationship to alliance-building and coalition cannot be taken for granted – despite tempting assumptions that applying intersectional thinking onto social movement politics would logically lead to coalitions' (Bilge 2016, 4). Moreover, coalitions incur power relations; for intersectionally marginalized groups, they may be viewed as necessary but also potentially subjugating (Bilge 2016). Others (Ward 2004; Townsend-Bell 2011) have reported problems of coalition building in the context of intersectionality and women's organizing. Issues identified include defining commonality as well as difference; negotiating power differentials (Cole 2008); agreeing salient axes of difference to include (Townsend-Bell 2011); and actor mobilization of additive and hierarchical understandings of oppression (Ward 2004).

Available literature is based on research primarily conducted in the US (with exceptions including Uruguay (Townsend-Bell 2011) and Turkey (Dursun 2022)). It predominantly looks at organizing within and among women's movements, rather than at cross-sector coalitions, with exceptions (Roberts and Jesudason 2013; Dwidar 2022). Indeed, the vast majority of literature on intersectionality, social movements and the NGO sector has focused exclusively on feminist organizations (Laperriere and Lépinard 2016; English 2019). I suggest that this may exclude an important part of the picture (in particular, the racial justice sector; see also Beaman and Brown 2019), as well as cross-sector intersectional work.

In the UK context, coalitions have been called for in order to operationalize intersectionality (Hankivsky and Christoffersen 2011; Hankivsky et al 2019), but prior to the research presented in this book, there had been no empirical examination of what happens in existing NGO sector coalitions regarding how they understand and use ideas of intersectionality.

Coalition is important because intersectionality theory indicates that experiences, identities and perspectives are particular and unique, that therefore social groups are never homogeneous, and there is no 'essence' of an aspect of identity/experience that holds true across all of its intersections. Within social groups, there will always be similarities and differences in identity and experience at the same time, and equality as a goal is, therefore, not principled on similarity but on coalition and solidarity, which account for difference yet recognize that there can still be common issues and interests (Mohanty 2003). However, intersectionality also illuminates how some interests are opposed. Many privileges can be understood as 'advantage privileges' which are in effect 'zero sum', meaning that to further equity requires people to lose advantages that they have (McIntosh 1998; McKinnon and Sennet 2017); in other words, they are 'positional goods': 'benefits of a political or status or cultural or "ontological" kind' (Mills 2017a, 134). In highlighting the simultaneity of privilege and oppression, intersectionality also illuminates where there may be entrenched privileges and opposing interests that pose challenges for coalition building and solidarity in the context of intersectional practice, and would need to be addressed in the interests of intersectional solidarity.

Solidarity

Coalition is related to 'solidarity' in complex ways. First, it is important to distinguish what type of solidarity I am referring to. Sally J. Scholz identifies three distinct uses of solidarity: civic solidarity, borne of shared national identity; social solidarity, driven by shared characteristic or similarity; and political solidarity, by common commitment to opposing oppression and injustice (Scholz 2008). Intersectionality challenges ideas of similarity in civic and social solidarity, while the concept of political solidarity is useful. Intersectionality signifies the interrelation of structures of inequality. It therefore facilitates identification of how and where political struggles overlap, which might otherwise be conceptualized disparately, and in doing so creates opportunity for political solidarity by making visible shared political goals. Solidarity is, however, also argued to be specifically 'acting on behalf of' in a relationship of deference to those receiving the solidarity (Kolers 2016). Scholz addresses this as participation of the privileged in political solidarity, arguing that this requires renouncing privileges; commitment to understand oppression; and active participation in resistance (Scholz 2008).

Coalitions may be premised on political solidarity, and/or may aim to create or increase solidarity. However, not all coalitions have solidarity. Actors may unite to further singular interests without a shared overall objective or commitment. Yet in parts of the NGO sector, 'solidarity both animates oppositional voluntary action and is the hoped-for outcome of this form of action. If solidarity is weakened within the NGO sector, the ability to mobilize at the intersections of different social justice agendas is undermined' (Bassel and Emejulu 2014, 133). Leah Bassel and Akwugo Emejulu find that solidarity is undermined in a context of austerity, thereby undermining the ability to make multiple axis claims, and to operationalize intersectionality (Bassel and Emejulu 2014).

From political solidarity we can further distinguish 'intersectional solidarity': 'an ongoing process of creating ties and coalitions across social group differences by negotiating power asymmetries' (Tormos 2017, 712; see also Cole 2008). Solidarity for intersectional justice necessitates reorienting agendas to issues affecting the most intersectionally disadvantaged groups (Tormos 2017). However, the particular historicized empirical relationships between solidarity and intersectionality across space and time are relatively underexplored (Kelliher 2018). More recently, intersectional solidarity has been further operationalized as a measure of group consciousness that helps to explain support for policies that disproportionately benefit intersectionally marginalized groups, for example Black women, in the context of the contemporary US (Crowder 2022). In the context of coalitions of organizations, intersectional solidarity can be further clarified in relation to how differences between organizations are reflected in the framing of issues, and whether coalitions try to redress imbalances in resources and representation (Ciccia and Roggeband 2021). The relationships between these two dimensions reveal four potential ideal types of intersectional solidarity (Ciccia and Roggeband 2021).

Patricia Hill Collins develops a concept of flexible solidarity borne from Black women's experiences of community work negotiating a broader Black solidarity. This is a critical solidarity that is not absolute, but rather subject to social context, because

> solidarity may be an admirable political goal, but can have within it entrenched social hierarchies that routinely privilege and penalize designated individuals and/or sub-groups. Instead, flexible solidarity can facilitate coalitions among groups who have a shared commitment to a social ideal … or to a shared social problem, yet who take very different paths into coalition building. (Collins 2019a, 190)

Building on this, Collins recommends as an avenue of inquiry the building of political solidarity between groups/collectivities, which are 'equally if not more significant in political action' than individuals (Collins 2019a, 187).

Summary and framework
Conceptualizing intersectionality
In this chapter, I first outlined definitions and concepts of intersectionality, with reference to selected key debates in intersectionality studies: the extent to which it is additive or constitutive; its levels of analysis; and attention to privilege as contrasted to focus on those who are most disadvantaged. I use these debates as parameters of how I employ intersectionality as a theoretical framework. First, I highlighted debates on the extent to which intersectionality is additive or constitutive. This distinction is central to my guiding definition of intersectionality. Moreover, this has been identified as intersectionality's *ontological project*, a 'reconstitution of relationships among categories of difference' (Hancock 2016, 28). Second, I have highlighted closely related debates concerning levels of analysis. Given the insight from the literature that intersectionality is predominantly used at an individual level in policy, I analyse the levels at which intersectionality is conceptualized in UK NGO sector equality practice. Third, I considered debates concerning *who* intersectionality is about. While intersectionality provides an important framework in which to study power and privileged social positions, practically

speaking, attention to those who are intersectionally disadvantaged is important to concepts of intersectional justice, affirmative advocacy and intersectional solidarity. In Chapter 4, I therefore analyse whether competing concepts of intersectionality attend to those who are intersectionally disadvantaged. Fourth, I outlined debates as to whether intersectionality is appropriated or co-opted, and the relationship between the social locations of Black women, women of colour and intersectionality. I employ an antiracist feminist framework throughout the book in which I analyse the relationships of competing concepts of intersectionality to these debates.

I have selected particular elements of intersectionality from a range of frameworks explicating components of intersectionality to employ as a theoretical framework, rather than employing one particular framework. This necessarily leaves out elements of some typologies. The framework that I employ is included in full in Table 4.1 on p 82. For instance, for Collins and Bilge, intersectionality has six characteristic themes, namely: relationality; social context; power; inequality; social justice; and complexity (Collins and Bilge 2016).

To employ this typology in full against my data, the bulk of which is interview data, would, I felt, ask too much of my participants. My objective has not been to deductively evaluate whether practice *is* intersectionality, but to explore what *practitioners themselves* understand intersectional practice as. For this reason, I similarly did not apply frame analysis to determine whether frames in use incorporated intersectionality or not (Cruells and García 2014). Nevertheless, I analyse competing concepts of intersectionality against a framework of key debates in intersectionality studies, not to necessarily conclude what is and what is not intersectionality, but to explore the implications (both normative and empirical) of practitioner concepts for intersectionally marginalized groups.

Applying intersectionality

I then turned to examine intersectionality's operationalization in distinct and yet related fields of practice: public policy, social movements and the NGO sector. Policy applications of intersectionality remain largely additive and individualized, although the equality policy context of the UK may provide potential for further exploration of intersectionality in policy (particularly in Scotland and the other devolved nations). In social movements and in the NGO sector, the literature points to some ways in which intersectionality may be used. Collins and Bilge argue that intersectional sensibilities can be manifested in organizing by: politicizing issues as a platform for differentially disenfranchised groups; efforts to create inclusive political identities (for example, the *Indignados* (Cruells and García 2014)); and building horizontal coalitions instead of federations (Collins and Bilge 2016). Bassel and

Emejulu find intersectionality to be deployed by French and UK NGOs in the making of 'multiple axis claims' (Bassel and Emejulu 2014). Others outline ways that intersectionality has been operationalized in and by specific organizations, conceptually and practically, including: mobilization of specific intersectional identities as a 'point of entry' (Chun et al 2013) to multi-issue, multi-site and multi-scale (Tungohan 2015) activism; mobilization of specific intersectional identities as transformative identities (Collins and Bilge 2016); through 'intersectional prefiguration' within organizations (Ishkanian and Peña Saavedra 2019); and building coalitions which attempt to balance existing asymmetries of power (Cruells and García 2014). In the US context, research has found that equality advocacy and lobbying organizations disproportionately represent on issues affecting advantaged sub-groups of constituencies (Strolovitch 2007; English 2019). Those that do represent on issues affecting intersectionally disadvantaged sub-groups do so through 'affirmative' or intersectional advocacy, or extra representation to disadvantaged groups.

While there is a growing literature on intersectionality's uses in public policy and in social movements, I have identified that there are particular gaps in research and literature on: (i) intersectionality's application in the NGO sector; (ii) the UK context; (iii) how practitioners *themselves* understand intersectionality; (iv) intersectional practice in 'intersectional' organizations as compared with single identity-based organizations; and (v) cross-sector, rather than intra-sector, coalitions (particularly those beyond the feminist sector).

Finally, I reviewed literature concerning issues in practice that form the themes of Chapters 5 and 6: representation, and coalition and solidarity. After reviewing relevant literature, I argued that intersectionality's ontological project (Hancock 2016) reveals the near impossibility, and inherent imperfection of many existing concepts of representation, including descriptive, substantive and group representation. Yet, intersectionality scholarship highlights the epistemological and political importance of representation of perspectives of intersectionally marginalized people when 'doing' intersectionality. However, this representation faces discursive and material challenges. Coalition has been consistently identified as important to intersectionality in practice, while the latter can be conceptualized as both political solidarity and as intersectional solidarity.

The politics of knowledge

Finally, this book also draws on theory more generally interested in the *politics of knowledge*, or the role of ideas in policy and practice. Researchers have highlighted the importance of knowledge to intersectionality's application: 'new types of expertise are required to move beyond the status quo of specifically focusing on single or even additive approaches (e.g., gender + age + race) and instead capturing multiple and intersecting locations and social structures' (Hankivsky et al 2014, 14); applying intersectionality 'will require a more embedded intersectional thinking among equality professions than is apparent to date' (Krizsan et al 2012a, 239). The importance of new knowledge and new framing for intersectional work is highlighted in the available literature on intersectionality from the NGO sector, for instance reframing types of violence against women disproportionately impacting women of colour away from essentializing, othering discourses (Larasi 2011).

In seeking to understand how intersectionality is conceptualized and operationalized, I asked what competing knowledges of intersectionality there are, how these came to be, how practitioners know them, and what the relationship is between knowledge (or theory) and practice. In particular, I explore knowledge of intersectionality that is 'embodied' in practitioners and 'enacted' at points of practice (knowledge generated in their action and interaction) (Freeman and Sturdy 2015), but that is not necessarily 'inscribed', that is, written in documents. I also seek to understand whether this embodied/enacted knowledge, and 'hidden transcripts' of equality policy (Scott 1990), can lend themselves to theorizing approaches to intersectionality's operationalization.

PART II

3

Contextualizing Intersectionality: Equality Policy, Austerity and Relations with the State

'The Equality Act ... didn't solve these problems around intersectionality, so people have got together and said, "How do we actually make this happen?"'
Julie, Director, refugee organization, England

Having identified gaps in knowledge about intersectionality's operationalization in Chapter 2, in this chapter I set out an analysis of the terrain in which equality NGOs in cities located in England and Scotland conceptualize and operationalize intersectionality.[1] This terrain is comprised of: (i) equality policy and discourse; (ii) austerity; and (iii) the sector's relationships to the state. The chapter is in three sections. I first situate equality organizations' work within public discourses arising from UK and Scottish equality policy, and analyse the implications of equality policy for intersectionality. While the organizations in my sample predominantly work at local level, I situate this work in national- and UK-level policy contexts, since local governments are subject to UK law and equality regulations and accompanying public discourses of 'equality/equalities', and given that the particular cities in which I researched are anonymised in order to protect the identities of participants. Though intersectionality's application in policy internationally thus far has been limited, scholars have argued that the UK has been attempting to apply intersectionality in policy (Squires 2009; Hankivsky and Christoffersen 2011; Hankivsky and Cormier 2011; Hankivsky et al 2019) in the context of the Equality Act 2010. Applications of intersectionality thus occur in the context of wider equality policy. Though intersectionality is relevant to all areas of policy, not solely equality policy, in the UK it is within the field of equality policy that understandings of institutionalized oppressions are inscribed, and that drivers and reference points to apply intersectionality in other policy areas would be found. However, as I will show, the Equality Act 2010 does not provide equality policy makers, practitioners, organizations or networks with a secure basis on which to proceed to understand or to operationalize intersectionality. Yet, the term 'intersectionality' is increasingly used in equality policy in the UK. This increasing use is reflected in Great Britain-wide and national equality policy documents published by Westminster and Holyrood, respectively. After analysing the implications of equality policy in relation to intersectionality, I report findings of policy document analysis to better understand the relationship between equality policy and NGO sector equality practice, that is, how intersectionality's conceptualization and application in the latter is influenced by the former (Christoffersen 2019). Specifically, this is accomplished through exploration of intersectionality's take-up, uses and meanings in English and Scottish equality policy documents.

Second, I discuss the external barriers that equality NGOs face when seeking to operationalize intersectionality in two sections (Christoffersen 2020a). While my research sought to explore, describe and understand *how* equality NGOs operationalize intersectionality, much of the data that I collected speak to how, and in what ways, they are *constrained* in doing so. This is important information to contextualize the following chapters, which focus on how organizations understand and use intersectionality (within the constraints of these barriers and challenges). Amid the backdrop of equality policy and discourse, in seeking to apply intersectionality, equality organizations face significant external barriers. First, they face challenges relating to neoliberal austerity: lack of funding for intersectional work, and competitive funding environments. Second, they face barriers concerning power: specifically, relations between equality organizations and local government and public sector actors, limiting NGO sector independence. These barriers and challenges influence the way that equality organizations operationalize intersectionality.

My argument in this chapter is threefold. First, *in equality policy, there are a range of definitions of intersectionality decontextualized from its origins, and its deployment is largely individualized, excluding consideration of the intersections of macro structures of inequality; merely descriptive; additive; and superficial, leaving its potential unrealized.* Moreover, there is a gap between academic debates, and the way that intersectionality is used in and by government: *meaningful engagement with race and race/gender as central social organizing logics, and key categories of intersectionality theory is lacking in policy documents not specifically concerning race equality.* Third, in a sector which has been predominantly organized around single issues/identities, efforts to take account of intersectional marginalization, where the political will is there, are crucial.

Yet *equality NGOs are significantly hampered in their attempts to operationalize intersectionality by the low status they occupy vis-à-vis the state and by neoliberal austerity contexts.*

First, I introduce equality work and discourse as being distinct to discourse of social 'inequality', and the implications of this for equality NGO conceptualization and operationalization of intersectionality.

Equality and inequality

Within UK policy, there is a curious discursive separation between 'equality/ equalities', meaning identity-based markers, and 'inequality/inequalities'[2] meaning indicators of socioeconomic disadvantage; the latter usually undifferentiated by identity markers. When seeking to operationalize intersectionality, equality organizations face challenges concerning not only this discursive separation in itself, but also attempts to integrate the two. These discourses and sectors have historically developed separately from one another.

At UK level, socioeconomic inequalities were included under the PSED of the Equality Act 2010 by the then Labour government, but subsequent governments have not brought this provision into force. However, more recently in Scotland, similar provisions have been enacted,[3] with recognition that 'those who share particular protected characteristics are often at higher risk of socioeconomic disadvantage' (Scottish Government 2018, 13).

In the lead-up to this development and more generally, there is policy interest particularly in some local authority areas in better integrating 'equality' and 'inequality'. In the case of one equality network, for example, policy makers set a remit covering both. Its membership, therefore, includes self-organized,[4] identity-based equality organizations, as well as NGOs focused on socioeconomic disadvantage, which do not tend to be led by and for their target group.[5] Most equality networks found in my UK-wide mapping, in contrast, are exclusively identity-based. However, often identity-based organizations, particularly those that identify themselves as 'intersectional' organizations, do seek to serve and represent those within equality communities who are socioeconomically disadvantaged: that is, they work at the intersection of both recognition and redistribution (Fraser 1997). Yet the reasons that these sectors are largely disparate are several. There is a long-standing history of sectors mobilized around socioeconomic disadvantage ignoring identity-based inequalities (Emejulu 2015) and of wider Left politics being dismissive of 'identity politics', viewing concern with racism, sexism and so on as divisive and separate from class-based organizing. By not taking account of identity-based inequalities, these sectors can be argued to have reproduced domination along axes of oppression. These dynamics were reflected in post-2008 mainstream anti-austerity activism, as activist women of colour reported (Bassel and Emejulu

2017). Many equality organizations have roots in autonomous breakaway groups from wider Left politics which they found to be exclusionary and discriminatory. Discourse around socioeconomic disadvantage in politics and the media is heavily racialized, in concepts of the 'white working class' and 'the left behind' (Bhambra 2017).[6] In this context, there is mistrust of these sectors among equality organizations, and a lack of solidarity between the two.[7] There are also material inequalities of funding between these sectors.

Therefore, equality NGOs do not, by and large, identify with organizations focused exclusively around undifferentiated socioeconomic disadvantage. One equality sector participant, for example, described the inclusion of organizations working around poverty/socioeconomic status in an equality network as 'problematic', because in their view those organizations do not 'get' or 'see' identity-related inequalities, or reach equality groups. This history, which produces a lack of solidarity, does not appear to be appreciated by policy makers keen to integrate these disparate policy areas, and to create structures which include both types of organizations before any relationship building takes place.

Among the equality networks that I studied, the one that expressly seeks to combine identity-based and socioeconomic sectors has the lowest level of engagement from self-organized equality organizations. The combination of identity-based and socioeconomic sectors is a contributory factor to the low level of engagement. This has important implications for understanding and practising intersectionality, since the network lacks in specialist knowledge related to markers of identity because it lacks engagement from organizations who specialize in identity-based inequalities. I have also not observed any solidarity or notable coalition working between these sectors as a result of the inclusion of both. These findings resonate with tensions between community development aimed at redistribution, and that focused on recognition, observed in the US (Emejulu and Scanlon 2016).

Therefore, equality policy and accompanying discourses of 'equality/ equalities' are distinctive to wider discourses of social inequality/inequalities, which often omit key markers of inequality along lines of identity, including race and gender, and race/gender; both this separation, as well as attempts to integrate the two, form part of the context in which equality organizations conceptualize and operationalize intersectionality.

Next, I discuss UK and Scottish equality policy's relationship to intersectionality, and analyse definitions and uses of intersectionality in equality policy documents.

Equality policy and intersectionality

The way that the UK Equality Act 2010 brings together equality categories into one piece of legislation has been variously argued to create opportunities for applying intersectionality, that is, to consider the interactions between inequalities, or has in and of itself been conflated with intersectionality. However, comparative empirical research has found that 'particular institutional and legislative frameworks neither ensure nor rule out intersectional practices' (Krizsan et al 2012b, 3). Furthermore, contradictions between the Equality Act and an intersectional approach have also been observed (for example, Solanke 2011).

Though opportunities to explore the interactions between inequalities, and therefore potential for intersectionality's application, may have been facilitated by this joining up of previously separate axes of discrimination into one Act and the creation of a unified 'equality architecture' to enforce it, in current law, there is no framework for addressing intersectional discrimination.[8] This is true not just of the UK but of 'Europe' as well (Kantola and Nousiainen 2012; Babouri 2014; Solanke 2021). Moreover, the joining up of equality infrastructure has not necessarily led to intersectionality's operationalization.

Equality organizations from across the NGO sector were heavily engaged in consultation and lobbying on the Act, and many felt that the regulations to support it, revised by a newly elected Conservative-led coalition government not long before they were due to come into effect, did not go far enough in creating greater equality for marginalized groups, particularly in England and within UK government (Trades Union Congress 2012). During consultation on a single equality bill, at Great Britain level, some equality NGOs campaigned for recognition of intersectionality in the Act. As a result, the Act includes a provision for 'dual discrimination'. In April 2011, after the so-called 'Red Tape Challenge' which consulted on whether the PSED should be 'scrapped altogether', a decision was made that the power within the Equality Act for people to make claims of 'dual discrimination' on the basis of two combined protected characteristics would not be brought into force. The government wrote, 'bringing this power into effect would duplicate the burden to businesses unnecessarily' (Cabinet Office 2015). In any case this provision would allow for only two grounds and was limited to direct discrimination (Babouri 2014). Because of this, international bodies including the UN CEDAW committee have expressed concern that the Equality Act 'does not adequately protect women against multiple discrimination' (United Nations CEDAW Committee 2013).

Not only is intersectionality not addressed by equality law, it is also profoundly in tension with it in its current form. In the Equality Act itself, what are best conceptualized as mutually constituting social divisions are described as separate 'protected characteristics'. In the language of the Act, everyone in the UK 'has' some of the protected characteristics (for example, an age, race, gender, sexual orientation, and so on); so discerning structural inequalities and power relations in this framework is not straightforward. Furthermore, the inclusion of human rights in the UK equality policy context poses additional challenges for operationalizing intersectionality (Gedalof 2013).

Moreover, the Act has not prevented siloing of equality areas: in some organizations, and in UK government departments, the strands remain largely separate. Walby et al (2012a) analyse the ways that multiple inequalities are conceptualized and treated within the UK equality policy arena (the EHRC, GEO and other units). The EHRC itself is not primarily internally organized around separate equality strands, though it does have some dedicated positions and committees. In the EHRC's approach, 'there are intended to be common instruments for perceived common problems … [at the same time] specialist expertise (reports, representation) is deployed in relation to specific inequality issues, and [there are] some elements of … special treatment to specific small groups at specific intersections; in short, hybrid' (Walby et al 2012a, 462). At government level, the 'model of relations between multiple inequalities in most of the governmental policy units concerned with equality is a combination of "multiple parallel" since there are different units for different equalities … there is thus a significant lack of alignment between the governmental policy units and the merged single equalities Commission' (Walby et al, 463), one which endures. The joined-up equality infrastructure assumes a similarity of response across equality areas (Krizsan et al 2012b).

More recently, in 2019, however, the government established an 'Equality Hub' in the Cabinet Office which brings together the still distinct Disability Unit, Government Equalities Office, Race Disparity Unit and the secretariat to the Social Mobility Commission (concerned with 'inequality'). The Hub's 'top overall priority is improving the quality of evidence and data about disparities and the types of barriers different people face', and it also seeks to work across 'equality' and 'inequality'. There was an earlier nod to a particular version of intersectionality in discussion of the formation of the Equality Hub (Government Equalities Office 2019) while no subsequent use of the term by the Equality Hub is in evidence, and its website describes equalities only singularly (HM Government 2023). The work of the Equality Hub has thus far not been explored in depth.

The UK legal framework lends itself more to an additive approach than one that accounts for mutual constitution, and creates a context where equality practitioners in both the NGO and public sectors navigate a landscape delineated by separate 'equality strands'. While 'cross strand' work has been undertaken within the context of, for example, the EHRC, this is not necessarily an intersectional approach. However, it has been argued that the PSED could be a vehicle for addressing intersectionality (Hepple 2010; Babouri 2014).

Scottish equality policy and intersectionality

In Scotland, intersectionality's entry into the policy arena was distinctive, and objectives among key actors seem to have differed from those at Westminster. The actors involved may have influenced the particular meanings and uses of intersectionality in Scottish equality policy. There is evidence to suggest, for example, that relatively powerful, predominantly white organizations in the Scottish women's sector were, at the time, opposed to a wider equality agenda represented by the creation of the EHRC, the Equality Act and PSED, and as such championed particular ways of thinking about intersectionality that perhaps were easier to assimilate into policy making. A leading organization, for example, opposed the inclusion of religion in the PSED and wrote, 'in practice, the diluted focus on gender under the PSED amounts to regression' (Engender 2014, 13); and in 2014 reiterated a call for a gender mainstreaming approach to equality overall (Engender 2014). Another organization wrote, 'although it is clearly important for public authorities to be aware of intersectional issues, the specific equality duties were designed and implemented to address institutional racism, sexism and exclusion of disabled people. The system [sic] inequalities that provoked the establishment of these duties have not been dismantled' (Close the Gap 2010, 5). The political legacies of women's sectors have been identified as important to whether and how they use intersectionality (Lépinard 2014). Moreover, the women's sector has tended to enjoy a relatively privileged position vis-à-vis the Scottish government, as compared with other equality sectors (see also McCabe 2023; Christoffersen and McCabe forthcoming). For example, the Scottish National Equality Improvement Project, established in 2014 by the Scottish government to help drive improved performance on the PSED, had only a women's organization on the core project team, to the exclusion of other equality strands. In contrast, research has found that the (more racially diverse, though not uniformly) women's sector in England was broadly supportive of the wider equalities agenda (Hermanin et al 2012).

Gender has been a priority consideration of the Scottish government as compared with other equality areas since devolution. This prioritization is evident in the regulations or Scottish 'specific duties' which support the Equality Act, as well as in new legislation. For instance, public authorities are required to publish their pay gaps relating only to gender, and the Scottish government published the first national action plan on the gender pay gap in the UK in 2019. Development of an Ethnicity Pay Gap strategy formed part of the 2021 Programme for Government, nearly 10 years following the introduction of the requirement to publish gender pay gaps. The government also legislated for the introduction of a gender quota for public boards (2018). Quotas have been suggested and are now in place only in relation to gender. In relation to other protected characteristics, public bodies are not required to publish their board composition or to reach a representation target, rather they should show evidence of 'diversity succession planning' for board appointments. This is in spite of racial justice organizations raising concerns around the implications of the sole focus on gender for women of colour in particular (Scottish Government 2016a), and the government noting that it could be perceived as unfair (Scottish Government 2016c). The organization CEMVO Scotland wrote,

> Whilst we welcome the opportunity for Public boards to become more representative of the diverse community that we live in, we have concerns that by developing this approach through the lens of gender that the wider implications for other protected characteristics have not been considered. There have been attempts to tackle gender inequality before for example the first Scottish Parliament had 50:50 representations; however this failed to have any impact for [Black and minority ethnic] BME women … without actions that would support women of all backgrounds these [measures] will be limited and therefore the impact of achieving true gender equality will remain minimal. (Scottish Government 2016a)

The government's response to the full consultation notes 'responses to the consultation felt it to be unclear as to why gender balance was being prioritised in relation to board diversity when many groups are underrepresented and this could be perceived as unfair' (Scottish Government 2016c). However, following the consultation, the amendments were passed with minimal changes. As has been argued elsewhere, 'when differences are … treated as constituting an add-on to the variable of gender … [this] perpetuates policy privileges to affluent, educated, white women' (Hankivsky and Cormier 2011, 218). In short, policy interest in intersectionality in Scotland sits uncomfortably alongside new gender-specific measures where women are treated homogeneously. Moreover, in contrast to wide acknowledgement of gender inequality and policy prioritization of gender, in Scotland meaningful policy engagement with structural racism is relatively recent.

Research on equality mainstreaming in the UK also found an ambivalent relationship between intersectionality and Scottish equality policy, with mixed perceptions among NGO sector, government and academic respondents as to whether intersectionality has influenced equality mainstreaming efforts, confirming 'an uncertain relationship between the UK's joined-up equality legislation and intersectionality' in Scotland as well as the other devolved nations (Hankivsky et al 2019, 10). While government respondents were more positive about the extent to which intersectionality has been taken up in the context of equality mainstreaming, equality NGO sector respondents tended toward scepticism (Hankivsky et al 2019).

Meanings and uses of 'intersectionality' in equality policy documents

Overall, analysis of equality policy documents reflects divergence between England and Scotland in terms of policy commitment to equality, particularly since the UK election of 2010. This is evident, for instance, in the regulations to support the Equality Act, known as the specific duties, which are greater in number and far more robust in Scotland than in England. This divergence likely contributes to accounting for differences in the relative volume and type of documents that intersectionality appears in across the two countries, according to my analysis of documents published between 2003 and 2017. In Scotland, 'intersectionality' was included in government publications, including high-level documents such as equality statements accompanying draft budgets (Scottish Government 2010, 2011) and the government's equality outcomes and mainstreaming reports (Scottish Government 2013a, 2017b). In contrast to England, there was evidence of the term being used in parliamentary committees on a number of occasions, including by the Cabinet Secretary for Equalities.

At Westminster, the same search largely returned department and agency blog posts and documents related to intersectionality in the context of international development, rather than domestic equality policy.

Intersectionality in England: a curtailed engagement

In England, the Equalities Review (Cabinet Office 2007), which foregrounded changes in equality law culminating in the Equality Act, indicated that it wished to capture issues of intersectionality across the 'equality strands'. Yet in my search, I did not find the term 'intersectionality' in government publications, such as the equality strategy or parliamentary records, but rather in EHRC documents (for example, Equality and Human Rights Commission 2015a).

Definitions: lacking

Intersectionality was defined less frequently in EHRC documents than in publications of the Scottish government. At times 'intersectionality' was used interchangeably with 'multiple identities' (for example, Equality and Human Rights Commission 2009a), when intersectionality theorists argue that it means something quite different, that an understanding of identity as mutually constituted by intersecting factors is antithetical to an additive approach (suggesting that equality areas, rather than being mutually constituting, can be separated from one another) (Yuval-Davis 2006).

In one document, 'intersectional group concerns' were defined as 'those that cut across different characteristics' (Equality and Human Rights Commission 2016a, 5). This suggests a perception of intersectionality as looking for common issues across equality strands still ultimately in some way separately conceived, rather than examining how strands are mutually constitutive. In another, intersectionality was considered as '[multiple disadvantage] across the statutorily recognised equality strands' (Equality and Human Rights Commission 2010, xii), suggesting an individualized and additive view of intersectionality.

Uses: intersectionality deferred, denied

In these documents, intersectionality was used in different ways: intersectional analysis was called for (rather than undertaken) (Equality and Human Rights Commission 2012b); as an analysis that should be done, but was not because of time and resources (Equality and Human Rights Commission 2012a); intersectionality was viewed as something on which literature and evidence are limited (Equality and Human Rights Commission 2009b; Department for Work and Pensions 2012); intersectionality was viewed as a complication that makes targeted intervention to remove barriers impossible (Bowes et al 2015); and as something that has not been empirically demonstrated: 'this review concluded that there is currently little in the way of statistically significant evidence of increased inequality by multiple characteristics' (Equality and Human Rights Commission 2015b, 23).

Intersectionality in Scotland: a nominal growth?

In contrast to England, in Scotland 'intersectionality' appeared in all equality-related strategies that I found, and in fact, the Scottish government has evidenced some engagement with the term 'intersectionality' since at least 2001 (Scottish Government 2003). A shift in terminology from 'multiple' identities/discrimination, to intersectionality, is in evidence. For instance, in the equality statements accompanying the draft budgets, terminology shifted from 'multiple characteristics' (Scottish Government 2010) to 'intersectionality' (Scottish Government 2011); and in the Equality Evidence Strategy 2014, 'intersection' was favoured over 'strand' or 'characteristic' (Scottish Government 2014).

Here, where intersectionality was taken up to a greater extent, in contrast to a visibility project concerning women of colour (Hancock 2016), intersectionality was used in pursuit of a more generalized or generic 'equality' and applied to an array of marginalized social groups, specifically the nine protected characteristic groups named in the Equality Act, as well as others not protected by the Act. Following Hancock (2016), among others, depending on whether race/gender continues to be a central focus, intersectionality's uses in Scottish policy could be read as an expanded application, or an elision of Black women, women of colour and the particular intersection of race and gender. While when the term intersectionality was used, 'ethnicity' or race was often listed in documents among equality areas to consider, meaningful engagement with race was inconsistent and often lacking.

Definitions: shifting, individualized and additive

In Scottish equality policy documents, I found several definitions of intersectionality and, similar to England, these evidence an individualized view of intersectionality, as well as an additive one. In the Equality statement on the Scottish spending review 2011 and draft budget 2012–13, for example, intersectionality was defined as

> a means of understanding how various categories such as gender, race, class, disability, and other axes of identity interact on multiple and *often* simultaneous levels, contributing to systematic social inequality, emphasising that individuals cannot be analysed through a single identity lens ... we remain aware of the importance of understanding the intersectionality of equality characteristics that individuals *carry*. (Scottish Government 2011, 90; emphasis added)

This inscribes an understanding of intersectionality as something that happens sometimes, as well as something descriptive of the facets of identity that individual people 'carry' or have, rather than corresponding to the relationship among structures of inequality in which we are all located. I found similar uses in other documents (Scottish Government 2014, 6), including in the equality outcomes, arguably the most important document governing equality policy (Scottish Government 2013a).

In these definitions, intersectionality was considered primarily as a descriptive attribute of individuals, wherein equality characteristics can be added and subtracted, rather than constructing one another. In none of the documents that I examined was intersectionality contextualized as originating within Black women's thought and activism.

Uses: degrees of engagement

Related to the meanings employed, a superficial use of intersectionality was apparent in the documents. For example, the document 'Rights to Reality: A Framework of Action for Independent Living in Scotland 2013 to 2015' states 'this document has been designed to take account of all equality characteristics and intersectional issues, to ensure independent living becomes a reality for all disabled people in Scotland regardless of age, race, gender, religion or sexual orientation' (Scottish Government 2013b, 8). However, other equality characteristics were mentioned only in one paragraph of the 91-page framework.

Similar to England, intersectionality was at times treated as something that should be considered but was not (Scottish Government 2010, 2011, 2014). Intersectionality was identified as an area for learning and development on the part of equality policy makers in the Scottish government's equality outcomes 2013–17, to meet an outcome to increase policy makers' confidence and knowledge on equality and diversity (Scottish Government 2013a). The document stated that by the end of 2016 a targeted programme of information sharing and development around areas including intersectionality would have been rolled out. Though it mentions specific training undertaken by policy makers, the progress report on these outcomes did not mention the delivery of any development around intersectionality (Scottish Government 2017b).

The greatest engagement with intersectionality was found within the only document with a primary focus on race: The Race Equality Framework for Scotland 2016–2030, co-produced with the Coalition for Racial Equality and Rights (CRER), where intersectionality is an overarching guiding principle (Scottish Government 2016b). A similar strategic engagement has not been found in England. This was Scotland's first strategic document related to race equality since 2008. In relation to intersectionality, it stated:

> The voices of women and young people were particularly strong in engagement activities and positively informed the Vision and Goals. We recognise that racism and gender inequality are not mutually exclusive forms of discrimination. Indeed, too often they intersect giving rise to compound or double discrimination. We therefore intend to pay particular attention to gender alongside race so that the framework is effective. (Scottish Government 2016b, 12)

However, throughout the document, women of colour were not pulled out as a group for analysis, with the exception of the discussion of health policy and interventions; and no specific actions were targeted to women (Scottish Government 2016b). Yet, intersectionality was mentioned in the implementation approach published the following year (Scottish Government 2017a), which stated that further consultation with specific groups was or will be undertaken to inform implementation, and a minority ethnic women's network has been established with events held to link into the Race Equality Framework actions. It is understood that there were key individual intersectionality advocates involved in developing this consultative strategy, influencing the focus on gender along with race.

Discussion

Overall, findings indicate policy divergence between England and Scotland around a political commitment to applying intersectionality. Only in

Scotland did it appear in recent government publications, parliamentary records and equality-related strategies concerned with domestic equality policy. Moreover, only in English documents was intersectionality dismissed as a complication or as something which has not been proven. Yet among both EHRC and Scottish government documents, the greatest level of engagement with intersectionality was found in the most recent of these, so nominal engagement with it appeared to be increasing. However, in policy documents in both countries, decontextualized, individualized definitions largely foreclose consideration of structural or institutional inequalities, including structural or institutional racism, as they are constructed by other systems of inequality. This is consistent with previous research where it has been argued that the dominant approach to intersectionality in policy is to consider it at the personal identity level, as an attribute of individuals (Parken 2010; May 2015).

I also found that inequalities were considered additively, so that equality factors including race were envisioned as being able to be legitimately subtracted from consideration of other equality areas. Moreover, I found uses of intersectionality overall to be largely superficial, with little meaningful engagement of the mutually constituting nature of inequalities in general, and race in particular. Furthermore, I have highlighted a discrepancy between debates in intersectionality theory, as to the centrality of race and the social location of women of colour, and intersectionality's meanings and uses in policy documents. This resonates with literature in the field (May 2015).

Intersectionality's definitions and uses vary across specific equality policy areas. The Scottish race equality strategy – the strategy examined that is based most on co-production with the NGO sector and on community engagement, and involved key intersectionality advocates in its development – showed the greatest level of engagement with intersectionality. In general equality policy in contrast, and that focused on gender and disability, engagement with intersectionality and the intersection of race was superficial and employed depoliticized definitions.

While from an intersectional perspective little progress on equality will ever be made without 'doing' intersectionality, in the UK the policy problem is largely framed as whether or not we will get to intersectionality, with intersectionality positioned as a kind of luxury, resources and time allowing. This is in spite of the Equality Act 2010 having been heralded as providing opportunities for operationalizing intersectionality. It was in this context and within these public discourses that equality practitioners in the NGO sector gave meaning and application to intersectionality, within further challenges of austerity and their position in relation to the state.

Having explored the implications of equality policy in England and Scotland for intersectionality, I turn to contextualize the chapters to follow in contexts of 'austerity', here used to mean post-2008 economic recession policies pursuing deficit reduction through cuts to public spending and tax increases in the UK.

Austerity

With the Equality Act 2010, equality policy may, on the surface, seem to have grown to be more facilitative to considering intersectionality than it was prior. However, during the same period that the Act has been implemented, the contexts of austerity and Brexit have contributed to a significant deepening of inequalities. Austerity has disproportionately affected those who were already intersectionally marginalized, including the overlapping groups of women of colour (Bassel and Emejulu 2017), disabled people (Committee on the Rights of Persons with Disabilities 2017) and migrants. This politics has also propelled intersectional activist and social movement resistance (Bassel and Emejulu 2017; Emejulu and Bassel 2018, 2020; Emejulu and van der Scheer 2021).

Moreover, austerity has decimated the equality NGO sector, an important agent of policy influence and implementation (for exploration in specific sectors see Colgan et al 2014; Vacchelli et al 2015), and particularly impacting intersectional organizations (Bassel and Emejulu 2014; Hankivsky et al 2019). Furthermore, austerity has depleted the EHRC as well as dedicated equality posts in the public sector, including local councils, and education and health services. Diminished resourcing for all of these groups, as well as for policy action on inequalities means that although the term 'intersectionality' may be increasingly used, intersecting inequalities are not being effectively addressed, and in fact, intersectionally marginalized groups are bearing the brunt of austerity (Bassel and Emejulu 2017; Committee on the Rights of Persons with Disabilities 2017; Women's Budget Group et al 2017).

Despite a different political context, austerity has had similar effects in Scotland, though not as severe on the equality NGO sector; here, in contrast to England which has seen a cutting back of infrastructure funding for NGOs, and equality NGOs among them, from both public and private sources, the Scottish government has taken responsibility for funding many equality organizations (Chaney 2012a). Importantly however, in this context of fewer dedicated resources for equality as well as equality 'mainstreaming', Scottish equality NGOs perceive a 'generic' approach to equality in policy, replacing the previous stranded approaches. Equality organizations in Scotland pushed back against this generic approach:

> The response from public authorities to the public sector equality duty has essentially been to treat protected characteristics in an undifferentiated way, glossing over or ignoring the specific

disadvantage and discrimination faced by specific groups of people. Public bodies increasingly attempt to consider multiple characteristics at the same time, and without adequate data or characteristic-specific competence ... contrary to the warning of the three predecessor equality bodies, our collective sense is that the publication and process requirements of the public sector equality duty are now almost universally carried out using a highly genericised approach that spans all of the protected characteristics. (Inclusion Scotland et al 2017, 4)

In both countries, the context of austerity presents barriers to operationalizing intersectionality:

The current political and economic climate has increased the fragility of our member organisations who occupy a space that has historically been a socio-political wasteland; one that exists in the intersection between gender and marginalised ethno-cultural identities. Where practitioners attempt to address other areas of structural inequality, for example around sexuality, they have rarely been able to do so in any meaningful, systematic way as they often become anxious about adding further layers to their marginalization. (Larasi 2011, 5)

Similarly, Leah Bassel and Akwugo Emejulu argue that:

The ability of actors seeking to represent 'intersectional interests' within the NGO sector is under threat because these claims may be silenced and/or misrecognized due to the prevailing marketized logic of the sector ... it is difficult for these organizations to inflect agendas with multiple-axis (race, class, legal status, and gender) concerns because these may well delegitimize their efforts and weaken their competitive advantage vis-à-vis other organizations vying for the same funding. (Bassel and Emejulu 2014, 133)

Operationalizing intersectionality in the context of austerity

In seeking to operationalize intersectionality, equality NGOs face challenges relating to neoliberal austerity: lack of funding for intersectional work and competitive funding environments. While some of these challenges pre-date post-2008 austerity politics (particularly funding issues), austerity has exacerbated these. The first of these challenges is particular to equality organizations and intersectionality, while the second has particular implications for intersectionality related to possibilities for coalition and solidarity building.

Austerity funding

Equality organizations have tended to be funded by both public and private sources, the latter particularly in England where there is a greater number of private trusts and foundations than in Scotland. In recent decades, funding from both sources has become more and more restricted, tied to short-term projects contingent upon delivering outcomes agreed with funders, or received as contracts to deliver public services. In response, some organizations have successfully broadened their funding to include more independent, unrestricted sources such as individual donors and social enterprise. Yet the most successful at this were often already relatively large and powerful organizations in their sub-sectors, and able to draw on more economically advantaged constituencies. However, for other organizations, equality 'causes', particularly intersectional ones, are often not popular, and the support to smaller organizations to enable successful enterprise has often been lacking.

While the equality sector and specific sub-sectors and intersectional organizations within it have long been underfunded compared with much of the rest of the NGO sector (Small 1994; Kairos in Soho 2012), austerity has exacerbated these inequalities. Diminished funding associated with austerity has had devastating impacts for equality organizations (CEMVO (Council for Ethnic Minority Voluntary Organisations) 2010; Colgan et al 2014; Vacchelli et al 2015). Moreover, austerity has made it more difficult for equality organizations to make funding asks, or tenders in the case of service providers, based around multiple-axis needs or priorities: when intersectionality is conceptualized as work by and for particular intersectionally marginalized groups, it is viewed as 'niche', having few beneficiaries and, therefore, not value for money, as Anika,[9] director of a small, funded women of colour organization in England, explains: "Invariably what happens is that the [women of colour] sector doesn't get the funding because most local authorities … want to fund a generic service." Therefore, much intersectional work is actually unfunded, according to Emma, practitioner in a small funded racial justice organization: "The nature of funding … is that it is very constricted what your funding could do … which means a lot of the [intersectional] work that's done is done on goodwill." Funding is also increasingly short-term, with some networks funded for only one year at a time, with no certainty that they will be able to carry on resourced after that point.

In this context of scarcity, the funding environment becomes increasingly competitive, which is generally negative for coalition building and for political solidarity (Scholz 2008) between members; a finding also supported by previous research (Bassel and Emejulu 2014). In network organizer Nicola's words: "Ultimately, we're all friends until, we're losing funding, right?"

Raka, director of a small, funded, racially minoritized women of faith organization agreed: "When funding is kind of skint ... [people think] 'I don't want to share with somebody else in case they take my ideas'."

Having contextualized the research within austerity and its implications for the equality NGO sector, in the last section of this chapter I discuss the sector's relationships with the state in contexts of both equality policy and discourse, and austerity, in more detail.

Equality organizations and the state

One challenge facing the equality NGO sector, as well as the NGO sector more widely, is the increasing policy move to include individuals as political actors in equality policy. In the case of one network which was conceived by local government, government actors specifically sought to bring individual community members onto a level footing with equality organizations, an approach supported and taken on by network organizers. In another city, the local government, similarly, is now seeking to engage individuals as 'civil society' actors. On the one hand, this is viewed positively by some participants, and can be perceived positively for intersectional practice: this potentially facilitates inclusion of radical individual activists and campaigners who may not be affiliated with organizations, as well as those marginalized by or excluded from organizations. On the other hand, some equality organizations view themselves as to some extent representative of equality communities (and indeed, some are membership organizations with sizeable memberships). Practitioners also view themselves as having *specialist knowledge* built not solely from their identifications within equality communities, but from their experience of working in equalities. The inclusion of individuals as political actors by virtue of their having 'protected characteristics' on a par with equality organizations destabilizes the place of organizations' specialist knowledge and representativeness, and ultimately collective action, as Diane, a practitioner in a small, funded women's organization in England explains: "Civil society in all its forms, apart from the existing established [equality sector organizations] ... but, as a group we can achieve more, have more protection. That's disappearing. Yeah, a little bit frightening."

Power relationships

When seeking to operationalize intersectionality through policy influence, equality NGOs are hindered by barriers of power imbalances with local government and public sector actors. 'Power' is perceived by participants, and used here, in two senses: (i) the ability to enact meaningful policy change and participate as equals with policy makers; (ii) as relations constructed by intersecting axes of inequality (Collins and Bilge 2016). I argue that equality organizations are significantly constrained in their ability to use ideas of intersectionality by the subordinate positions they hold vis-à-vis both local government and the public sector, which are reflected in feelings that they have minimal influence, material inequalities, curtailed independence, and interpersonal relationships structured by power inequities.

As background, in the UK, successive governments have enacted legislation and regulations eroding NGOs' abilities to freely engage in campaigning. Few funders will fund organizations for this purpose and charities in receipt of UK government funding are prohibited from using this funding for 'political lobbying'.[10] Furthermore, participants report that some public service commissioning prohibits NGOs with public service contracts from engaging in advocacy. As network organizer Elizabeth notes, while there are "opportunities to [challenge embedded institutional inequalities] … it's making sure that you take them and then there are sometimes sort of tensions within where your funding comes from."

Yet, equality organizations recognize that the social change intersectionality demands requires state action, and they have a vital role to contribute to the state addressing intersectionality. For example, Linda, director of a small, funded, disabled people's organization in England has been involved in training police to identify hate crimes across multiple axes; not an easy task: "They'll look at you and say, 'I can only flag [the crime] as one [thing]', you go, 'Just try it, just try it'. And they go, 'Ooh I didn't know I could do that!'."

However, participants feel their capacity to effect change is extremely limited. While in Scotland NGOs have much closer relationships with policy makers than in England, here too at local level practitioners perceive that though they are the experts at working with and understanding the experiences of those who are marginalized, recognition for this is lacking, and nonetheless their influence is minimal; as Yvonne, director of a small, funded women's organization in Scotland explains:

> 'We are the kinda coal face workers dealing with these issues and I think that that's sometimes forgotten … we've always been trying to drive the agenda as opposed to respond to their agenda. That's where you get that sense of powerlessness. It is that no matter how hard we try to be drivers we're not we're not, we're not.'

Another participant feels similarly: "We have a lot of answers. What we can't do is actually make any fucking difference whatsoever because we have no power" (attribution omitted).

This marginality in relation to the state is reflected in networks' experience of providing input into local equality strategies, a key way in which they perceive themselves as operationalizing intersectionality, discussed in detail in Chapter 6. While experiences varied, in some cases involvement of equality organizations in formulating these strategies was last minute, and not experienced as meaningful, in the words of one network organizer.

> 'I feel that we don't get involved as fully as we would like or as fully as the legislation expects the communities but the civil servants, it's almost like we're a hindrance to getting a piece of work done… it's like, "You know, we're just getting this out, it's a high-level thing. Of course, when we're implementing the equality [strategy], we'll be in touch," nobody's been in touch and it's a year later.' (Attribution omitted)

Many organizations also engage strategically without being funded to do so. Often, in order to engage in policy concerning equality and intersectionality, equality organizations are, in effect, asked to give up time, unpaid since this work is not funded, to sit at a table in a consultative role in a context where the others present, civil servants and decision-makers, are remunerated and hold decision-making power. Therefore, "The [NGO] sector are still at the bottom rung and until we are equally funded … and equally respected, that's not really going to change" (Yvonne, director, women's organization, Scotland).

Sometimes, practitioners feel they are used instrumentally, reported to only after the decisions have been made, so that public sector organizations can say that they have met Equality Act duties to consult with 'protected characteristic' groups.[11] In some of these interactions, attention to inequalities and especially to the interactions between them are framed by decision-makers as a luxury which austerity cannot afford; equality organizations feel they are at times constructed as 'greedy'. The unpaid time that equality organizations contribute is scarce since in the funding environment organizations' time is strictly allocated to meeting outcomes agreed with funders. Alternatively, some that are funded to engage strategically are not made effective use of by relevant public bodies. Reflecting on participation in these spaces, one network organizer felt:

> 'These are not spaces of change … this is not the space where there's a robust, full and frank sharing of views … the decision-making has been done prior, and these committees – it's about: "Here's your paper, do you agree three proposals, accept the things that they put, get a working group set up, okay", few questions are asked.' (Attribution omitted)

Participants further perceive that the extent of their influence is very dependent on political parties in power at local level. Yet, equality organization efforts to effect policy change to take account of intersectionality are crucial. Policy makers report that the efforts that they have made in this regard have been due to equality sector influence. However, in trying to influence policy to take account of intersectional marginalization, equality organizations face institutional inequalities that compound marginality experienced by other NGOs.

Many participants value NGO sector independence from the state highly. At times, this is quite deliberately curtailed by local government. Some local equality networks that were established by policy makers were set up to be essentially governed by state and public sector actors. These were referred to by one participant as 'puppet structures'. While other networks are able to act as 'critical friends' to state actors (to an extent, given that they may be funded by them), seeking to influence policy and service provision, and challenging decisions that have been made, there is little evidence of those governed by state actors having played a similar critical role. This is significant since few others have access to policy making structures to offer any critical input.

Beyond these structural issues affecting how racial justice, feminist, LGBTI, disability and refugee rights organizations and networks of them are perceived and treated, at an interpersonal level participants report cases of disrespect, and direct and indirect discrimination, from civil servants towards intersectionally marginalized colleagues (particularly women of colour) trying to engage the state around issues of intersectionality. Since equality networks tend to be made up of relatively powerful organizations within their respective sectors, if this account is reflective of their experiences engaging with the state, more grassroots, voluntary and radical organizations of intersectionally marginalized people are sure to be yet further marginalized.

Conclusions

In this chapter, I provided an analysis of the context in which equality NGOs conceptualize and operationalize intersectionality. This context is characterized by: distinctive equality policy and discourse, and intersectionality's relationship to it; austerity, which has significant material implications for equality organizing; and equality organizations' relationships to the state, wherein they perceive that they have minimal influence, and experience material inequalities, curtailed independence, and at times discrimination in interpersonal relationships with policy actors.

The term 'intersectionality' is growing in popularity in equality policy. Yet, analysis of intersectionality's meanings and uses in equality policy documents reveals that a range of definitions of intersectionality are in use which are decontextualized from its origins, and which are also largely individualized: merely descriptive, additive and superficial, leaving its potential unrealized. Furthermore, meaningful engagement with race and race/gender as central social organizing logics and categories of intersectionality theory is lacking in policy documents not specifically concerning race equality. In other words, when research indicates policy engagement with and commitment to intersectionality, it is important to pay particular and close attention to the specific meanings and uses of intersectionality inscribed in the specific policy context. These findings echo my reading of the literature on intersectionality and public policy in Chapter 2.

My analysis of equality policy documents raises questions including: is this inevitable? Is it true that, as Collins and Bilge note, 'the growth, acceptance and legitimation of intersectionality within ... some public policy venues necessarily changes its composition and purpose' (Collins and Bilge 2016, 198)? Moreover, what is the relationship between representation among decision-makers and definitions of intersectionality? In Scotland, there had not, up until 2021, been a woman of colour elected to Parliament, and representation of equality groups, particularly people of colour among both those elected and civil servants, remains lacking (in spite of positive action measures enabled by but underused in the context of the Equality Act). Who is creating policy documents influences the understandings of intersectionality contained therein. While a coalition of equality organizations[12] is working with political parties to effect change in this regard, relations of power and privilege generate vested interests in maintaining the status quo.

The meanings and uses of intersectionality in equality policy are both influenced by and influence understandings of intersectionality among NGOs. The equality NGO sector can be viewed as a resource for policy makers interested in working intersectionally: my analysis of equality policy documents has found the most meaningful engagement with intersectionality to be concomitant with NGO sector co-production. Yet, this may depend on which sub-sector within the equality NGO sector we mean. Intersectionality's particular meanings and uses in policy, including those which fail to engage race, are related to the aims of the specific actors involved in influencing equality policy, and the relative power between them. In Scotland, predominantly white national feminist organizations which have historically done little work around race themselves (Squires 2008a), and have opposed a wider equalities agenda, have had a disproportionate influence on equality policy. Here, inscribed understandings of intersectionality are often as an attribute of marginalized individuals. This is not necessarily helpful, and may, in fact, exacerbate stigma and marginalization. In short, the Equality Act and its accompanying discourses do not provide equality practitioners, organizations and networks with a secure basis on which to proceed to understand or to operationalize intersectionality; in fact, they are characterized by a superficial engagement with intersectionality given shifting meanings, which thus leaves intersectionality underdetermined. In other words, there are not only shifting theoretical meanings of intersectionality in the literature (Chapter 2), but also empirical ones in the policy context, suggesting a need to further examine meanings of intersectionality in practice to inform intersectionality's growing interpretation by policy makers.

Equality organizations in my sample, working predominantly at local level, operate in these national policy contexts, and are significantly hampered in their efforts to operationalize intersectionality by neoliberal austerity contexts and the low status they occupy vis-à-vis local governments and the public sector. Nevertheless, they seek to do so, in competing and contradicting ways which the following chapters will discuss in detail.

4

Perceptions and Practices: The Spectrum of 'Intersectionality'

'I think [intersectionality is] a word that could come under … virtue signalling … there's not like ever any analysis into what intersectionality means … it's a word that people know that has got to be ticked off.'

Nicola, network organizer

Intersectionality theory typically includes the elements that I identified in Chapter 2: mutual constitution of inequalities; different levels of analysis; relationality; and focus on those who are intersectionally marginalized (in particular Black women and women of colour).[1] However, as I will show, in practice, different meanings are adopted. While past studies have documented how intersectionality is practised in specific movements, organizations and contexts, my research explored what *meanings* of intersectionality are related to these practices, in the UK equality NGO sector. Intersectionality presents a huge challenge to the status quo of siloed equality work, and while some organizations and practitioners engage with this challenge, others subvert intersectionality for other purposes, or seek to merely incorporate it into the status quo, emptying it of its transformative potential in the process. Competing meanings are important because each has different implications for intersectionally marginalized groups and intersectional justice.

In the chapter that follows, I will outline five 'applied concepts' of intersectionality derived from my data (Christoffersen 2021a). When embarking on this research project, I maintained a separation between how intersectionality is 'conceptualized' on the one hand and 'operationalized' on the other, reflected for example in my interview discussion guide. During analysis, I initially coded 'conceptualization' separately from 'operationalization'. However, I found that participants tended to articulate their understandings of intersectionality, that is, what it meant to them, by expressing how they apply it, or would apply it, in their equality sector practice; or similarly, by the implications of what it means for how policy makers and the public sector should act. In other words, the distinction between conceptualization and operationalization reflected in my interview discussion guide more or less collapsed in the process of data analysis. This makes sense when we think about intersectionality as being largely a 'praxis' (Collins and Bilge 2016). It is for these reasons that I refer to these as 'applied concepts'.

I asked participants directly what intersectionality means to them, and sought out meanings in their wider narratives, as well as in documents. I also observed understandings at work in meetings and events. Many different meanings of intersectionality were ultimately identified based on all of these data. Yet, particularly when looking at the networks as a whole, and then across them, five emerged as being particularly prevalent, in some cases, opposing, and generally having a range of significant practice implications driving networks, projects and other equality work. These concepts are:

1. generic intersectionality;
2. pan equality intersectionality;
3. multi-strand intersectionality;
4. diversity-within: work within an equality strand;
5. 'intersections of equality strands': work at the intersections of equality strands.[2]

Some, but not all, of these concepts are conceptually exclusive to one another. Notwithstanding this, in practice, the same networks, organizations and even individuals may employ multiple concepts. In fact, contradicting concepts were at times used within the same conversation or interview. Use of competing concepts may be instrumental, to gain funding for example; it is also done in interaction with wider discourses. However, my sense is that for many participant practitioners who employ contradicting concepts, this is because they are still exploring what intersectionality does mean and how to use it in practice. As Nicola explained: "It's one of those words you wonder if everybody quite knows what it's all about."

For each of the five concepts:

1. I will explain what it is and provide examples of how it works in practice. In some ways, these concepts follow from organizational structures, and they also each have implications for which organizational structure would be best suited to operationalize (this understanding of) intersectionality.
2. I will analyse who holds the understanding, and why: how did they learn about intersectionality, what do they identify as the sources of their knowledge?

3. Next, I will ask, how did this meaning of intersectionality gain prominence? Are there salient differences between England and Scotland?
4. Perhaps most significantly, what are the implications of this understanding for intersectionally marginalized groups? What are the wider implications? Is there any resistance to it?
5. Furthermore, what is the relationship of this meaning to key concepts in intersectionality theory identified in Chapter 2?

In considering questions 3 and 4, I will also draw on a co-construction workshop held with participants after my fieldwork was completed.

I will argue that the term 'intersectionality' is understood and used in multiple, contradicting ways. Some of these uses are likely to be more effective than others at furthering equality for intersectionally marginalized communities, while some, in spite of being described as intersectionality, further entrench inequalities, at times in insidious ways.

I will outline each concept of intersectionality in turn, and then move to a general discussion. Concepts are also included in Table 4.1.

Intersectionality as generic equality

'Generic intersectionality' is a concept of intersectionality wherein there is no focus, or very little focus, on any equality strand or strands in particular. The same or similar work is delivered to benefit 'all'. Crucially, work aims to address issues that affect 'everybody', that is, not only, or even primarily, marginalized equality groups (Christoffersen 2021a, 2022).

One network in particular employed an understanding and application of intersectionality that I characterize as generic. For instance, network organizer Leanne identified that one way the network practises intersectionality has been to structure work around issues, rather than protected characteristics/equality strands:

> 'We made the decision to have discussions around themes rather than equality strands or communities of interest. That was a very conscious decision to have that intersectional focus without calling it an intersectional focus ... [because] ... those areas affect everybody from all groups ... an intersectional approach ... [is] ... issues that do affect everybody ... all people are at an equal standing in the network.'

In employing this understanding, the network sought to avoid an essentialist framing of issues as belonging to certain groups, by recognizing the overlap between groups. Framing discussion around issues is very different from a multi-strand understanding of intersectionality, discussed later in this chapter, in which discussion is framed around each equality strand,

Table 4.1: Applied concepts of intersectionality

Name	Meaning	Practice examples	Relationship to intersectionality as a theoretical framework			
			Additive vs. mutually constitutive	Individual vs. structural level of analysis	Relationality/ simultaneity of privilege and oppression	Focus on those who are most disadvantaged
Generic	No focus or very little focus on any equality strand or strands in particular: the same work is delivered to benefit 'all'. Addressing issues that affect 'everybody' (that is, not only or even primarily marginalized equality groups).	Work is addressed at and intended to benefit 'everybody', so intersectionality is envisioned as being 'mainstreamed', or a general approach to the work. Since this concept treats everyone the same, work on specific inequalities is not consistent with this understanding of intersectionality.	Since this concept has no recognition of specific inequality structures, these are considered neither additively nor constitutively.	There is no recognition of inequality structures.	There is no recognition of inequality structures, which would need to be in place before recognizing how they relate to one another.	Does not focus on disadvantaged groups.
Pan equality	Addressing issues that affect all/most marginalized equality groups.	Issues include mental health, hate crime.	Does not necessarily recognize mutual constitution. Issues may be viewed as though they happen to be common to distinct groups; or as being common because of the synthesis of structures of inequality such that the groups overlap.	More structural view than other concepts.	Does not necessarily recognize the interrelationship of structures.	Some networks/organizations seek to focus on those who are intersectionally marginalized within these wider issue campaigns, but not always.

Table 4.1: Applied concepts of intersectionality (continued)

Name	Meaning	Practice examples	Relationship to intersectionality as a theoretical framework			
			Additive vs. mutually constitutive	Individual vs. structural level of analysis	Relationality/ simultaneity of privilege and oppression	Focus on those who are most disadvantaged
Multi-strand	Addressing equality strands in parallel, separately, simultaneously and equivalently.	Some network collaboration and engagement on the development of local equality strategies.	Additive.	Either, but structures would be conceptualized as separate. When conceptualized individually, multi-strand is synonymous with 'diversity'.	Does not recognize the interrelationship of structures, and consequently views people as solely oppressed or privileged.	No particular focus. Inclusive of an idea that all strands should be included and treated equally, that no strand is more important.
Diversity–within	Addressing intersections within an equality strand, for example, differences among women. One strand/inequality viewed as primary.	How intersectionality is often addressed within single-strand organizations: inclusion projects targeted at intersectionally marginalized groups.	Additive.	Mainly individual; neglects interactions of structures of inequality, since it views one inequality as fundamental.	Not recognized insofar as it is additive. Views groups as solely oppressed/ privileged along the primary axis. Belonging to other equality strands usually thought about as 'additional barriers'.	The primary inequality is predefined.

(continued)

Table 4.1: Applied concepts of intersectionality (continued)

Name	Meaning	Practice examples	Relationship to intersectionality as a theoretical framework			
			Additive vs. mutually constitutive	Individual vs. structural level of analysis	Relationality/ simultaneity of privilege and oppression	Focus on those who are most disadvantaged
Intersections of equality strands	Work of/with specific groups sharing intersecting identities, for example, women of colour, disabled women. No particular strand is primary or more in focus than the other(s).	'Intersectional' organizations.[a] Intersectional alliances (formal and informal partnership projects across equality strands; relatively equitable partnerships).	Tends to capture ideas of mutual constitution.	Multiple levels.	Recognized.	Does focus on issues of who is felt to be disadvantaged, though specific markers may be predefined.

[a] Used to mean organizations constituted at the intersection of equality strands, for example, a Black LGBT organization, as distinct from single-strand organizations. This structure is reflected in mission statements as well as whom the group is led 'by and for'. This is a specific definition of an intersectional organization, while many single-issue organizations (that are not focused on serving and/or representing a specific group experiencing intersecting inequalities in their mission statements, and are led by and for a singularly defined group such as 'women'), may claim to be 'intersectional' organizations. This distinction is well established in the NGO sector, and previously dominant terminology in England was 'community of identity' organizations. An LGBT organization is a community of identity organization, while a Black LGBT organization is an *LGBT* community of identity organization. Moreover, as I discuss in Chapter 5, intersectional organizations are also importantly distinctive in having arisen precisely because single-issue organizations did not represent the interests of intersectionally marginalized people.

and these are addressed separately. Yet other networks have adopted an issue-led approach and still maintained a focus on marginalized, and particularly intersectionally marginalized, equality groups. In seeking to avoid essentialism, the network seemed to lose sight of structures of inequality and relationality between them, where not all issues do affect everybody in the same way. Moreover, working on issues that affect only the most disadvantaged is both foreclosed upon, and constructed as being *not intersectional*.

Speaking of another project, Leanne described how their intersectional approach seeks to avoid essentialism, amounting to treating everyone the same.

> 'We weren't grouping people by characteristic, or community of interest. It was just [undertaking the same work with everyone] ... the idea was for that to be intersectional and also inclusive and accessible. ... We didn't go to a group of people with disabilities and say, you know, "Well, talk to us about your disability?" We ... went to a group of ... BME young carers, and none of them mentioned their BME, or young carer identity. That's not how they're defined in the world and that was really nice.'

On one hand, it may be viewed as positive practice not to expect people to be (solely) defined by their equality strand/s; on the other hand, it seems problematic to celebrate the fact that people of colour talked about equality without mentioning race. The responses given will also be influenced by who was doing the asking – in this case, white practitioners.

An understanding of intersectionality as generic equality has several implications for practice. Work is addressed at and intended to benefit everybody, so in contrast to other understandings that employ targeted projects, intersectionality is envisioned as being 'mainstreamed', or a general approach to the work. Since it treats everyone the same, work on specific inequalities is generally inconsistent with this understanding of intersectionality. Yet within a generic understanding, intersectionality is also mobilized to displace specific attention to racial justice *in particular*, in spite of intersectionality's origins in theorizing the synthesis of race, class and gender; thereby reconstructing 'gender' and 'women' as white.

Who holds this understanding?

The meaning of intersectionality as generic equality was found among policy makers in some contexts, and the overlap between policy makers, the public sector and NGO sectors; I did not find it in more grassroots (unfunded) organizations. In other words, this understanding is limited to more powerful actors. It was prevalent in networks that work at the intersection of 'equality' and 'inequality' (as discussed in Chapter 3).

In terms of individual positionality of participants, this meaning was less prevalent among those with marginalized aspects of identity, and more prevalent among those with privileged ones. It was only associated with white participants (the significance of which will be highlighted in the following discussions). Those who hold this understanding mainly report learning about intersectionality in academic environments.

How did this meaning gain prominence?

Since this concept is so removed from intersectionality's original meanings, and therefore presents serious negative implications for intersectionally marginalized groups, I contextualize it in more detail than the four subsequent concepts that I will discuss.

UK and national levels

At UK and national levels, meanings of intersectionality as 'generic' arose in contexts of 'cohesion', that is, policy fear of racialized minority faiths and divestment from concepts of institutional racism, and a multi-strand equality policy framework. To construct this meaning, intersectionality needed to be emptied of its association with race and race/gender; ideally, racial justice needed to be dispensed with altogether. To this end, amid growing popularity of intersectionality across cities in both England and Scotland, I observed a unique pressure on organizations dedicated to racial justice to relinquish their specific focus on race, in other words, to broaden their areas of work.

From the late 1990s/early 2000s, accelerating following social uprisings of predominantly minority ethnic people in the northern English cities of Bradford, Oldham and Burnley, there was a policy shift away from 'multiculturalism' toward 'cohesion' and 'integration' (Afridi and Warmington 2009; Meer and Modood 2014), that is assimilation (Lewis 2005). As part of this transition, there was a government policy against 'single group' funding (Cantle 2001), later successfully challenged by a key Black[3] feminist organization, Southall Black Sisters. This policy meant that, for a time, organizations led by and for particular minority ethnic communities were not entitled to government funding, as this was constructed as counterproductive to cohesion and integration. Therefore, some equality organizations were forced to place less emphasis on working with their specific target communities (Bhavnani 2005; Afridi and Warmington 2009; Mills 2009).

In 2010, the then Communities Secretary, Labour MP John Denham, stated that it was 'time to move on from the one-dimensional race agenda'

(Craig 2011, 381), in the context of the Equality Act 2010 which, as discussed in Chapter 3, entrenched a move to a united, multiple equalities or 'multi-strand' policy framework. Here, Aziz, director of a funded racial justice organization in Scotland, explains the concerns that they had about the Act in the race sector, which viewed legislation on race as being comparatively strong:

> 'One of the issues with [the Equality Act] and all the race community, race organizations that were dealing with race stuff did have some reservations about the legislation and it's come true in terms of race. What was said at that time is they wanted to bring everybody together so everybody got the same service and all that. The race dealing community was very fearful that the 1971 act [sic] then the amendment act was very strong. It was a strong piece of legislation. We as organizations or practitioners, we were very, very clear that the new legislation should bring the rest to par rather than dumb down the race and it happened. You can see now, the race is nowhere to be seen and where race used to get resources, nobody gets resources now.'

Fears of dilution seem to have come to some fruition as far as race is concerned. In both England and Scotland, since the establishment of the EHRC, which replaced the Commission for Racial Equality (CRE), race equality councils have become less widespread. Many of these councils, first constituted under early race ('community relations') legislation, have closed due to lack of funding which used to come from the CRE. Of those that are left, many now work in a way where race equality is not the focus (for example, through rebranding to 'equality councils' rather than race equality councils). In England, this is not uniform. For those for which this is the case, the Equality Act was cited by participants as the reason for this rebranding. In Scotland however, pressure was more acute, reportedly coming in the form of a directive from the Scottish government for race equality councils to relinquish a dedication to race, and to change their names, as a condition of funding (interview with policy maker, 2018). Moreover, here previous research found that following the closure of the CRE, the EHRC (when it still had funds to disburse to equality organizations) did not fund any racial justice organizations in 2009/10, while in the preceding financial year the race sector had received the largest share of funding, and other strand sectors continued to be funded (Campbell 2014). A director of a former race equality council explained,

> 'EHRC came along which then totally there was no funding ... name-wise because there was no core funding, a lot of [the race equality councils] had to close down. ... We have to move with the times.

Whether we liked it or not. So, therefore the name changes and also our way of working changed.'

The finding that race equality organizations experience various pressures to relinquish a focus on race is very significant, since other strand organizations/sectors (women's, LGBTI, disabled people's) did not report the same pressure to lose the focus on their strand, nor did I observe it. In other words, there seems to have been a clear double standard at play wherein, in the new multi-strand policy context, race equality organizations were expected to immediately begin working on other equality areas, a standard that white-led and predominantly white sectors were not held to in the same way. One reason for this discrepancy is that by policy makers and funders, and equality organizations and practitioners in other sectors also, race equality itself, and the racial justice sector, are constructed as being very specific in a way that, by way of comparison, other (predominantly white, and white-led) single-strand sectors are not (women's, disability, LGBTI). In other words, institutional racism is at work, at the same time that institutional racism is constructed as passé. The equality areas that other sectors work in, always already constructed as white, are concurrently by necessity also (re)constructed as such and as separate from race. This, in turn, effaces the overlapping groups of women of colour, and disabled and LGBTI people of colour.

I found that, further, intersectionality (as generic equality) is used as a rationale for this relinquishment of a focus on race and racism. Moreover, since race is constructed as very specific, and intersectionality as generic, *racial justice organizations are constructed as uniquely incapable of doing intersectionality*, compared with other equality sectors. The following quote is a reflection on these organizations at the time my research was conducted, a good eight years following name changes and broadening of work into 'equality' organizations among the former race equality councils: "I don't think they could generally even now call themselves [intersectional] … organizations" (Peter, policy maker).

Racial justice organizations were viewed as incapable of intersectionality not only by policy makers, but by other (white) equality practitioners employing a generic concept of intersectionality: one similarly stated that they did not feel that a particular organization was intersectional; though it had changed its name to a regional equality council, it was still really doing race (not 'intersectionality'). After a pause, they said, "That obviously is important" (fieldnotes, 2018). This is in spite of the fact that some race equality councils had dedicated work concerning the intersection of race and gender, even before this directive to change focus came about.[4] In fact, the policy maker quoted earlier reflected that they did so, but nevertheless felt that these organizations were incapable of doing intersectionality.

Here, intersectionality is conceptualized generically, firmly distanced from race/gender, and women of colour. Intersectionality is used generically to delegitimize work on race specifically and, in so doing, it reconstructs race as separate from other strand work, reinforcing siloed thinking.

To summarize, there was a perceived hierarchy of grounds before the Equality Act, with race secondary to other inequalities (notably gender, constructed as white; see also Christoffersen, 2024). Thereafter, in contexts of cohesion and the Equality Act, 'intersectionality' has come to be appropriated and instrumentalized to give a new name to generic approaches to equality. These approaches uniquely target racial justice organizing as passé, and as incapable of incorporating intersectionality. Since the events described here, in some ways the 'one-dimensional race agenda' returned. In Scotland there are some intersectional approaches within the Race Equality Framework for Scotland. In England, however, among prominent figures in the 'race disparity' initiatives begun by Theresa May in 2016, intersectionality was constructed as a luxury that might come later (conversation with policy maker, 2018), and there were no clear intersectionality advocates among them (key leaders were also men). Notably this policy approach has since been largely replaced by a dominant one denying that racial inequalities exist (Meer 2022). While intersectionality may not be given the meaning of generic in these new contexts (and is virtually non-existent in the English one) the construction of this meaning has stuck elsewhere.

Local level

At local level, meanings of intersectionality as generic arose in contexts of austerity. Contemporary equality networks usually superseded strand-specific networks that were resourced by local government (race, LGBTI, women's and disabled people's networks). In times of austerity, local governments stated that they no longer had the capacity or resources to administer the strand-specific networks: in the case of one equality network, for example, a stated aim of establishing it was to reduce costs associated with local government fulfilling its legal obligations around equality. Intersectionality has been used as a rationale for dismantling siloed networks, a rationale which obscures the material reasons of austerity (Anonymous Document (AD) 2).[5] Clearly, it is much less expensive for local government to fund one 'intersectional' network, than it was to fund three to nine strand-specific networks. Here again, intersectionality is given the meaning of generic, where no equality strand is addressed in particular, and the aim is constructed to be equality for 'everybody' rather than for marginalized or disadvantaged groups.

Susan, director of a small, funded disabled people's organization in Scotland, for example, perceived that 'intersectionality' is at times instrumentalized to mean generic equality:

> 'I think funders do take the approach that intersect – putting [all inequalities] together is usually about rationalization. It's usually about saving money ... I think there's good things about having the approach in your head of including everybody, but I think the way that it is being approached can actually take away from the benefits.'

This meaning of intersectionality is not, however, only imposed top-down by policy makers. Networks themselves recognize and use the intersectionality-as-value-for-money argument in a context of austerity: "I suppose the advantage of intersectionality is this, that you can say we're a one stop shop [laughs] for anything that you have a problem in terms of discrimination ... I'm just wondering about – I suppose there's an economic advantage to the concept in that you can do that" (Christopher, network member).

Comparing England and Scotland

Generic understandings of and approaches to intersectionality were more prevalent in Scotland than England. In Scotland, policy and NGO sector meanings and uses of intersectionality are closely intertwined, to a greater extent than in England given that it is a smaller country and that the political system is characterized by greater openness and engagement (Hankivsky and Christoffersen 2011; Chaney 2012a). The term intersectionality is used more in government in Scotland (as established in Chapter 3), which is due in part to NGO sector influence, and in turn, policy makers and the public sector influence understandings and uses of intersectionality within the NGO sector.

A contributing factor to the prominence of generic understandings in Scotland is the context of equality 'mainstreaming', one of the Scottish-specific duties to support the Equality Act discussed in Chapter 1. While in theory it could be individual stranded or intersectional (here used to mean 'intersections of equality strands') approaches that are mainstreamed in an organization, in practice mainstreaming in a context of austerity often amounts to generic approaches. Equality organizations describe a generic approach as follows: 'to treat protected characteristics in an undifferentiated way, glossing over or ignoring the specific disadvantage and discrimination faced by specific groups of people' (Inclusion Scotland et al 2017, 4).

A generic approach to *equality* was perceived by scholars and equality organizations since the lead-up to the Equality Act and its mainstreaming duty in Scotland, and they attempt to fight back against it. What I identified is the way that *intersectionality* is instrumentalized in and constitutive with this perceived approach. *Intersectionality* is mobilized to give a new name to a generic approach to equality, and a very particular meaning to 'intersectionality'.

Implications for intersectionally marginalized groups

A generic concept of intersectionality effaces intersectional marginalization, including of Black women and women of colour, which I explore further in the final section of this chapter. Some of its implications were highlighted by research participants employing alternative concepts of intersectionality.

Some participant practitioners and organizations resist intersectionality as generic equality, in response pointing out that although different equality groups may be affected by the same issues, they are likely affected by them differently. Here, Emma, practitioner in a small, funded racial justice organization, criticizes a generic approach:

> 'In order to say that everything is intersectional, you need to have an equality, discrimination or disadvantage in mind. Even if it is a shared disadvantage, it will still look different for different groups. You need different actions, you cannot just have one statement and expect that to make everything better for everyone. You're always going to have people disproportionately benefiting if that's the way you go about it.'

She argues that in a situation of inequality, applying a generic approach will reproduce and exacerbate those inequalities.

Within a generic approach that targets everyone, spaces and activities are created which are open to those who are privileged in relation to most aspects of identity, as well as those who are marginalized. Some raise concern about this: "If you start mixing particular identities that have been ... part of the problem ... then ... the same [domination] happens" (Christopher, network member). Emma, a practitioner in a racial justice organization, agreed: "Activists tell us all the time that they feel ... that by bringing [all inequalities] under the same umbrella it marginalizes some of the most vulnerable people and some of the most discriminated against people."

Moreover, several participants contended that a generic approach itself can actually increase siloed attitudes, themselves a barrier to practising intersectionality. When everyone is treated the same, people may start advocating for their own corner, emphasizing difference of 'their' group from those 'others', including who is 'more discriminated against'. These attitudes further entrench an idea of equality groups as being mutually exclusive. Stephen, director of a small, funded racial justice organization in England, explained.

'If you create a spurious equality between different protected characteristics, for example, say they're all equally worthy of study and being addressed, then I think you're actually going to end up with the opposite of what good intersectionality does. Which is to say that actually these are multiple and you'll end up with a situation where people will end up constructing their own hierarchies of oppression if you're not careful.'

A further implication relates to resourcing. Some view generic understandings and approaches as a policy-led attempt to simplify and save costs, particularly in austerity contexts; and one that ultimately will fail to meet any stated aim of reducing inequalities. Susan likened a generic approach to a 'short cut':

'The short cut, I really firmly believe that does not work. I think it's a funder and a policy maker's short-cut approach to ticking boxes. I think it's crass and it doesn't take account of people who need a great deal of support and investment to develop their voices to overcome barriers.' (Susan, director, disabled people's organization, Scotland)

Claire, director of a small, relatively unfunded disabled women's organization identified the superficiality of some uses of intersectionality, and the complementarity of this with austerity.

'People like intersectionality as long as it doesn't cost more money. If you can say you can do intersectionality, you're not asking for more money, yay. If you suddenly say, "Hang on a minute. To be intersectional, we need to be providing information in Bengali or we need to be hiring wheelchair accessible spaces that cost 50% more or we need to do this or that", that's not so interesting anymore. People like intersectionality as long as it doesn't cost more money ... people like cheap intersectionality rather than true intersectionality.'

Generic approaches imply a lack of resourcing allocated to reducing inequalities, which is borne out when they are employed.

Finally, a key implication of generic understandings is the threat they pose to intersectional organizations and to work employing alternative, competing concepts of intersectionality.

While recognizing it particularly among public sector colleagues, most participants strongly rejected this concept of intersectionality, viewing it as a departure from intersectionality's 'real' meaning, as a funder-driven co-option of intersectionality that serves to devalue 'intersections of equality strands' work and intersectional organizations. They also perceived generic intersectionality as closely related to policy reduction of equality to inequality and poverty (discussed in Chapter 3).

Intersectionality as 'pan equality'

The second applied concept that I identified is intersectionality as pan equality. This means addressing broad issues that are common to all, or most, equality strands, or in other words, addressing issues that affect all, or most, marginalized equality groups. The focus on marginality is what distinguishes this concept from the generic understanding (interested in issues that affect 'everyone') discussed previously, and is reflected in issue selection. The extent to which issues are perceived as common to equality groups is what, in turn, distinguishes it from multi-strand understandings, the concept explored next. Network organizer Nicola, for example, defined intersectionality as: "The commonalities of barriers and disadvantage faced by different protected characteristic groups."

While many practitioners conflated pan equality and intersectionality, others made a conceptual distinction between them. For example, network organizer Catriona reflected on the difference between the two.

> 'I think obviously the difference is [between pan equality and intersectionality], effectively they're the opposite of one another, in a way. Within any kind of pan equality say campaign or policy desire, really if you're trying to reduce inequalities or reduce discrimination then actually the most effective way to work on that is to support intersectional communities within that pan equality issue to highlight their needs or lobby.'

Here, Catriona feels that while pan equality and intersectionality are distinct concepts, they also can complement one another, and she views both as necessary for equality work.

Julie, director of a small, funded refugee organization in England, expressed a similar view: "In some ways a lot of work around equality is about looking at smaller and smaller and smaller [intersecting] groups, but at the same time it has to be balanced, by looking at the bigger and bigger more fundamental issues ... but neither one nor the other is quite right."

To illustrate how this works in practice, a prominent example employing this concept of intersectionality was work on hate crime, perceived as a common issue affecting marginalized equality groups, and worked on in networks and other coalitions. Hate crime was an example given by several participants as being a site of intersectional work, including Jacqueline, practitioner in a small, funded disabled people's organization in England: "That's one of the areas [where] we're very aware of intersectionality." While some participants made a conceptual distinction between pan equality and intersectionality, others saw pan equality work (for instance, to campaign for legal parity in hate crime legislation across strands) as their intersectional work.

Who holds this understanding?

This was the second most prevalent of the five concepts of intersectionality among my research participants. Yet it was not found at all among strictly service-providing organizations (given that these operate within individualized discourses, while this is a more structural meaning of intersectionality). In terms of individual positionality, it was particularly prevalent among white participants (though not exclusively, as is the case with generic intersectionality). Those employing this concept predominantly reported learning about intersectionality from personal experience and diverse staff within organizations, in equality networks and online.

How did this meaning gain prominence?

According to Catriona, a network organizer, pan equality is perceived as an important concept because "[w]hilst the issues of different intersectional communities, or the experiences might be quite different, in terms of maybe the things that they want or need to improve their rights or access into services or appropriate services, quite often might be the same or similar".

Pan equality has a longer history as a term in the sector than 'intersectionality', particularly in England. Pan equality work is an outcome of networks and coalitions of single-strand organizations, the formation of many of which coincided with the lead-up to the amalgamation of disparate equality legislation into one Act. As intersectionality has grown in popularity, it has assumed the meaning of this term. When asked what intersectionality means to them, many participants articulated this applied concept: addressing issues that are common to marginalized equality groups.

One possible explanation for why this meaning of intersectionality has gained prominence is that, similar to generic approaches, pan equality approaches can appear cost-effective to funders. One network organizer made this argument, that pan equality work is the best 'value for money' for funders. In contrast, many across the networks commented on the lack of dedicated funding for, and difficulty in acquiring funding for, 'intersections of equality strands' intersectional work.

Implications for intersectionally marginalized groups

The concept of intersectionality as pan equality creates space for organizations working across different equality issues to come together, develop joint work and pursue policy change collectively, potentially heightening their impact. Yet the particular agendas of groups of intersectionally marginalized people may be lost when this understanding of intersectionality is employed on its own; common issues may be watered down in content to the lowest common denominator (see also Ciccia and Roggeband 2021). Similarly, when practitioners employ arguments that pan equality work is good value for money, this suggests that work employing 'intersections of equality strands' understandings is not. Yet this concept may also ultimately facilitate intersectional working:

> 'If we identify the big pan equality concepts so we know what many of them are, power and structure and hostility and hate and abuse and those things, then it becomes possible to work intersectionally ... the pan equality stuff ... provides a connecting mechanism for people who are working with ... intersections between what in our minds are still separate issues.' Julie, director, refugee organization, England

Multi-strand intersectionality

The third distinct applied concept of intersectionality that I will discuss is multi-strand intersectionality. This is addressing equality strands in parallel, separately, simultaneously, and often seeking to do so equivalently. It is distinct from generic understandings focused on 'everyone' effacing specific inequalities, in that equality strands remain very important and in primary focus. It is inclusive of an idea that all strands *ought* to be included, and treated equally, or at least, accorded the same level of attention and resourcing.

This can be interpreted as an additive understanding of intersectionality: equality strands are conceptualized alongside one another, but not as affecting one another. As such, some with this understanding view intersectionality as interchangeable with multiple discrimination, for example Aziz, director of a racial justice organization in Scotland:

> 'My understanding [of] intersectionality is more about the different strands coming together. So you might be facing more – it's just like multiple discrimination that's the word we used in the past, multiple discrimination. That's easier to understand than intersect – I think it means the same but it's a new word.'

A multi-strand understanding of intersectionality is also evident in the following example shared by a participant, which she identified as a 'passive aggressive' use of intersectionality. When she was talking about issues pertaining to the equality strand she specializes in, someone from another strand sector said, "We need to consider intersectionality here", and then proceeded to talk simply about 'their' strand in a singular way, rather than the intersection of the two. This is emanating from an understanding of intersectionality where it simply means all equality strands.

Networks themselves are structured according to this concept, to greater and lesser degrees. Some are composed wholly of single-strand equality organizations aiming to cover all of the protected characteristics, which would be closest to a multi-strand model. Others include intersectional organizations. Others are broader still, including organizations that work on poverty and socioeconomic inequality. Yet in addition to being a form of equality organizing, multi-strand intersectionality is more importantly a practice.

A key example of this is equality network collaboration to input into local equality strategies. Across networks, a substantial number of participants identified this as a good example of their network's intersectional work. Yet on careful analysis of the processes and documents constituting this, it often followed the definition of multi-strand intersectionality elaborated here. These processes will be explored in detail in Chapter 6.

Who holds this understanding?

This understanding was more prevalent among service-providing organizations than other types of organizations (most of which are single-strand organizations). It was particularly prevalent within one city, wherein the equality sectors had developed in particularly siloed ways. Similar to generic intersectionality, it was more prevalent among those with privileged aspects of identity and less prevalent among those with marginalized ones. This is significant because this concept serves to further the interests of singularly disadvantaged groups.

How did this meaning gain prominence?

This meaning of intersectionality is clearly related to the Equality Act, which created a multi-strand equality policy framework. Indeed, during co-construction sessions, participants recognized this approach in government templates for equality impact assessments, in which there is space dedicated to consideration of each strand separately (with no dedicated space to consider intersections of them). This concept was prevalent in a city that has a particularly siloed equality sector characterized by siloed attitudes (discussed further in Chapter 6), due in part to an especially competitive funding environment, and to the workings of intersecting inequalities to silence intersectional organizations, including Black women's organizations. In this context it may be that organizations are 'stuck' at multi-strand understandings of intersectionality. Within this network, multi-strand understandings were particularly correlated to diversity-within ones: so at a collective level, intersectionality is addressing equality strands in parallel, separately, equivalently and simultaneously, while at an organizational level, it is about diversity-within, but in which one inequality remains primary, considered to be more important than others.

It has been theorized within intersectionality literature, and felt by some of my participants, that bringing equality strands together, whether into one law as with the Equality Act, or into one network, creates opportunities to explore the interactions between inequalities, and thus to operationalize intersectionality. In contrast, single-strand and siloed working are viewed as barriers to intersectionality. Multi-strand intersectionality may then, given the current siloed configuration of equality work, be a necessary first step to practising intersectionality collectively. Yet, for some, it seems to stop there: *because this is in and of itself conflated with intersectionality*.

To understand intersectionality as something else would be to admit that equality networks, organizations and practitioners are not actually doing intersectionality. While bringing equality strands together into one law or network may *create* opportunities to consider the relationships between them, it is clear from my data that this does not automatically follow, or necessarily happen.

Implications for intersectionally marginalized groups

Within this understanding, intersectionality is constructed as something that happens *after* equality strands (understood singularly), both conceptually and temporally. This effaces an 'intersections of equality strands' understanding and work employing it, discussed later. More significantly, it effaces intersectional marginalization per se, since equality strands continue to be conceptualized singularly. There is little in this concept of intersectionality that challenges the status quo of single-strand equality work, and the siloed thinking behind it. Yet, multi-strand fora are important places of learning about other equality issues, out of which other approaches to intersectionality can develop.

Intersections within a strand: diversity-within

The fourth concept of intersectionality that I will outline is 'diversity-within'. This is addressing intersections within an equality strand; for example, differences among women. A particular strand remains the focus, and is viewed implicitly or explicitly as more important than others; this is the key distinction between this understanding and the final one, 'intersections of equality strands', which I will discuss next.

This concept of intersectionality follows from single-strand equality organizing, and is how intersectionality is often addressed within strand-specific organizations; but not always. These organizations also at times employ 'intersections of equality strands' understandings, discussed next, as well as, in coalition with one another, pan equality and multi-strand ones. In other words, while this concept of intersectionality is related to single-strand organizing, it is not determined by it.

Here, Diane, a practitioner in a small, funded women's organization in England, explains what intersectionality means to her. Since this exemplifies much of what there is to unpack in this understanding of intersectionality, it is worth quoting at length.

> 'Intersectionality is the new word … it has relevance … to the work that I do and that I'm focused on, so … obviously from my side it's more about sort of women and those things that are happening around women and particular groups of women as well and how those things work, and I'm sort of quite interested in sort of gathering and articulating how a response to that or almost sort of the baseline of any work that we go forward doing, how that impacts on access to services, how organizations stay sustainable, there are lots of issues that are emerging now that, are, forgive me if I just keep going on about women-specific things, but the generalization of services, about funds being cut, and how that recognition of intersectionality impacts on women's lot. It's quite, it's insidious. The, the prioritizing of the individual I think is seriously damaging to women as a group. And those intersectional points, I think is why we need to be clear and articulate, how and when that affects, and keep the case going strongly for keeping those visible. That's, that's my focus.'

Intersectionality is constructed as something 'new' that has relevance *sometimes*, so not all the time; as well as something which is inherently individualistic, involving 'prioritizing of the individual'. Recognition of intersectionality is 'insidious' for women 'as a group'. It is their task to narrow down exactly 'how and when' intersectionality affects 'women', implying that oftentimes, it does not. In other words, they consider intersectionality reluctantly.

This highlights a similarity that this definition of intersectionality shares with multi-strand intersectionality: its additive nature. Instead of being mutually constitutive with other strands, other strands are perceived as being only nominally relevant and only sometimes.

It is important to note that very few participants employing this understanding were openly reluctant about intersectionality. Indeed, most were enthusiastic. It is only through analysis and contrast of participant narratives that this reluctance becomes apparent.

In practice, use of this concept often involves developing projects targeted at particular intersections within the strand. Which intersections are targeted is a matter for analysis. For example, there is a clear pattern in my data of white-led/predominantly white organizations (LGBTI, women's, networks) developing work around disabled people/disability/ access which they describe as their intersectional work. My interpretation is that these organizations feel more confident, and perceive it as in some ways easier,[6] to develop focused work on this than it is to address issues of race, racism and gendered racism. In other words, they may be more willing to acknowledge ableism than white supremacy; perhaps ableism is easier to accommodate within this deficit model where other inequalities are constructed as 'additional barriers', given discourses of paternalism relating to medical models of disability well documented by disabled scholars (Shakespeare et al 2009). A concomitant pattern is white-led/predominantly white organizations (LGBTI, women's, disabled networks) commenting that race is the 'one area they struggle with', that is, focused work on race and projects targeted toward people of colour. Some organizations offer problematic 'cultural' narratives that they use to rationalize why particular minority ethnic groups will not engage with them, thereby relieving their organizations of responsibility to acknowledge and address white supremacy. These patterns together mean that disabled people of colour are particularly excluded from targeted projects; there is a particular silo around race and disability.[7] In contrast, some organizations, cognizant of the origins of intersectionality, describe as their intersectional work either their own work with Black women (in the case of racial justice organizations), or seeking to widen their work with Black women and/or racially minoritized communities. For example, Anya, a practitioner in a small, funded racial justice organization said: "We would look at [intersectionality] more from a point of view of having Black women's organizations involved ... we would be looking to make sure that their concerns were not drowned out by the majority and always came to the fore."

Because of the additive nature of diversity-within understandings of intersectionality, projects are conceptualized singularly. Even in a white-led organization that was perceived as being 'good on race' by some racial justice organizations, a project developed on disability seemed to forget this inequality: imagery depicted only white people, race was not highlighted in the documentation, monitoring information revealed that the project beneficiaries were around 95 per cent white while none were Black, and outreach reported did not include any racial justice or minority ethnic organizations (AD 42). This was possible, in part, because within this understanding of intersectionality, inequalities are conceptualized as being legitimately able to be added and subtracted at will, rather than being viewed as mutually constitutive. Some single-strand organizations may therefore have targeted projects/programmes that may be deemed successful, but these are not always 'layered', and can be conceptualized and managed entirely separately within an (even quite small) organization. This effacement of disabled people of colour within the equality sector adds to their marginality in the wider social world.

Who holds this understanding?

This was the most prevalent applied concept of intersectionality among those in the women's sector (see also Christoffersen and Emejulu 2023). In contrast, this was not the case for any other single-strand sector (refugee, racial justice, disabled, Deaf, LGBTI), nor was it true of any of the intersectional sectors included in my sample. It was more prevalent among single-strand organizations than intersectional ones. In terms of individual positionality, it was associated with dominant identities (like multi-strand intersectionality, diversity-within serves to further the interests of singularly disadvantaged groups). Out of the main sources of intersectional knowledge that participants identified,[8] this understanding was most associated with professional learning about intersectionality (professional development and on the job training) and within the NGO sector. Single-strand organizations train new staff with this particular understanding of intersectionality.

How did this meaning gain prominence?

This concept of intersectionality emerges from within single-strand, siloed working. Similar to multi-strand understandings, intersectionality stops here, or else organizations and practitioners would have to admit that they are not really doing intersectionality. The development of projects targeted at particular groups within the strand has often been driven by demographic analysis of service users by equality characteristics, frequently instituted as a funding requirement in light of the Equality Act. Jaqueline, practitioner in a small, funded disabled people's organization based in England, describes how her way of thinking changed when she realized the extent of crossover among constituents of LGBT and disabled people's organizations:

> '[An LGBT organization] told us that I think it's 45 per cent of the people that [are users of the organization] are disabled, 45 per cent. So a very high percentage and that's when it really ... the kind of the penny – not penny dropped because I'd been already aware, but ... how [intersectionality] was really integral to our work here.'

This lays bare the contradictions and ultimately the inadequacy of singular single-strand equality work.

Single-strand organizations have not then, always embraced intersectionality and developed projects out of goodwill. They have often been driven by equality monitoring requirements of funders revealing their exclusion of intersectionally marginalized people, though they are funded to serve 'all' in a given geographic community of identity.

Comparing England and Scotland

Taken together with multi-strand intersectionality since these are correlated, these concepts of intersectionality are more prevalent in Scotland than in England. One reason for their prevalence in Scotland may be who the influential proponents of intersectionality have been, and the understandings of intersectionality that they have, as explored in Chapter 3 (see also Christoffersen and McCabe, forthcoming). According to participants, the Scottish government's Equality Unit has been influenced, in particular, by the women's sector, and especially the violence against women sector, to develop work around the term and the concept intersectionality. This source is unsurprising given that the (white) women's sector enjoys a privileged relationship with the government. The women's sector was relatively opposed to a widening of the equalities agenda (to include, for example, faith). It championed particular ways of understanding intersectionality as "the further complications, the further disadvantages and further discrimination that you can experience … if you fall into more than one group" (interview with policy maker, 2018), wherein one inequality (gender) is considered primary (see also McCabe 2023; Christoffersen and McCabe, forthcoming). There are key Black women's organizations in Scotland, however because of gendered racism these do not have the same relationship to policy makers and, as such, were not identified by policy makers as sources of their knowledge of intersectionality. The government has absorbed particular meanings of intersectionality from specific NGO sector actors, and especially since the Equality Unit is a key funder of equality organizations, these meanings then constitute a discourse in which other actors take them on.

Implications for intersectionally marginalized groups

This understanding bears all of the implications of gender-first approaches to equality which efface women of colours' experiences that are widely critiqued elsewhere (Crenshaw 1989, 1991; Hankivsky 2005). Within it, it may be possible to incorporate other aspects of identity as 'additional barriers', but this tends to be limited to one, and the deficit model employed is not affirming nor is it concerned with enabling participation. Moreover, inclusion of intersectionally marginalized people as service users does not mean that there is any change in the issue agendas of single-strand organizations (see also Laperriere and Lépinard 2016). In the context of the women's sector, this concept of intersectionality serves to further the association of 'women' with whiteness; in other words, the construction of 'woman' as always already white (Lewis 2017).

While many participants viewed this as a valid concept of intersectionality during co-construction sessions, not all participants agreed that single-strand or diversity-within work is intersectional. One of the networks has a project employing this approach, while its other projects more closely align to either pan equality or 'intersections of equality strands' approaches. For one of the members of the network's inner governing circle, the diversity-within project was described as a 'failure of intersectionality'. This participant did not agree that this strand of work was appropriate for the network or see it as intersectional.

Intersections of equality strands

The final applied concept of intersectionality that emerged is 'intersections of equality strands'. This is work of and with specific groups sharing intersecting identities, for example, women of colour, disabled women, among others. The key distinction between this understanding and approach, and the diversity-within concept discussed previously, is that no particular equality strand is primary, or more in focus than the other (or others). In sharp contrast to those employing generic, pan equality and multi-strand understandings, those with this understanding perceive their intersectional work as that with those who are intersectionally marginalized, belonging to particular overlapping equality groups.

Here, network organizer Elizabeth contrasts this approach to generic ones: "Lots of local authorities have this, 'We'll only fund services which are open to all', which is fine for some things, but doesn't really give the opportunity to do a project that's really *intersectional* that fits [a] particular need that you've identified about a specific community." (emphasis added). This approach to work may be taken with the view that getting it right for the most marginalized will benefit 'all', the target of generic intersectionality; but in the long term, as network organizer Catriona described.

> 'I think I've always felt that if you can work with and support the most marginalized, then really that should be able to be applied to any other community. If we get stuff right for disabled refugees and asylum seekers, then it should work for all other vulnerable refugees. It should work for all other disabled people. It should work for all other people. Ideally.'

This approach is sharply distinct from, and most marginalized by, a generic use of intersectionality that has no particular equality group or groups in mind.

Key practice examples employing this approach include 'intersectional organizations', focused on multiple mutually constitutive equality issues at their core, and partnership projects between single-strand organizations, which I describe as 'intersectional alliances'. Kya, practitioner in an intersectional LGBTI refugee organization in England, explains the difference between single-strand, 'diversity-within' approaches and this approach: "We already knew about the different challenges, the intersectional challenges that people have. This is what our work originally sought to address ... so it's not a concept that is new to us but it is something that our work is already set on for a very long time."

While intersectionality is something that comes later for single-strand organizations, and is similarly constructed as being 'after' strands in multi-strand understandings, here it is felt to be present at the outset. While some organizations may seek training in intersectionality, or actively try to work 'intersectionally', others perceive themselves to have always done so. For organizations that are single-strand, intersectionality is often constructed as something that comes after the organization temporally, as something that perhaps challenges the organization, or something that demands some (at times reluctant) change of the organization. For intersectional organizations, intersectionality is constructed as something that has always been present in the organization/its work, though this particular term may not have been used. For example, a participant from one such organization viewed challenges to taking up and addressing intersectionality as being located solely outside of the organization, in their relationships with other (non-intersectional) organizations; while single-strand organization participants would often narrate challenges that were internal as well as external. However, participants from intersectional organizations recognize that there are issues that they know less about, that they get things wrong and are continuing to learn and develop.

I will describe the work of one intersectional organization, which shares many similarities with that of others in my sample. It is self-organized around the intersection of four markers of inequality (gender, race, ethnicity and minority faith), and has targeted work which also takes account of age and disability. It has taken steps to develop learning on LGBTI identity. It is a mixed type organization, providing community development and community services as well as engaging in policy and campaigning work. It works holistically across multiple issues, including employment, education and training, and health and well-being. This multi-issue approach resonates with research on how intersectionality is applied in social movement organizations (Chun et al 2013; Tungohan 2015). The organization views itself as meeting needs that are not met by mainstream services, as well as advocating for policy change to further the rights of its constituents. The organization also provides an important bridge to accessing other mainstream public and NGO sector services, for example, domestic violence services, through signposting, referrals and one-to-one support to women accessing such services. Finally, it provides cultural awareness training aiming for other services to become more accessible to their constituents.

Beyond intersectional organizations, this concept of intersectionality is also employed in intersectional alliances, or partnership projects between strands. I use the term 'intersectional alliances' to encompass both formal partnership projects (joint funding to jointly deliver a project) between strand-specific equality organizations, as well as more informal partnerships. An 'intersections of equality strands' understanding implies an aimed-for equitable partnership or relationship, since no strand is given primacy, whereas a 'diversity-within' understanding does not.

One example of an intersectional alliance is a disabled LGBTI group, which emerged fairly organically from disabled LGBTI people, and was then supported administratively and financially by a disabled people's organization and an LGBTI organization and LGBTI infrastructure. The network in the city also provided support to the initiative.

Intersectional organizations and alliances can 'mainstream' intersectionality rather than it inhering in particular projects, as in a 'diversity-within' model. However, this is a very different mainstreaming from that of a generic approach to intersectionality.

Who holds this understanding?

This was the most prevalent of the five concepts of intersectionality among my participants, but by a small margin, and there are important differences among organizations and practitioners related to whether they hold this understanding or not. Unsurprisingly, this was the most prevalent understanding among those from intersectional organizations by a wide margin. It was more prevalent in England. In terms of individual positionality, it tended to be associated with those having marginalized aspects of identity: it was the most prevalent concept among racially minoritized, disabled and LGBQ participants and those of minority faith. This is the only concept that positions intersectionally marginalized people as agents. Out of the main sources of intersectional knowledge that participants identified, this understanding was most associated with those who learned about intersectionality from their own personal experiences and diverse staff within organizations, and within equality networks.

How did this meaning gain prominence?

This is the applied concept identified that most closely resonates with wider academic and popular understandings of intersectionality. Yet among my research participants, it competes with the four other concepts identified in this chapter. Intersectional organizations are increasingly laying claim to the term 'intersectionality', recognizing their work in the concept though the term itself may be newer to them. The formation of intersectional alliances is often driven by desire to work in more intersectional ways.

Implications for intersectionally marginalized groups

There are two key challenges for work employing this concept in relation to furthering equality for intersectionally marginalized groups.

The first is individualization. Similar to 'diversity-within' approaches, work employing this concept can be disproportionately aimed at alleviating symptoms, rather than addressing causes of inequality.

The second challenge for 'intersections of equality strands' approaches is meaningfully accounting for the range of markers of inequality, particularly given that this is not the approach favoured in policy and resourcing. Andrew, director of a funded LGBTI young people's organization, reflected that: "Just because we're a specialist, equality and diversity organization on a couple of strands of diversity doesn't mean that we're, we've got our act together on, on all of them. We've still got work to do on other aspects of equality." As I stated previously, it is frequently race that is left out of the picture among white-led sectors.

Due to the workings of intersecting structures of inequality, intersectional organizations and alliances have been particularly hard hit by austerity; many intersectional organizations have closed. This was identified by participants as a significant barrier to operationalizing intersectionality.

Conclusions

Tensions between concepts

As I mentioned in the introduction to this chapter, some participants employ several of these concepts, or in other words, describe multiple ways of practising intersectionality. At times, there appeared to be some confusion and tension, as participants tried to work out how to go about their work in a way that takes intersectionality into account. This tension can be related to single-strand working: if an organization is constituted around one equality area, how can it apply intersectionality?

One example of this is an equality month marked in one city and led by a single-strand LGBTI organization. In interview with the director of this organization, tensions were evident in the organization's approach to the focus of this month: whether this would be specifically about inequality experienced by LGBTI people, across intersections among LGBTI people, or more broadly focused on issues, using a pan equality approach. The participant seemed unsure, and contradicted themself on this point. They also expressed a lack of confidence and knowledge in taking a position on debates concerning aspects of inequality (constructed as) outwith the LGBTI strand (for example, race). The approach subsequently taken was a multi-strand one: the organization divided the month into strands, so for part of it the focus would be on disability, another LGBTI, and so on. This example evidences the tensions inherent in operationalizing intersectionality in the context of strand-specific sectors and a siloed policy context (wherein although strands may have been brought together into one Act, within it they are still conceptualized separately). The multi-strand approach they opted for clearly fails to take into account mutual constitution of strands, or intersectional marginalization, in a meaningful way; indeed, intersectional marginalization was effaced.

In addition to practitioners employing multiple concepts, I suggest that policy makers employ, and accept the validity of, whichever of these concepts of intersectionality suit their interests at particular junctures.

Some of these concepts are opposing, while others may be considered as complementary: this will be discussed throughout the book.

Relationship of concepts to intersectionality theory

The elements of intersectionality theory that I discussed in Chapter 2 include mutual constitution of inequalities (vs. additive approaches); levels of analysis; relationality and the simultaneity of privilege and oppression; and focus on those who are intersectionally disadvantaged (Table 4.1).

Generic understandings of intersectionality can scarcely be analysed in relation to these theoretical elements. Since equality strands are not in focus, these are conceptualized neither additively nor constitutively. This concept fails to engage structural levels of intersectionality, since it has no grasp of inequality structures, so it similarly lacks understanding of relationality and the simultaneity of privilege and oppression. It does not focus on those who are intersectionally disadvantaged.

While a pan equality concept is perhaps most reflective of a structural, as opposed to individual, conceptualization of intersectionality, it does not necessarily reflect the mutual constitution of inequalities, and can thus verge into multi-strand concepts of intersectionality meaning all strands, as well as generic ones targeted at 'everyone'. It does not necessarily incorporate relationality nor focus on intersectional marginalization.

Multi-strand intersectionality is additive; it tends not to recognize relationality and the simultaneity of privilege and oppression, since inequalities are conceptualized singularly. For this reason, equality groups tend to be viewed as solely oppressed. It precludes focus on those who are most disadvantaged, since it is inclusive of an idea of equivalence between strands. Ultimately, this is a limited and limiting conceptualization of intersectionality, a concept synonymous with 'diversity' when applied to groups of individuals, and a merely descriptive concept when applied to individuals ('person x is intersectional'), wherein some may be conceptualized to 'have' more intersectionality, as an attribute, than others ('person x has a lot of intersectionality'), meaning 'multiple identities'[9] (coinciding with many uses of intersectionality in equality policy documents, discussed in Chapter 3). This conceptualization therefore neglects intersectionality's attention to structural inequalities, obscuring understanding of it as the 'fusion of social structures that creates specific social positions' (Bassel and Emejulu 2010, 538), evidencing and reinforcing an additive view that these structures can be separated from one another. This fusion of social inequalities, while in constant process, can also be conceptualized temporally as happening prior to person x occupying social position y, but this is invisibilized by this conceptualization of intersectionality.

The 'diversity-within' concept fails to recognize relationality and the simultaneity of privilege and oppression insofar as it is additive. For this reason, it tends to view marginal groups as solely oppressed, and those with marginalized intersecting identities as having 'additional barriers' in a deficit model. Projects may be articulated as service delivery to the 'hard to reach' with little apparent thought to agency or structural change. This concept does not focus on those who are most disadvantaged insofar as the main focus, the primary inequality, is predefined regardless of issue area or context.

The 'intersections of equality strands' concept of, and approach to, intersectionality captures the mutually constitutive nature of inequalities. It lends itself to consideration of multiple levels of intersectionality. Relationality and the simultaneity of privilege and oppression are often accounted for. This is important, since this is the only concept of the five identified which conceptualizes intersectionally marginalized people as agential. This approach does focus on issues for those felt to be disadvantaged, though specific markers of inequality may be predefined, as with 'diversity-within' approaches.

Debates in literature: race/gender and women of colour

None of these approaches privilege the intersection of race/gender, though some organizations and projects with 'intersections of equality strands' concepts of intersectionality do. To the contrary, within a generic understanding of it, intersectionality is mobilized in order to *displace* specific focus on racial justice. Focus on race, gender and race/gender, Black women and women of colour, may be absent from pan equality approaches, and, as I have discussed, are frequently absent in 'diversity-within' ones. Multi-strand concepts include consideration of race and gender, but separately.

This is all significant particularly in light of academic debates (re)locating intersectionality in the intersection of race/gender, with women of colour its key subjects (see, for example, Hancock 2016). It also resonates with critiques of the erasure of Black women and race in intersectionality research (Alexander-Floyd 2012; Bilge 2013; Jordan-Zachery 2013), or in other words, white appropriation of/colonization of (Tomlinson 2013a) intersectionality, indicating similar erasures in equality policy and practice.

The use of intersectionality to theorize social divisions other than those positioning women of colour is controversial among intersectionality theorists, and in wider popular (Black) feminist culture. Yet, in the equality policy and NGO sector environments in England and Scotland, there is little detectable awareness of these debates among powerful actors. Here, intersectionality tends to be used in an unspecified way, across the up to nine protected characteristics named in the Equality Act 2010 (as explored in Chapter 3). Intersectionality is also growing in popularity. While at times locating intersectionality in Black feminism, the approach to centrally considering race when thinking about and using intersectionality varied among my research participants. For those that do centrally consider race, it is important to note that a focus on race, in itself, does not necessarily do justice to intersectionality's primary concern with *women of colour*. Some organizations have taken on language and concepts of intersectionality, to describe an array of social positions across both race and gender. Indeed, within my sample intersectionality as both a term and a concept has been embraced by and for work with a range of groups: disabled women, LGBTI refugees, disabled refugees and asylum seekers, to name just a few examples. Women of colour are among all of these groups, yet this is not the identity highlighted in these projects and organizations, and they work across race while the latter two work across gender. This does not mean that that identity falls to the wayside necessarily, though, as I have discussed, other inequalities are likely to when additive 'diversity-within' models are employed. Employment of an 'intersections of equality strands' model is one way to try to do justice to intersectionality's origins and the range of intersectional marginality in intersectional work, though there are further divergences in approaches to difference that impact upon intersectional praxis (Luna 2016). Another related way concerns representation, which is the focus of the next chapter.

Meanings and uses of intersectionality

While elements of this typology (particularly the concept that I have identified as multi-strand intersectionality) are consistent with US-based literature revealing where intersectionality is used as synonymous with diversity, as an apolitical and non-intersectional concept (for example,

May 2015; Nash 2019), or what Rachel E. Luft and Jane Ward describe as 'misidentification' of intersectionality (Luft and Ward 2009, 9), it also departs from it in identifying very *generic* uses of intersectionality. Where diversity may connote difference in individualized and singular ways, and may be used in the US context in particular to mean racial or ethnic diversity, in generic understandings, difference is flattened, and intersectionality becomes a new word for equality as liberal sameness (Christoffersen 2022).

Yet, in line with critiques of intersectionality as diversity, across the typology, participants consistently defined and described intersectionality at an individual level, to the exclusion of other levels. In the literature, different levels of intersectionality have been defined (these are various, but examples are structural, symbolic, individual/interpersonal), and we have been warned of the risks of conflating these (Yuval-Davis 2006). I tried different ways of asking about structures/structural inequalities, with limited success. At times this dominant articulation at individual level was likely because the participant lacked a structural understanding of inequality generally, which may be the case, for example, in strictly service provision organizations, and shows how far sectors now are, in many ways, from any social movement origins they might lay claim to. However, articulation on an individual level is also related to policy- and funder-driven discourses that the sector operates within, including having to quantify work in project outcomes that are frequently measured as changes in individuals.[10] Furthermore, it may also simply be that the concept of intersectionality is easier to grasp when articulated at this level.[11] One implication of the research presented here is the need for better articulation and awareness raising of intersectionality as the fusion of structures of inequality. One exception to individualization is the pan equality concept, which lends itself more to a structural understanding of intersectionality. However, on its own it does not engage mutual constitution of inequalities at an individual level. Issues may be viewed as though they *happen* to be common to distinct groups (in which case, this verges into multi-strand understandings), or they may be viewed as common issues because of the synthesis of structures of inequality, such that these groups overlap and issues are interrelated. As I have discussed, one network explicitly combines this understanding with an 'intersections of equality strands' concept to overcome these limitations. This is important since even 'intersections of equality strands' work is often individually focused, though this is not an inherent feature of it.

Since meanings tend to be articulated at individual levels and pertain to how they would be applied in practice, again across the typology with the exception of pan equality, the detail of practice is often related to inclusion and access. Within generic understandings, this amounts to inclusion of *everyone*, including dominant and intersectionally privileged groups. Within multi-strand ones, this is inclusion of 'diverse' people or organizations, singularly defined; and 'diversity-within' and 'intersections of equality strands' share a focus on inclusion of those marginalized at points of intersection. Notwithstanding the similarity of focus on inclusion and access, there are important differences related to these concepts concerning this attention to representation (of who, how, why and at which levels), which will be explored in the next chapter.

In this chapter, I have outlined five distinct applied concepts of intersectionality that I found employed by equality sector practitioners, organizations and networks in England and Scotland. Given that intersectionality is understood in multiple, contradicting ways, it can be interpreted as a 'floating signifier' which in different contexts has come to mean what different equality sector actors use it to mean. However, these meanings are sites of contestation. These actors have varying social positions and interests, and so struggles over intersectionality's meanings are political.

There are now several studies exploring how intersectionality is practised in specific organizations and contexts. Few, however, explicitly explore what *meanings* of intersectionality are at play. Where take-up of intersectionality may be celebrated and become subject to investigation when it appears nominally or where researchers infer it (in so doing, at times conflating it with multi-strand or pan equality work (Parken and Young 2008; Parken 2010; Verloo 2013)), my research shows that when we look closer, we may see that intersectionality is not being used in the ways that we may assume that it is – not just in policy and institutions, but even among feminist, racial justice, and disability, LGBTI and refugee rights advocates. Which concept of intersectionality is at play is important since each has very different implications for intersectional marginalization, and intersectional justice.

PART III

5

Representation: The Politics of Intersectionality in Practice

'To always be inclusive in every sense of the word, is ensuring that no one is left behind and that everyone is always at the table, and if you're not on the table, then you're probably on the menu, so ...'

Kya, practitioner, LGBTI refugee organization, England

This chapter explores issues of representation (who is represented, and whether and how to represent) in efforts to operationalize intersectionality. Representation was identified by many of my participants as inseparable from intersectionality in equality organizing. Equality organizations themselves arose because of issues of representation: perceptions and realities of not being represented elsewhere. These organizations seek to counter misrecognition and misrepresentation and to achieve recognition. Organizational practice often centrally involves making representative claims (Saward 2006): this is true in policy and campaigning, and community development, on behalf of whole communities; and in service delivery, on behalf of service users (and by implication, other members of the target social group). The status quo of equality claims has been to speak for whole equality strands, singularly conceived.

Intersectionality presents a challenge to the status quo of equality sector representation, as well as to the literature on political representation (reviewed in Chapter 2), in three ways. It complicates the concept of 'descriptive representation' (Pitkin 1967) in highlighting that the complexity of identity means that no one can directly represent an equality group (indeed, that there are no singular equality groups). It further complicates 'substantive representation' in highlighting that essentialist single-strand claims tend to privilege the interests of the advantaged within-groups (Smooth 2006; Strolovitch 2007; Hancock 2014). Finally, it problematizes representative claims (Saward 2006) that constitute a singular 'represented'. Nevertheless, descriptive representation of intersectionally marginalized people is normatively, politically and epistemologically (Collins 1990) important to intersectionality.

At issue in the literature on the appropriation of intersectionality (Alexander-Floyd 2012; Bilge 2013; Jordan-Zachery 2013; Lewis 2013; Tomlinson 2013b; May 2015; Hancock 2016) is a politics of representation and knowledge: in what ways does it matter *who* uses intersectionality, and *for* whom? What relationships do the identities of knowers and doers of intersectionality have with the meanings employed, and the interests that those meanings further? What are the politics of the take-up of the term 'intersectionality' by those privileged in relation to its original concerns of the intersection of marginal race/gender? Empirical research has found that among academic knowledge producers, there are relationships between the social locations of women of colour, and LGBTI identity, and emphasis on race and sexuality in intersectionality research, respectively (Mügge et al 2018). In the preceding chapter, I similarly found that individual positionality influences which applied concept of intersectionality participants employ. 'Generic intersectionality' and additive 'multi-strand' and 'diversity-within' concepts were more prevalent among those with privileged aspects of identity, while 'intersections of equality strands' understandings tended to be associated with participants having marginalized aspects of identity. I found similar patterns in terms of the types of organizations that participants work in (single-issue vs. intersectional). Moreover, representation is closely related to sources of knowledge about intersectionality. The most prevalent source of knowledge identified by participants was either their own personal experience, or knowledge derived from experience shared within organizations.

Many participants identify having experiences of intersectional marginalization (that is, representation) within organizations as important to their learning about and doing intersectionality, providing impetus to do so. When asked about intersectionality, participants often inevitably discussed representation: they narrated issues of who is represented and who is misrepresented/and or excluded, whether within their organizations or in their outward-facing work. In so doing, they draw a trajectory between experience and knowledge that is also central to intersectionality theory. While intersectionality departs ontologically from standpoint theory in positing the simultaneity of privilege and oppression, it nevertheless similarly epistemologically privileges knowledge of inequalities and the fusion of these gained through experience. Many participants value personal experience of group experience in order to know about and to represent a group.

However, with regard to the spectrum of intersectionality outlined in Chapter 4, *perspectives on the significance of representation conflict, depending on which applied concept of intersectionality is employed.* In the preceding chapter, I observed that across most concepts of intersectionality, participants tended to express intersectionality in individualized ways, and therefore to articulate practice in terms of inclusion and access. Yet, there are very different ways of 'including' and representing. The ongoing need for representation to further intersectional justice claims (Howard and Vajda 2017), and the complexity of intersectionality which highlights the imperfection of representation, together raise questions of how practitioners might go about representation to advance intersectional justice – both in terms of who is represented descriptively, and how they are represented in practice. What is acceptable, and what is less so (Alcoff 1992)? More specifically: when practitioners seek to enable the participation of others, or to develop others as representatives, is this really another way of 'acting for'? What kind of participation is deemed essential: participation in activities, and/or decision-making about what these activities are? What understanding of intersectionality is at the root? Are there ways of 'acting for' that can be understood productively, as acts of allyship or solidarity, and ways that cannot? If we are acting *for* others, are we really practising intersectionality?

In what follows, I explore empirical problems of representation that emerge in UK NGO sector equality practice in three sections. I look first, as background and context, at key issues of representation and equality organizing: self-organization, and the extent to which single-strand equality organizations and networks of them represent equality 'communities' and those who are intersectionally marginalized within them. Next, I explore the relationship between representation and intersectionality in equality organizing, including internal representation and intersectional organizing, and varying approaches to representation in outward-facing work, ranging from enabling participation to acting *for* others. In other words, I consider issues of representation at different levels: those who run and staff organizations, as well as their wider constituencies. Finally, I explore conflicting perspectives on representation.

I will demonstrate that while equality organizations and networks fall short of being representative in various ways, many participants perceive that intersectional practice is fundamentally about: (i) representation of those who are intersectionally marginalized, and previously excluded, and (ii) the question of representation, namely: whether, and how, to represent. I argue that *competing concepts of intersectionality create conflicting views on, and approaches to, representation.* In particular, those employing generic understandings of intersectionality construct ideal representatives at odds with both those employing other concepts of intersectionality, and with intersectional justice. At the other end of the spectrum, participants employing 'intersections of equality strands' concepts value equitable and meaningful representation of intersectionally marginalized people highly.

Background: representation and equality organizing

A crucial distinction concerning representation among equality organizations is the extent to which they are self-organized, rather than being led by those more privileged than the organization's target group. Self-organization is important to perceptions of the validity of knowledge claims.

Self-organization

Self-organization refers to the extent to which organizations are 'led by and for' the group that they aim to serve or represent. Many participants perceive fundamental differences of knowledge, legitimacy and authenticity between such organizations and organizations that are not self-led. It is notable that the expression 'nothing about us without us' emerged from the UK disabled people's movement, and that contemporary disabled people's organizations are one outgrowth of this. The principle of autonomous self-organization has been similarly important in the feminist, racial justice, LGBTI and migrants' rights movements, and intersectional combinations of these, also institutionalized into NGOs. Equality organizations have roots in perceptions of not being represented elsewhere, in struggles for recognition (Benhabib 2002).

Here, Catherine, a practitioner in a small, funded disabled people's organization in Scotland, describes what working in a 'led by and for' organization means to her, in a quote representative of feelings in the disabled peoples' sector.

> '[I worked for a] user-led network … it was a brilliant job … I really [liked] the fact that the power in the organization was in the right place. It was with the members. It was a membership-led organization as is [my current organization … which] was started by disabled people … the board of management is still all disabled people. It's still controlled by disabled people … very much that's what people say is "I feel like I'm coming along and participating in an organization that's for me, that is mine." It's not the same as having things done to you and going along because there's some kind of imagined deficit … that needs to be fixed.'

In contrast, in equality organizations that are not user-led where she had previously worked, she perceived "power differences between workers and people who were being supported and within organizations".

Susan, director of Catherine's current organization, felt: "Disabled people trust us because we're disabled people. It's that peer to peers thing." Yet, Susan also recognized that despite sharing an identity as disabled, she did not share other aspects of identity with many of the organization's constituents.[1]

The value placed on being led 'by and for' is reflective of a belief in the central role of experience in knowledge production. Organizations that were not led 'by and for' their target group were not perceived to be able to act in the interests of marginalized groups in the same way, or to have the required knowledge. Eilidh, practitioner in a small, funded disabled people's organization, was frustrated at the lack of recognition of this distinction and the lack of value sometimes placed on experiential knowledge by other practitioners.

> 'There are … organizations which don't necessarily have any specific community equalities expertise, particularly around disability and who then start [to] try to move into speaking for disabled people. We … actually got a really hilarious email from someone asking us to be part of a forum that they were going to set up to identify what the issues are for disabled people in their area. And, and um, yeah, that was quite infuriating and I think we just ignored it.'

However, practitioners also perceived themselves to have specialist expertise that is not merely a product of their experience of marginalization or identification in particular equality communities, but importantly also from their experience of *working* in equalities. Practitioners who belong to multiple intersecting equality communities recognize that they do not necessarily share the expertise of those who work in equalities concerning other aspects of their identity. Similarly, practitioners with a multi-strand remit reflected that they do not have the same expertise in particular areas as those working in particular sub-sectors. This common reference to specialist knowledge resonates with what has been argued elsewhere, that politics does not follow from experience, but that experience needs to be analysed within a structural context to produce a political commitment to social change (Brewer 2011; Hemmings 2012; Phipps 2016; see also de Jong 2017). Moreover, it is important not to conflate social position, identity and political values since these are analytically distinct (Yuval-Davis 2006).

Yet, self-organization has material as well as symbolic implications. While there are different ways of measuring self-organization in use in the sector, in general, it implies that decision-making power in the organization is with those who identify as part of the communities whom it seeks to serve and represent. There are alternative structures, for example disability and refugee organizations that are not led by disabled people or refugees, or projects targeted to LGBTI people in organizations that are governed by straight and cisgender people. As I noted previously, organizations focused on socioeconomic disadvantage are not usually 'led by and for' their constituents. Importantly however, most of my participants perceived self-organization as key to knowledge claims, organizational legitimacy and perceptions of authenticity.

Representativeness of single-issue equality organizations

Representative roles for equality organizations have been encouraged by policy makers (Afridi and Warmington 2009) as well as being sought by organizations themselves: equality organizations frequently make representative claims (Saward 2006) for equality communities. Yet, even among organizations that are 'led by and for' their target group, the extent to which they are representative is a matter of debate. However, the representativeness of organizations (the extent to which they have legitimacy to represent, and are representative of, equality communities) is often taken for granted and uninterrogated within those organizations and among policy makers (as well as among scholars of political representation). Representativeness is uninterrogated although: (i) wider societal relations of domination and attendant exclusions are replicated in the NGO sector, and the equality sector within it; and (ii) equality NGOs are not, by and large, democratic organizations (wherein decisions are made by a membership), and may or may not have formal, defined constituencies to which they aim to be responsive or are accountable. Even for those that are democratic organizations, their constituencies do not encompass the whole of communities.

However, equality organizations also experience an extra burden of representation, or in other words, a higher threshold of representation, as compared with other kinds of organizations: there are double standards at play reflecting institutionalized inequalities wherein they are expected to be extra representative, and their legitimacy hinges on this expectation. These double standards do not affect all equality sub-sectors equally; they are particularly applied to racial justice and minority faith (for example, Muslim) organizations (Jones et al 2015).

Some participants recognized problems concerning the extent to which their organization is 'representative', including Robin, from a small, funded trans organization in England.

> 'Although we represent trans people ... we're not always going to be the voice of trans people and we might not get it right for the community ... somebody from another, representing another group of marginalized people and they aren't, again, going to be the voice of that one group.'

Robin recognized that their organization is perceived outwith the trans community to represent 'all' trans people, and yet that the organization will not always be perceived by all trans people as representing their interests. They felt the same was true of all other equality organizations.

Here, Nicola, an organizer of an equality network, reflected on the network's role as *governance* rather than representation – demonstrating a criticality in this regard that was exceptional among participants: "That thing about us [the network] being the gatekeepers to change. And we're probably more conservative [than some community members we are meant to represent]." Nicola felt that by virtue of being institutionalized, the equality network tended away from the radical claims-making demanded by some constituents, thereby becoming 'gatekeepers' and at times preventing needed social change.

Yet ultimately, equality organizations, in spite of the fact that not all would say in their mission statements that they aim to represent the whole of their communities, are not merely representing those individuals to whom they are concretely affiliated to policy makers – they are serving as de facto representatives for whole social groups. This assumption of representativeness is driven by both policy makers and organizations themselves. Policy makers at times seem to be happy to treat equality organizations as representative when it is in their interest (for expediency) to do so, and equally happy to call the same organizations out as unrepresentative when they become too critical or too radical, or are not otherwise performing the governance role the state desires. There is an expectation that to be valid, equality sector contributions to policy debates require representational legitimacy beyond what practitioners perceive as their specialist expertise.

Representativeness of equality networks

Where equality organizations may aim to represent equality communities, equality networks aim to represent or are interpreted as representing the sums of both organizations *and* communities. My participant equality networks have policy intermediary, representative roles between communities and organizations, and local government structures.

Equality networks reflect intersections of privilege. They are predominantly white (some more than others), predominantly cis, older, and non-migrants. Reflecting on the make-up of NGO networks, Olivia, director of a funded racially minoritized women of faith organization, said:

> 'In terms of the work that's been done there's lots of different and some really good work being done ... but [those doing the good work] didn't have a seat at the table. That also makes me question who is being selected to – quite often with these things you find that it's the same people at it.'

While Olivia, a woman of colour, was critical of representation in networks, many white participants were less so. Beyond representing predominantly intersectionally privileged individuals, equality networks are also made up predominantly of powerful *organizations* in their respective sectors: larger, single-strand organizations, to the exclusion of intersectional ones.

Some networks are particularly constrained in their abilities to represent the interests of marginalized equality communities by a lack of independence from policy makers and the public sector. Myra, coming from a more grassroots (unfunded) perspective, was able to be critical of this: "How do you actually lobby for institutional change when really [the network], it's institutional? It's funded by institutions. If you know the councillors are going to be there, you can't be like, 'well [the] council's a bit rubbish'. They can never be grassroots" (Myra, director, women's organization, Scotland).

As I explored in Chapter 2, intersectionality complicates existing theories of representation. One network in particular was aware of competing views, and competing interests, among its members, and so struggled with its role: whether it is to represent *all* of these views, to attempt to represent a middle ground between them, or to take one position over others – and cease to be representative in this way. These tensions are explored further in Chapter 6.

Summary

In sum, although they may be 'led by and for' the group that they aim to serve/represent, and although representativeness is often taken for granted, single-strand equality organizations, and networks of them, claiming to be or interpellated as representative, fall short of being representative of the actual populations they represent. However, they are no less representative than many other types of organizations. The equality sector has disproportionate representation of intersectionally privileged groups and so is not representative of intersectionally marginalized communities, and is constrained in what interests it can represent by funding sources. Yet, organizations and networks are often perceived to represent equality communities by powerful actors, whether they intend to or not. This is particularly acute in the case of equality networks, which have formal representative roles. Some participants are reflective about problems of representation, and consider its complexities; this is an important precondition to taking meaningful steps to take account of intersectionality.

Equality organizations, representation and intersectionality

Intersectionality exposes the inadequacy of single-issue and equality network representation. At times, equality organizations' representative claims are recognized and challenged by intersectionally marginalized members of the community being represented/being constituted through representation. Here a participant describes one such case, how the organization was perceived, and how this had made them reflect on the privilege incurred to those working in organizations in relation to some members of communities they are supposed to represent.

'When I spoke to the complainant on the phone, it was very much, [they] saw us within the context of being part of the problem. Probably, I would say, liberal elites. "We're getting paid and sit at a desk," actually, I was thinking, "that's actually good for us to hear". It might not be very pleasant or have been delivered in the most like way that you would like, but we do get a salary to fight for folk that are fucking sitting in food banks and are not able to get out of their houses, actually. It can be quite cosy. And you know we go along to the council and we have a coffee, and we have a biscuit and we do our meetings. It will be good for us to have a reality check from a ... person who feels very marginalized. Huge lists of barriers and stuff going on in their life who feels unemployable has it like, "I will never ... get that job that you've got. I will always be an outsider, but I don't want to engage in this shit that you're all engaging in because it's meaningless".' (Attribution omitted)

Some equality organizations are constrained in the extent to which they can be representative of the interests of intersectionally marginalized people, by resourcing, funders and laws. Put bluntly, organizations are constrained in the extent to which they can take radical positions that would more closely reflect the interests of intersectionally marginalized constituents. For similar reasons, single-strand organizations report that it has been much easier to gain funding for singular equality work than work that is intersectionally focused.[2] This is an excerpt of Eilidh describing the delicate dance that they and other organizations have to do between representing what they perceive as the interests of their constituents, and avoiding being too political in a way that might imply promotion of a particular political party, which would be in contravention of the law. This quote is representative of other participants' comments on this issue. "We do have to take care that we're not, kind of presenting information in any kind of politically biased way, but that's just, you know, it's actually quite easily done when you're just presenting facts like that happened kind of thing."

Recognizing that they are not representative, and reflecting on this, many single-strand equality organizations are concerned with increasing representation of marginalized groups within their organizations: this is a central narrative of how organizations understand and use intersectionality. Myra described why she felt this was important, drawing a clear link between experience and knowledge:

'You need a mix of people who can help remind each other like have you thought of it from that perspective and once you have a good mix of that it doesn't mean you need to represent every kind of aspect of identity there is, but you need at least four or five different aspects before so that you can get that conversation going so at least somebody will always think about other aspects that you might have missed. ... if you have an organization that isn't diverse in that ... intersectionality is like an academic exercise for them then sometimes it can work, but it's a lot of hard work to constantly be thinking of those things it's really difficult. Why not just do it the relatively easier way to get people who think about [it] naturally anyway. That's the main thing I think is key.'

Susan described how they were able to increase representation of intersectionally marginalized people in their organization: "[LGBTI people] became involved in [our organization] ... because [we were] tackling homophobia. Naming it and putting it out there and creating a culture where people felt safe" (Susan, director, disabled people's organization, Scotland).

Other organizations have taken formal decisions to become more representative, to expand their areas of work to encompass a wider range of interests, as Julie, director of a small, funded refugee organization in England described:

'This [members] meeting, we basically raised the question are you as ... members willing to back us to become an equality organization? Which means raising issues and talking about issues like sexuality and religion and domestic violence and FGM [female genital mutilation] and all these issues ... the whole discussion we had ... is are we going to talk and be equally inclusive. That wasn't the language we were using, but it works for now, equally inclusive of ... LGBT refugees, and atheist refugees, and women refugees who don't have husbands. Are we going to be this or not?'

Some participants were critical of other organizations for lacking representation of intersectionally marginalized people. This lack of representation was viewed by some as a barrier to 'doing' intersectionality. Without it, network organizer Elizabeth perceived that practitioners:

'Are like completely focused on that [single] issue because it's so important and the impact of it is so great. And ... it may be impacting ... the person or group themselves, but other things aren't [so] the commonalities and the ... will to fight these structural things together isn't there.'

Participants reflected that representation drives concern with intersectionality, and that conversely when organizations lack representation of people experiencing other inequalities, the will to address them is also lacking.

'Intersectional' organizations

Thus far in this section, I have discussed the inadequacy of 'single-strand' organization representation, their efforts to become more representative, and how they relate this to intersectionality. Single-strand equality organizations are often not representative of intersectionally marginalized people. While single-strand equality organizations emerged from perceptions of not being represented elsewhere, intersectional organizations arose for similar reasons, of not being represented by single-strand organizations, in struggles for intersectional recognition. There are power differences between these intersectional organizations and single-strand organizations, reflected in representation in equality networks and other structures.

Here, Claire, director of a small, relatively unfunded disabled women's organization described how and why their organization was formed.

> 'We exist pretty much because ... the disability movement in the UK was gender blind. As a thing, women were very rarely talked about within disability dialogue and even now within the disability sector in the UK there is only a limited amount of work intersectionally across multiple identity fronts and in particular, as well as gender, not being adequately addressed, neither is racialization.'

In other words, issues of visibility, recognition and representation of intersectionally marginalized groups have been at the core of the inception of such organizations, responding to problems of political intersectionality (Crenshaw 1989). Raka, director of a small, funded racially minoritized women of faith organization similarly described the origins of her organization: "[The organization] was set up to meet the needs of a very marginalized group of ... women. We weren't visible to anybody. We weren't visible to the wider community. We weren't visible to the internal community. We were there and that was it."

Intersectional self-organization is key since participants feel that if intersectionally marginalized communities are not represented/present, no one else will speak in their interests, as Raka explained.

> 'Over the years then you begin to see that if you're not visible, you're not quoted. People can call it whatever they like but if you're not there, nobody will say, "Oh, and by the way, what about the ... community?" Or, "By the way what about the Chinese community because we don't have anybody here." Nobody will talk about them. Nobody will want to know what their issues are because everybody's there with their own agenda which is rightly so. You don't have the time to go and talk about somebody else's agenda.'

Raka's quote emphasizes the importance of representation, and she felt that substantive representation was not possible without the descriptive.

Anika, director of a small, funded women of colour organization in England, explored the link between representation and intersectionality, the difference that self-organization makes, and the challenges that these organizations face, in a quote representative of similar concerns among intersectional organizations.

> 'As an organization, we have values and we've got [a] policy statement that makes it clear what we're about. That includes stuff around intersectionality. In terms of the organization, we say actually it's led by and for BME women. All our board members, staff volunteers, everybody comes from- they're women and they come from those backgrounds ... most local authorities who want to fund have one contract, and they want to fund a generic service. They say, okay, we will also provide [a] service for BME women. What they don't understand is actually what it means to provide a BME service. When I was talking about being a led for, by, and all that, women only organization, BME women only organization. This is what it means. In reality, it's not just having one member of staff from a BME community who speaks one language. That's not how- what we see specialism as. What we're concerned about is that … the BME women's refuges are going to just not get the funding going forward and will end up closing.'

Anika's quote clearly demonstrates the perceived differences between intersectional organizations and other organizations, and their marginality to the rest of the sector.

Raka articulated what she perceived as their representative role.

> 'Over the years we have just become one of the probably are the only [such organization] in [the country]. We've kind of become the voice of the [community] in some way. If anything that comes through like consultation, we want to ensure that we get it out to as many people as possible. Now, whether they respond or not at least we know that we have got a response in there in some manner or form.'

However, this (being a 'voice' of the community) raises problems of representation. While we may take it as self-evident that single-strand organizations are not representative of intersectionally marginalized groups, the same questions may be asked of intersectional organizations: the extent to which they are representative of intersectionally marginalized groups beyond the intersection that they are constituted around.

Thus, intersectional organizations are also concerned to increase representation of excluded groups. Participants from these organizations described how changes in representation within their organizations had led to new knowledge and new issues coming to the fore. For example, Olivia explained this in the context of a racially minoritized women of faith organization of which she is director: "We were quite [a] diverse team at one point ... and actually that influenced the conversations ... we then, with a bit of research, started piloting, 'Okay, can we go out and can we engage? What's the need?' That would inform us putting in for funding and doing work around that as well."

While often not represented in equality networks and other structures, intersectional organizations are sometimes conversely inundated with requests to represent their communities, as Claire described.

> 'Yes, intersectional organizations, on whatever grounds, need to be in spaces. We need to have the invites and the opportunities to be in spaces. What you tend to find is that ... across the board, because of how civil society is failing to be intersectional, when an organization is found that is intersectional that ticks certain boxes. They will start being inundated with requests above and beyond what they can deliver through goodwill alone ... that makes it incredibly difficult because actually, most intersectional organizations have very limited capacity.' (Claire, director, disabled women's organization)

This is important since intersectional organizations are thus called upon to over-represent communities; they have a burden of representation that many single-strand organizations do not have (though they also have an extra burden of representation as compared with non-equality organizations). This burden can also lead to burn out among organizers, in contexts where intersectional organizations are underfunded and much work within them is voluntary.

In spite of the plethora of equality organizations that exist, there are some intersectionally marginalized communities that lack representation. Here, Julie explained how she had tried unsuccessfully to find a representative organization for D/deaf refugees: "I was absolutely shocked by ... how very, very little there is out there for D/deaf refugees. There isn't any organization that has specialist knowledge in working with D/deaf refugees" (Julie, director, refugee organization, England).

Based on the preceding discussion, we would not expect intersectionally marginalized people to be adequately represented by, in this case, either D/deaf or refugee organizations, so the implications of this lack of representation include a lack of recognition and visibility, as well as a lack of articulation of interests, issues and concerns, and exclusion from existing services.

Having discussed representation among those who govern and staff both single-strand and intersectional organizations, I now turn to consider issues of representation relating to organization constituents: namely, whether and how organizations seek to represent them.

Competing approaches to representation in practice

Thus far, I have discussed how participants view representation as it relates to people who run and make up organizations. Once an organization has representation of intersectionally marginalized people among those who run it, how does it aim to reflect this among those who engage with the organization? How does it seek to represent those people?

Among organizations there are different approaches to practice related to representation discussed in narratives on intersectionality. These are enabling participation; seeking to develop others to participate and/or to act as representatives; and acting on behalf of, or for. Some are also more closely associated with some concepts of intersectionality than others.

Enabling others to act for themselves

Beyond increasing representation of previously unrepresented categories of people among those who run organizations (staff, trustees/directors), enabling participation of intersectionally marginalized people in the outward-facing activities of the organization is often viewed as key to how organizations practise intersectionality. Diversity-within and 'intersections of equality strands' concepts of intersectionality share a concern with including intersectionally marginalized people. However, for the former, this often stops at inclusion as service users, while those employing the latter seek to enable participation in decision-making.

For Anya, practitioner in a small, funded racial justice organization, whose source of knowledge of intersectionality is Black feminism, intersectional practice is, foremost, about involving and representing Black women in racial justice work. One way that her organization seeks to enable participation is through having specific consultative fora with women of colour, and other groups including disabled and older people of colour, people of colour and faith, and LGBTI people of colour, when they are producing policy consultation responses. To organize these, they have recruited members of those communities to lead community engagement in them. Moreover, they also separately involve intersectional organizations working at the intersection of race, as well as single-strand organizations in other equality sectors. However, these efforts are also constrained by the siloed, path-dependent nature of equality policy, and are not often reflected in the policies that are the ultimate outcome.

Kya, a practitioner in a small, funded LGBTI refugee organization in England, described how the organization seeks to involve communities in decision-making.

> 'To address intersectionality, we always ensure that we work with ... refugees, at the centre of all delivery are refugees. It's not led by people who are not refugees, so refugees are also part of the team, and ... most of the services that we offer are actually requested by refugees themselves, so they're part of the planning or from conception to planning to delivery. Every step of the way, [intersectionality is] including the people that you serve or the people that you want to work with.'

Yet, this drive to facilitate participation and self-representation does not necessarily overcome the challenge of reflecting situated perspectives and conflicting interests within intersectionally marginalized groups.

Though they value participation, practitioners quoted here are clear that it should have an objective, and are critical where it is sought without a clear purpose. They point out, for example, that there have been numerous evidence-gathering exercises, consultations and so on, in which equality communities have put forward what the issues are, articulated experiences, barriers and demands or recommendations for change. Further, they point out that creating yet more spaces of participation can be experienced as disempowering and demotivating by participants in those spaces who do not see any outcomes of their prior participation in the same kinds of spaces, and who may stop engaging in trying to create social change to progress equality as a result. Eilidh described frustration around this.

> 'We had somebody from the council the other day ... one of the officers asking one of my colleagues here if [they] could come within the next two weeks to speak to disabled people to find out what the barriers are to transport for disabled people and we ... were along the lines of please don't come and ask them about the barriers. We've got thousands of pages of consultation documents that we've written. We've got, we know what the barriers are ... come and ask them what the solutions are and discuss what you're going to do about it ... for people to be asked the same thing over and over again to say over and over again and still not see any change ... people do get a bit frustrated with that.'

Organizations and practitioners have to negotiate taking advantage of the political opportunities that emerge with maintaining participation in a sustainable way.

Seeking to develop others as representatives

While some organizations seek to enable participation, others seek to develop others in order that they *are deemed able to* participate. In other words, there is a step perceived to be necessary prior to their participation and ability to represent others. Catriona, a network organizer, described experience of developing representative structures of intersectionally marginalized people.

> 'It was also a lot of developing some of those people who didn't feel they were at the same level as somebody else. To say, "No. We need to hear your expertise." Really it's almost like mentoring people because they haven't been mentored in school or they haven't had the confidence built in them in other ways.'

Catriona thus felt that some people require others to 'develop' them before they are able to participate and to represent others. However, others were critical of the presumption that community members require development and do not already organize and participate outwith the scope and knowledge of equality NGOs. For example, Emma criticized the work of one equality network to develop representatives:

> 'I do feel like it is quite arrogant to assume that these communities don't already organize themselves … that all of a sudden you need this organization that's popped out of nowhere to bring together the BME community rather than tapping into the structures that have existed for decades in [the city]. Yes, there is definite tensions there. … There's plenty of people who are perfectly capable of speaking on behalf of themselves. It is about having meaningful change; it's about having actions.' (Emma, practitioner, racial justice organization)

On the other hand, Susan agreed that some people might need support in order to feel able to participate meaningfully: "Often disadvantage does lead to people needing [to have] their confidence built, their connections built and their ability to make contributions and be involved in all of this. To be built and supported and peer support is just so important" (Susan, director, Disabled people's organization, Scotland).

Some participants employing 'intersections of equality strands' concepts sought to facilitate others' participation and representation of others through the creation of structures on which there is representation of intersectionally marginalized people, or the alternative category of 'experts by experience' (a term used by some participants, one that has emerged in part from mental health service user self-advocacy movements). Here experience is not solely related to membership of social groups, but to life experiences that members have had. Network organizer, Catriona, described a structure that includes strand-specific organizations, and intersectionally marginalized people positioned at the intersection of those strands. This structure advises on work around accessing rights, including guidance and campaigns. Relating to the role of those with experience, she said:

> 'I'm like, "You know the system. You've been through it. You lobbied for your rights, other people's rights. You know the realities." When [policy makers] say, "Well, that's a one-off case." He can say, "Well it's not," but that strategic group again I've tried really hard to have a three-way split of experts by experience and then D/deaf and disabled people's organizations with experience of refugees and refugee organizations with experience of disabled people but really to try and build it so that the people who are leading that are not the lawyers or the medics on either side but the people who really genuinely know: disabled refugees.'

Acting on behalf of

Often practitioners try to create spaces of participation, but experience challenges of people's lack of capacity to engage in those spaces, particularly acute in a context of austerity. Sometimes they see themselves as ultimately speaking *for* others when they intend to speak with a collective voice or to enable others to speak for themselves. Jacqueline, practitioner in a small, funded disabled people's organization in England, described this:

> 'I'm really responding … to government consultations national and [local] government and … if I can … I'm giving information to local organizations to respond individually; quite often I'm gathering evidence of … what is happening to disabled people … and put it in a response … which we send so it's a kind of dual thing either helping local organizations do their response. Though many are so hard stretched in order to do the frontline services. There's not many organizations that have got the capacity to do consultation responses. So I'm aware of that. So I'm kind of speaking for D/deaf and disabled people.'

In contrast to 'speaking for' unintentionally as in the above quote, some view themselves as speaking with intention for those who cannot have a voice. This perception is at times found among those employing 'pan equality' concepts of intersectionality, who see themselves as working on the wider issues. For example, Julie:

> 'I've spent the past 14 years talking about refugees but I'm not a refugee. I know a great number of people that, have had the privilege

to meet a lot of very interesting people and, also, a lot of people who are struggling and suffering very badly in those years who aren't going to be able to express that or find that voice … it's not an either/or, and people who don't have those experiences mustn't be excluded from the process because they can play very valuable roles as well as long as people are clear on what the potential is they have.' (Julie, director, refugee organization, England)

Others problematized this approach. Kya responded:

'You know, to always be inclusive of lived experiences, I understand that sometimes people think that people with lived experiences might not have that voice but they always do. It's finding them and bringing them to this space. They don't have access to different equality spaces is not saying that they're not able to speak about the issues they're facing or the challenges or how intersectionality is [affecting them], but no one is making an effort to reach out into their communities and bring them forward and safe … if you are out in the community, you might not know about [this network] and you may not know how to join and even if you're like a small group and you are working in silos, if no one makes an effort to outreach to you, you won't have access to that space and voices are left behind and marginalized communities are further marginalized, so is someone making an effort to outreach and bring people to the table?' (Kya, practitioner, LGBTI refugee organization, England)

Catriona expressed a similar view:

'I think it's as political a statement to put somebody on a platform and allow them to say their – and to do that every time. I don't accept that they're hard to reach or they don't engage with us. "No, you've not done your outreach properly." That's something we have to be really, really aware of.' (Catriona, network organizer)

In spite of these drives to enable participation and self-representation, inevitably equality organizations make decisions for the communities they represent. For campaigning and policy organizations, this might be in the form of deciding which consultations to respond to, or which research is a priority, or how to frame an issue. For community development or service delivery organizations, this might be more directly deciding what activities members or service users can engage in. Equality organizations make meaningful decisions on behalf of those they aim to represent or are taken to represent, many of which are very significant to intersectional practice and intersectional justice.

As described in the previous chapter, participants employing diversity-within and 'intersections of equality strands' concepts of intersectionality have articulated their intersectional practice in the form of specific projects targeted at particular intersectionally marginalized groups. A key distinction related to representation is whether these projects are 'led by and for' the group that they serve and/or represent. This is distinct from the earlier discussion of self-organization since usually these projects are not undertaken in this way – it would make little sense for a Black women's organization to develop a dedicated project for Black women, for example. Rather, projects are usually not self-organized in this sense, but developed in the context of an organization with a wider remit, often as a response to intersectionality. As such, the projects may be subject to representational criticism from organizations led by the same target group – and, in a competitive funding environment, larger organizations with wider remits may be at an advantage to secure funding for similar work to that of a smaller self-organized group.

While many projects are developed on behalf of, and are not led by, the target group, it was important to some practitioners to articulate that projects were led by the target group. Yvonne, director of a small, funded women's organization in Scotland described one such project:

'We got money and worked with D/deaf women ... and it was led by D/deaf women. And we did a consultation right before we did that and it had to be led by D/deaf women because that's what they were saying, "We were fed up with hearing people coming in here and then telling us what we need and then, we did and it's written for English-speaking people, it's not written for BSL [British Sign Language] [using] people".'

However, given that projects are located in organizations that often lack that representation in governance, the extent to which they can be truly self-led is limited.

In the preceding sections, I have distinguished between enabling participation; developing others before they *can* (or are deemed able to) participate; and acting *for* others. Yet although some approaches seek to equalize power more than others, ultimately regardless of approach, there is a power dynamic between representatives and the represented. This is reflected in abilities to 'put' people on platforms, and in doing 'outreach' *to* others. These different approaches raise questions of allyship and solidarity, that is, what roles (if any) those who do not share that aspect of identity, who are privileged in relation to it, might have in advancing equality for that group, in the context of the power relation between these. This will be discussed further in Chapter 6.

Thus far in this chapter, I have discussed the extent to which we can consider equality organizations and networks to be representative. I have explored how intersectionally marginalized people are represented in organizations, whether through self-organization into 'intersectional' organizations, or through efforts to increase representation of intersectionally marginalized people among those running single-strand organizations and among their constituents. I have outlined different approaches to representation in practice. I will now turn to examine in detail how the different concepts of intersectionality that I outlined in Chapter 4 are related to competing views of, approaches to and conflict about representation. I will highlight several understandings of intersectionality that are particularly salient, while all concepts are analysed with reference to representation in Table 5.1.

Representational conflicts

As discussed in the preceding sections, although equality organizations fall short of being representative, to most participants, representation is fundamentally important to equality work and to practising intersectionality. This is reflected in the principle of self-organization, and in efforts to increase representation of intersectionally marginalized people among those who run organizations, as well as among constituents. Participants are driven by a belief in the link between experience and knowledge, valuing personal experience to know about and to represent a group. They describe that this representation has better enabled them to do intersectionality. Beyond internal representation issues, in their outward-facing work, practitioners have different approaches to representation in practice, ranging from enabling participation, to acting *for* others. Not all participants, however, place the same value on representation and 'authenticity' for practising intersectionality.

The spectrum of intersectionality
Multi-strand intersectionality

Some equality networks do have representation of multiple (singularly) marginalized communities, and see this as closely related to intersectionality. Among other participants, Diane, a practitioner in a small, funded women's organization in England, made this link between representation and intersectionality.

Interviewer:	Can you say a bit more about how intersectionality is kind of relevant to the ... network from your point of view?
Diane:	At this stage. It's been more about ... who the collective round the [governing circle] are. So it's that representation that's happening.

Here, however, intersectionality and representation are being conflated.

Within multi-strand understandings of intersectionality, wherein practising intersectionality is viewed as addressing equality strands in parallel, separately and simultaneously, intersectionality and representation are often conflated. Therefore, practising intersectionality stops at representation, while representation itself is unproblematized. Having representation of different equality strands in a network, coalition or other forum is, in and of itself, considered to be intersectionality. Similarly, having a diversity of singularly defined individual people can be conflated with intersectionality, in this additive intersectionality model. This is significant because this conflation effaces intersectional marginalization, and reinscribes singular understandings of equality strands. It fails to engage the challenge of intersectionality in reducing it to diversity, of types of equality organizations and the people representing them. From this perspective, intersectionality is equated to addressing equality strands in parallel, so reflection on the extent to which 'representative' organizations of these strands represent intersectionally marginalized experiences and interests is precluded.

Diversity-within

Those operating from a diversity-within concept of intersectionality (as well as at times, generic and pan equality ones) can seek to practise what I describe as 'inclusion without representation', one way of 'acting for': attempts to include as members/service users/constituents without representation among those running the organization. Since this understanding of intersectional practice, as addressing diversity within an equality strand viewed as more important than others, constructs those within the strand who also belong to other equality groups as having 'additional barriers', enabling participation and agency is not central to practice. Overall, for those employing this understanding of intersectionality, representation of intersectionally marginalized people in decision-making is constructed as more of a 'bonus' than a necessity (Christoffersen and Emejulu 2023).

Comparison of three different projects addressing violence against disabled women illustrates varying approaches to representation that are related to competing concepts of intersectionality (AD 5–11, 42). These projects were all identified as intersectional by participants. Across them, this work has aimed broadly at increasing disabled women's use of, and access to, violence against women and girls' services, responding to the exclusion of disabled women from these services. These services emerged within women's organizations and have been subject to the exclusions of those organizations: they were not set up with disabled women in mind. For two of these projects, disabled women came to be identified as a priority because of equality monitoring: when looking at service user data, disabled women were found to be disproportionately lacking in representation. The projects have been initiated by non-disabled women's organizations seeking to increase representation of disabled women among service users.

In the two projects employing a diversity-within concept of intersectionality, representation of disabled women among those running and directing these projects was not viewed to be as important as it was in the project employing an 'intersections of equality strands' understanding. Moreover, building relationships with the disabled people's *sector* in developing and implementing projects was also not viewed to be as important. The diversity-within projects' focus was building capacity of non-disabled women's organizations to serve disabled women. Therefore, this is a version of 'acting for' or 'doing to', which fails to take into account disabled women's agency and can be interpreted as paternalistic. In other words, the intersectionally marginalized subject constituted through representation (Saward 2006) driven by diversity-within is non-agential and multiply marginalized.

'Intersections of equality strands'

In contrast to 'inclusion without representation', this understanding of intersectionality, as work of and with specific groups sharing intersecting identities, is associated with aspiring to equitable representation, and participation, of those belonging to the relevant strands/their intersections. In other words, representation and enabling participation of intersectionally marginalized people is overall viewed as important within this concept of intersectionality.

The disabled women's project led by a network and developed from an 'intersections of equality strands' concept of intersectionality involved both the women's and disability sectors from the outset, and aspired to be disabled women-led as a core guiding principle, as well as involving survivors of violence. The project grew out of conversations among these actors. It was also the only one of the three similar projects which centrally involved women of colour and integrated consideration of race, sexuality and trans status along with gender and disability, consistent with a constitutive rather than an additive understanding of intersectionality. The representation of disabled women's organizations and women of colour in decision-making capacities in these conversations was critical to the project developing in this way.

There were also differences in how representation is sought. Whereas disabled women report that they are often asked and expected to give their unpaid time to consultative roles, advisory groups or similar, disabled women participants in this project advocated for their participation to be remunerated as expertise. In contrast to focusing projects on capacity-building non-disabled women's organizations, disabled women in this project advocated for developing disabled women-led peer support services. In contrast to diversity-within, therefore, the intersectionally marginalized subject constituted through representation driven by 'intersections of equality strands' understandings of intersectionality is agential, and this social position is constructed as mutually constituted rather than additively formed.

Generic intersectionality

Equality networks employing generic understandings of intersectionality, wherein there is little focus on any equality strand or strands in particular and similar work is delivered to benefit 'all', fall particularly short of being representative of intersectionally marginalized people (Christoffersen 2022). One network had low levels of engagement overall (relatively few members, few of whom attended meetings, or participated in consultation exercises between equality communities and local government). In my fieldnotes, I reflected that the few people at meetings seemed to know one another (fieldnotes, 2017). Network staff described aspirations to be member-led as 'not really panning out', so decisions ultimately on behalf of whole communities were made by a small number of staff: "We are struggling a little bit for it to be really member-led, so we are tending to direct a little bit more than we would like" (Leanne, network organizer). However, in the knowledge that it was not member-led, the network nevertheless problematically desired to maintain its position as officially representing marginalized equality communities in relation to local government.

In that city, there is one formal equality representative in local government structures; this role has mainly been held by white men. Among my participants, this was not always problematized. In fact, by some participant equality practitioners, one such positioned person occupying the role was looked on favourably, since they were viewed as 'unspecific' or 'unbiased' as compared with marginalized others.

One meeting that I participated in/observed was dominated by this white male representative, who is also employed in the equality sector. This role was initially envisioned to be held by someone acting in a voluntary capacity (someone with 'lived experience' of in/equalities, notwithstanding the considerable power imbalance that would have existed between this person and all others occupying roles within this structure), but this has not happened. His dominance at the meeting was commented on by others whom I went on to interview, in addition to being observed in my fieldnotes (2017):

'Like that meeting that went – well, we went along and we listened ... most of the time, it was [him] that was doing all the talking. ...

> I thought to myself these events have to be inspiring, they have to be invigorating, so you come out of the event thinking, "Right." Rather than, "Oh, God".' (Christopher, network member)

It was difficult to imagine this meeting as an inclusive space for equality sector practitioners of colour, in particular.

In contrast to valuing representation of intersectionally marginalized people, participants with a generic understanding of, and approach to, intersectionality appeared to think it is preferable if those whom they perceive as more 'neutral' people do the representing in the interests of intersectionality. One network organizer, for example, felt that if symbolic equality roles were held by those from single-strand organizations, they would not be able to have an 'intersectional' view – in the context of this role being held by a white man, and other organizations being led by and for equality communities. I took the implication to be that from their perspective and within this understanding of intersectionality, the current (white male) representative was preferred (fieldnotes, 2018). Some seem to doubt the abilities of (some particular) others to think beyond their own experience and identity, to feel that siloed thinking is so engrained that it cannot be overcome, and that intersectionality stands a better chance of being practised by more 'generic' people and organizations. This is a view also shared by some funders and policy makers.

Here, a figure is being constructed as neutral, as generic, as capable of representing all others, as most capable of intersectionality. This figure is from those groups constructed as the majority, in other words from those groups that are dominant: white and British, non-disabled, cisgender, not too young and not too old, not too religious. This figure is constructed as capable of knowing about and doing intersectionality, while 'those groups who are subject to misrepresentation find that this serves to make them less credible knowledge claimants … the misrecognition of their social identity works to undermine their position as knowers' (McConkey 2004, 203). The intersectional subjects of Black woman and woman of colour are effaced and implicitly constructed as self-interested, specific and ungeneralizable, and untrustworthy.

This constructed ideal figure is also from a generic or a multi-strand *organization*. Here it is felt that single-strand organizations are not able to overcome their diversity-within understanding of intersectionality because of siloed thinking, which, based on my criticism of this approach in the preceding chapter, is a valid concern. Yet, intersectional organizations are effaced within this, and their knowledge is doubly constructed as too niche and specific to be able to know about and do intersectionality (conceptualized generically).

However, many in the equality sector have a low opinion of generic organizations, as David, director of a small, unfunded LGBTI organization in England, explained: "There's what I call … generic … organizations which are people who are not specialists but dabble in different communities.

Sometimes there's some resentment against them because they're seen as organizations that are not from the community but they come in and take community money."

Generic intersectionality and its implications for representation are illustrated in the following example. As discussed in the previous chapter, this concept is often found among policy makers and within the overlap between policy makers, the public sector and NGO sectors. In one city, as in both others, in the former equality policy environment the council hosted and administered strand-specific equality networks, including a race equality network. For reasons partly due to the new multi-strand equality policy context and largely owing to diminished resources, the strand-specific equality networks were dissolved.

The council also funded a former race equality council, at the time a rebranded multi-strand equality organization, for strategic equality input and infrastructure. Although now multi-strand because of policy pressure, these former race equality councils have tended to retain a strong focus on race as compared with other multi-strand organizations that lack this history – likely owing to continued substantial representation of racially minoritized antiracist advocates among the staff and in governance structures.

However, in order to establish a new local equality network, a network intended by the council to be 'intersectional' from the outset, funding was removed from this multi-strand equality organization, with a history and key focus on race. In other words, in the name of intersectionality, funding was removed from race equality to go toward generic 'intersectional' equality; funding was removed from a people of colour-led and predominantly people of colour organization (in part, on the basis that it was thought incapable of sufficient intersectionality) and given to a white-led and predominantly white organization (constructed as being capable of, indeed best positioned to do, intersectionality). Here, intersectionality is given the meaning of 'generic', namely: where no equality strand is addressed in particular, and equality is constructed as being for and about 'everyone' (white people) rather than marginalized groups.

'Acting for' becomes particularly problematic when those doing the acting do not have personal experience of the group that they are representing. In my field notes, I observed the whiteness of the equality network (space, meetings, events, member organizations) developed by the organization constructed as being capable of intersectionality. But this may or may not even be problematized in a discourse where race is constructed as specific and non-intersectional (qua generic).

As Anya observed in a different context,

'Some of them [public sector partners] don't really get what [intersectionality] is. They get it confused with sort of cross-strand approaches, or sometimes even worse they get it confused with blanket approaches, like "We need to be mindful of intersectionality so we'd better not focus on race"!? [laughs] and you go, "What!? Stop it".' (Anya, practitioner, racial justice organization)

Organizers of this network acknowledged that engagement from racially minoritized groups was low, and mentioned the possibility of doing targeted work around this; to my knowledge at the time of writing this had not happened, due to alternative structures emerging (explored later).

In this context, practitioners working on racial justice in some capacity felt that race had been marginalized, as Raka explained.

'All the tokenism and everything like that seems to be going out of the window as well now. It's kind of like at the barefaced level of we've got rid of the race – we're an equality … based thing – and that works across all six [sic] strands. … Now, it's just an equality network. Race has fallen off the agenda.' (Raka, director, racially minoritized women of faith organization)

Raka's perspective is particularly noteworthy, since according to some literature on intersectionality and public policy (for example, Parken 2010; Hankivsky and Christoffersen 2011), it would be organizations such as this that might be expected to benefit from establishment of a multi-strand network, as opposed to single-strand networks. In a single-strand network model, intersectional organizations may: (i) feel compelled to participate in more than one network (for example, a race and a women's network), which would take twice the resources to do; and (ii) they may feel that their issues and experiences are compartmentalized, and inadequately addressed. However, this is precisely opposite to the view of this organization, within which some were supporters of the new equality network at its inception, but changed their perspective when they felt that race was marginalized by the network's generic approach to equality and to intersectionality.

Alternative organizing by women of colour

Generic approaches to equality and intersectionality engender resistance from women of colour. Some of those who felt that race had been marginalized from policy agendas with both the dissolution of the council-administrated race equality forum, and within the new equality network itself, established a new racial justice forum. This forum brings together practitioners from different organizations to focus on strategic engagement with key policy makers. This forum is not funded by the council or other funders, so it is voluntary (although those involved may work in the sector, the time they spend on this is outwith their jobs). Participants describe it being made up predominantly of women of colour. This forum arose as a direct response to what practitioners perceived as the marginalization of race in the funded equality network, as Emma explained:

> 'I must say that that's part of the reason that the [forum] was set up. It's because they felt that the council had taken funding from lots of different organizations and just created this body that was apparently meant to address all protected characteristics ... we did feel that [the new "intersectional" network] wasn't looking at race.' (Emma, practitioner, racial justice organization)

Raka agreed: "There was quite a discussion amongst quite a few people that have been involved in [racial justice work] for many, many years to see that there is nothing now to challenge [the] council about what's happening around the race agenda. This [alternative forum] has been formed" (Raka, director, racially minoritized women of faith organization). In other words, when they did not feel included in or represented by the new network operating with a generic understanding of intersectionality, intersectionally marginalized women of colour organized to represent the interests of racially minoritized communities. Given the lack of funding, however, there was some concern in participant narratives that this forum may not be sustainable. Yet it is highly unlikely to be funded by the council, since the council seeks generic intersectionality as value for money in the context of austerity, and has funded the development of the new network accordingly. At the time of research, participants were trying to gain funding for the forum:

> 'This informal group are really active and then everybody's working ... people think that everybody wants to be paid all the time but sometimes these jobs or these organizations do need somebody that's paid. Everybody is doing everything voluntary. But, if you're tied up with other things then that's when it falls off the edge. If we create something it should be something that has a sound base. Even if you have one person that is full time. That's able to collate the information, put it together, call the meetings, have a space. Then these kind of things will work. But if everything's part time and piecemeal, we'll never have the same clout as something that's as organized from a base.' (Raka, director, racially minoritized women of faith organization)

Representation and opposing understandings of intersectionality

I identified that there are competing understandings of intersectionality in circulation among research participants, as well as in wider academia and popular (feminist) culture; that in fact, intersectionality is imbued with meanings that are so opposed to one another, that its utility at all in this context is a matter for debate. Some concepts of intersectionality are particularly opposing.

The first of these is intersectionality as generic equality, firmly distanced from the 'specificity' of race, and serving to efface Black woman as both figure or intersectional subject, and embodied being (Lewis 2017). Equality networks employing this meaning see themselves as representing 'everybody', and make representative claims that constitute this everybody:

> 'We're representing all the protected characteristics … and not one is more important than the other. We just wanted to sort of pre-empt any issues around that with working with organizations that have a sole focus, and will naturally see that as the most important, but we needed everyone to kind of get together and be on a level.' (Leanne, network organizer)

Moreover, here 'intersectionality' itself represents or signifies everybody.

Within a generic understanding, it is either deemed irrelevant who is doing the representing, since the aim is to represent 'everyone'; *or*, it is felt preferable to have figures constructed as occupying 'neutral' social positions as representatives. This understanding of intersectionality is firmly present in the construction of racial justice organizations as incapable of doing intersectionality, discussed in the preceding chapter, and in the policy decision to remove funding from one such organization in order to fund intersectionality. It is in sharp contrast to intersectionality's focus on women of colour and those who are most disadvantaged. Yet, others with alternative understandings of intersectionality, and of the relationship between experience and knowledge, feel that: "Without having knowledge on the ground, without having key experts around the table, I don't know how you can claim to represent all protected characteristics" (Emma, practitioner, racial justice organization).

One understanding of intersectionality in particular can be described in opposing terms to generic ones, as one grounded in the specific social group/location of Black women (for example, Hancock 2016) or women of colour. From this perspective, intersectional representational practice relates to women of colour, and organizations employing this meaning see themselves as being led by and for women of colour. Emma felt that the alternative race equality forum was intersectional, insofar as it was predominantly women of colour involved: "Most of the network members are Black women. I think from that perspective [intersectionality] comes up a lot. In terms of what we've been looking at doing and because of structural issues it's looking at structural issues on race. There's an implied intersectionality but nothing's explicit" (Emma, practitioner, racial justice organization). This understanding is directly opposed to *generic* understandings of intersectionality. Within the former, it is very relevant who the representatives are. This distinction is important because in the city where this story unfolded, generic understandings of intersectionality have much more power than others.

Conclusions

In this chapter, I have explored broadly the concept of representation, and how it relates to participant meanings and uses of intersectionality. I have shown that though some equality organizations and networks strive to be representative, as a key part of how they view themselves to use ideas of intersectionality, overall, they are not representative of intersectionally marginalized people within their constituencies. This lack of representativeness is imbued with implications for intersectional practice and intersectional justice, particularly in relation to powerful equality networks. This is because, regardless of aims to be representative or representativeness, equality organizations are interpellated as, and cultivated as, representatives by policy makers. However, there are important differences among organizations and networks, including to the value placed on representation, and how it relates to intersectionality. Most participants believe that representation of marginalized groups is important, which is reflected in self-organization. They also believe that there is a strong relationship between experience and knowledge. Participants feel that knowledge of inequalities derives from identification with and experience of inequalities, but that in working in equalities, additional expertise is gained. In a similar vein, knowledge of intersectionality is often derived from (i) experiences of intersectional marginalization, and (ii) at a more collective level, the joining together of single-strand expertise in networks and coalitions. Participants described how changes in representation at different levels led to more intersectional working.

Next, I analysed different approaches to representation in day-to-day outward-facing practice. Some practitioners seek to equalize power, and to enable participation, so that people might act for themselves (thus doing away with a need for representation). While laudable, this approach has inherent limitations, since enabling participation of whole social groups or constituencies is not logistically conceivable. Others seek to develop others (usually conceptualized as more marginal than themselves) to act as representatives. This approach raises disagreement as to the power dynamic involved, the need for such development, and prioritization of representation over policy change. Still others reflect that, in spite of efforts not to, they ultimately end up speaking *for* communities, which has been theorized as epistemic violence (Alcoff 1992). Other acts of what may be interpreted as 'acting/speaking for' include the creation of new projects targeted at particular intersectionally marginalized communities, another prevalent way in which organizations narrate their use of intersectionality. Here the value given to self-organization by participants in relation to their own single-strand organizations is at times curiously forgotten. Yet some practitioners are keen to encourage community leadership of such projects, insofar as that is possible in organizations governed by those who are more intersectionally privileged.

I argued that *conflicting perspectives on representation hinge on competing concepts within the spectrum of intersectionality*. In other words, competing concepts of intersectionality are at the root of conflicting views on who is best positioned to do and represent intersectionality, as well as having implications for how representation happens in day-to-day practice. Multi-strand understandings tend to problematically conflate representation with intersectionality, singularly essentializing equality groups in the process and effacing intersectional marginalization. Acting for others takes different forms, and networks employing generic concepts of intersectionality that do so are particularly problematic. Less obviously and more insidiously, acting for others by way of 'inclusion without representation', named as doing intersectionality among participants practising it as diversity-within, also falls far short of what intersectionality demands. Conversely, projects developed with an 'intersections of equality strands' understanding are associated with high levels of value placed on representation, and with efforts to equalize relationships (see also Laperriere and Lépinard (2016) who observe a similar distinction among Canadian women's organizations). Enabling participation, and making space for self-organization of intersectionally marginalized people (or 'intersectional recognition' (Lépinard 2014)) concerned with the intersections of equality strands provides a more promising model for how practitioners might operationalize intersectionality to advance intersectional justice.

Within generic understandings of intersectionality circulating among relatively dominant and privileged practitioners, intersectionally marginalized, misrecognized and misrepresented people, in particular people of colour working on racial justice, are constructed as non-credible knowers about and doers of intersectionality by their equality sector 'colleagues'. This is important, since proponents of this view include powerful political actors. Also within generic understandings, I found subtle indications of belief in the desirability of representation in the name of intersectionality to be 'non-specific', which has been both implicitly and explicitly constructed as those occupying dominant social positions; and not representing a specific equality 'interest' or organization, but rather, 'everybody'. In response and resistance to generic understandings, intersectionally marginalized women of colour organize to represent themselves. The relationships between competing concepts of intersectionality and representation are further specified in Table 5.1.

I have aimed to demonstrate that operationalizing intersectionality in equality practice is fundamentally about representation: self-organization among intersectionally marginalized people, and increasing representation of intersectionally marginalized people within organizations and among constituents, driven by belief in the relationship between experience and knowledge. Importantly, I have also aimed to demonstrate that using intersectionality in practice also often centres on questions of representation: *whether, and how, to represent*.

In Chapter 2, I reviewed literature on intersectionality and (political) representation, finding that the literature broadly concludes that: (i) representation of marginalized groups is important symbolically for recognition (Phillips 1995); (ii) though substantive representation does not necessarily follow from descriptive representation, there is some relationship between the two; (iii) determining 'substantive interests' is challenging and risks essentialism; (iv) the process of representation is constitutive of who and what is being represented; and (v) there is a need to be critical of the possibilities, normative desirability and unintended consequences of representation. I demonstrated that intersectionality complicates existing concepts of representation. Conversely, some existing intersectionality theory fails to adequately contend with representation (wherein it is reduced to an analytic/empirical practice; see, for example, McCall (2005)).

My findings resonate with literature on the symbolic importance of representation, and support a relationship between descriptive and substantive representation. Participants from *both* single-strand and intersectional organizations employed essentialism strategically (Spivak 2003), and they also view themselves as having expertise that goes beyond identifying with the groups that they serve and represent. Put another way, participants were not immobilized by concerns around essentialism.

My findings indicate the difference representation can make, and the need to consider intersectional organizations distinctly from 'single-strand' organizations, whereas some literature considers the former as sub-categories of the latter (Strolovitch 2007; English 2019; Marchetti 2019) (if they are not omitted entirely). Moreover, equality organizations complicate literature on political representation per se, with many focusing on enabling participation and developing representatives and *not* 'acting for' others (dependent on which understanding of intersectionality they employ). In a broader context of epistemic injustice that devalues intersectionally marginalized women of colour as non-credible knowers, they organize to represent *themselves*, rather than placing faith in single-strand or generic organizations to do so; they declare themselves present (Lewis 2017). While some literature on representation has urged focus on the claims made rather

Table 5.1: Representation and applied concepts of intersectionality

	Applied concept of intersectionality	Representation
Generic	No focus or very little focus on any equality strand or strands in particular: the same work is delivered to benefit 'all'. Addressing issues that affect '*everybody*' (that is, not only or even primarily marginalized equality groups).	Preference for 'neutral', 'unspecific' and 'unbiased' representatives (that is, belonging to dominant social groups); constructed as the only ones capable of knowing about and doing intersectionality, and as representing all others. Intersectionally marginalized people (and organizations of them) constructed as non-credible knowers about and doers of intersectionality, unable to think beyond their own experience and identities.
Pan equality	Addressing issues that affect all/most marginalized equality groups.	Varying approaches; representation of intersectionally marginalized people not necessarily viewed as important. Some employing this concept justify acting *for* others.
Multi-strand	Addressing equality strands in parallel, separately and simultaneously.	Intersectionality and singular representation are conflated: practising intersectionality stops at representation; effaces intersectional marginalization. Intersectional representation constructed as being the presence of all singular equality strands.
Diversity-within	Addressing intersections within an equality strand, for example differences among women. One strand/inequality viewed as primary.	Acting *for* intersectionally marginalized others constructed as non-agential: 'inclusion without representation'. This is seeking representation of intersectionally marginalized people as service users or constituents, but not meaningfully in decision-making. Implicitly, therefore, constructs privileged sub-group members as ideal representatives.
'Intersections of equality strands'	Work of/with specific groups sharing intersecting identities, for example women of colour, disabled women, and so on. No particular strand is primary or more in focus than the other(s).	Representation and enabling participation of intersectionally marginalized people viewed as important. Intersectionally marginalized people constituted as agents.

than the claims-makers (Saward 2006), when thinking about and using intersectionality, my participants view these as closely interrelated and remain deeply concerned with who is making claims, and for whom. Finally, my findings confirm the importance of careful exploration of the understandings of intersectionality that are employed in practice, and their implications.

Given that equality organizations are not often representative of (all) intersectionally marginalized sub-groups of their constituents, one solution is a plurality and diversity of organizations focused on multiple identity axes. Many of my participants value this plurality, since they are not otherwise represented, and see it as under threat in austerity. Yet, arguably, social change in the interests of intersectional justice demands a higher level of organization, which organizations currently approximate through networks and coalitions. The next chapter focuses on the challenges and possibilities for intersectional solidarity of these relationships.

6

Coalition: Solidarity and Intersectional Practice

'It suits definitely the powers that be, I hate using that term, but that … whole divide and rule thing. If we link up across different groups and realize that actually … things are set up to favour certain people and not others and that actually, the more we work together to challenge those structures, the better.'

Catherine, practitioner, disabled people's organization, Scotland

In Chapter 4, I outlined five distinct applied concepts of intersectionality held by equality practitioners, organizations and networks. In Chapter 5, I analysed how these concepts shape approaches to representation, which emerged as a core issue in narratives of understanding and using intersectionality. Issues of representation also influence which concepts *of* intersectionality are employed by participants, in a cyclical relationship.

My research confirmed the importance of a second key issue to understanding and using intersectionality, one identified in the literature and utilized in my research design: coalition (Strolovitch 2007; Cole 2008; Bassel and Emejulu 2014; Collins and Bilge 2016), within which I also consider relationship building and solidarity. Consistent with previous research (Strolovitch 2007; Roberts and Jesudason 2013; Collins and Bilge 2016), many participants described intersectional knowledge and practice, and commitment to it, as emerging from political intersectionality formations/multi-strand equality networks: equality networks were identified as an important source of knowledge about intersectionality. Alternatively, desire to work intersectionally was also a key driver for coalition building and network membership. In the context of intersectionality, participants often spoke of other coalitions and networks that they were part of, without being prompted.

There are different ways of considering 'coalition'. From an intersectional perspective, identity-based work can itself be understood as coalitional work, because of the vast differences within identity groups (Crenshaw 1991; Chun et al 2013; Carastathis 2016; Collins and Bilge 2016). The extent to which equality organizations recognized and reflected this varied. My research specifically focused on another level of coalition, that between organizations. The networks that I worked with differ from some definitions of 'coalition' in that they are not necessarily temporary, but are coalitions in the sense that they involve some 'direct coordination of claims between two or more previously [or otherwise] distinct actors' (Tilly and Tarrow 2007, 16). They also host and generate more temporary formations to achieve distinct goals.

Yet coalition building among equality organizations is hampered by what is often a lack of shared beliefs (Meer 2019) within the equality sub-sectors that I researched in and with (racial justice, women's, disability, LGBTI, refugee and intersectional combinations), often along intersectional lines. There are competing perspectives on: whether policy priorities relate to privileged sub-group members or intersectionally marginalized ones; whether the approach is 'diversity-within' wherein one inequality is considered primary, or whether it is 'intersections of equality strands'; whether equality groups are conceived of as overlapping and thus having shared issues ('pan equality intersectionality'), or not ('multi-strand intersectionality'). This lack of shared beliefs is clear when we consider intersectional organizations and not only single-strand organizations to be key members of equality sub-sectors. These intersectional fractures, in turn, intersect with competing perspectives within equality sub-sectors as to whether to frame inequalities as relating to institutional discrimination, or to deficits within equality groups (Meer 2019). These competing perspectives influence the issues that equality networks seek to address.

Coalition building can be related to solidarity. Goals of building solidarity motivate network membership for many members, and the networks aim to further build solidarity. The way that the networks come together across difference for shared political goals, namely to cooperate in order to advance equality in their respective cities through practice and policy influence, provides moments consistent with 'political solidarity': a form of solidarity based not on similarity, but on common commitment to opposing oppression and injustice (Scholz 2008). The specific goals of the networks fluctuate, but many can be located in opposing injustice in policy. In coming together, network members have committed to a broader concept of equality than that subscribed to by their own, mainly single-strand/issue, organizations, broader than what the organizations work toward on a day-to-day basis. They have committed to seeking equality beyond similarity or shared experience. Yet, across all three networks, equality and intersectionality remain vaguely defined; and not surprisingly, building and extending solidarity across difference raises challenges. Within political solidarity we can further distinguish 'intersectional solidarity': 'an ongoing process of creating ties and coalitions across social group differences by negotiating power asymmetries' (Cole 2008; Tormos 2017, 712; Ciccia and Roggeband 2021).

The networks

Beyond desiring and aiming to achieve greater equality for marginalized groups, and having some contingent shared interests in, for example, increasing funding for equality work in general, networks are not necessarily united by shared beliefs or values, and these fractures are often closely related to intersectionality. In this context, network organizers (staff of the networks) have the challenging task of building unity and managing competing perspectives in order to develop and achieve particular policy objectives.

Funding for equality networks goes to one organization, which hosts the network and is accountable for it, or to the network itself, if it is formally constituted; it is not split among the organizations in the network. Yet, across all three networks, membership implies some commitment and aims at cooperation and collaboration. Network members (equality organizations) maintain organizational autonomy yet come together to cooperate and collaborate, notably on policy engagement.

Across the three networks that I studied, the how and why of network formation varies. There tends to be only one equality network in a city, and some are members for that reason: because it is the only equality network with official influence into local policy structures, and so they wish to have a seat at that table. The first network aims to enable individuals and organizations to work with the public sector to advance equality, promote human rights and address poverty. This network was established by local government, and although active membership offers access to local policy making structures that most organizations would not otherwise have, NGO sector engagement with the network is low, and alternative coalitions have been formed. The second network aims at cross-sector cooperation on equality issues, and policy influence into local structures. This network was initiated by some equality organizations and, to others, offers access to local policy making structures that on their own they would not have. The third network aims to bring together equality and human rights organizations to facilitate learning and collaboration, as well as to influence policy and public services. This network has been maintained independently by equality organizations. There are thus differences between the networks: coalition formation is more successful, and there is greater scope for solidarity building, when organizations come together willingly out of desire to work together, and a desire for solidarity, than when top-down structures are imposed by local government. Whether networks have been formed relatively organically by their members seems to be more important to engagement in them than what participation might offer instrumentally.

Equality networks are made up predominantly of powerful organizations in their respective sectors: larger, single-strand organizations. Participants from less powerful organizations identify a range of barriers to their participation in such structures. Some networks are inclusive of less powerful actors (for example, intersectional organizations). Where less powerful organizations are included, they are in a minority and may struggle to have their concerns come to the fore (see also Bilge 2016). They often also have different motivations for participation in networks, including gaining access to policy structures, other organizations and relationships that they would not otherwise have.

In this chapter, I ask, when applying intersectionality together in coalitions, what do networks do, and how? How do competing applied concepts of intersectionality circulate, and with what effects for intersectional solidarity and intersectional justice?

This chapter is in four sections. I will first discuss barriers to coalition and solidarity. Foremost among these barriers are engrained siloed thinking and attitudes, which are particularly associated with additive multi-strand and diversity-within concepts of intersectionality. Second, having explored barriers *to* coalition and solidarity, I will turn to a more detailed examination of coalitions at work, through analysis of network engagement on local equality strategies. This analysis further explicates all of the concepts of intersectionality discussed in this book, and the tensions between them and their proponents. Third, I will look in more detail at challenges and conflicts that emerge in these coalitional collaborations. Siloed thinking extends to outright discrimination within and among equality sectors. As I discussed in Chapter 4, diversity-within and multi-strand concepts of intersectionality lack recognition of relationality and the simultaneity of privilege and oppression because they are additive. Since they view members of equality groups as solely oppressed along a singular axis, they can engender resistance to recognition of the interlocking nature of other inequality structures and the acknowledgement of privilege and complicity that that would entail. This recognition also unseats diversity-within's premise that one inequality is always, or ever, primary. *This resistant refusal to recognize the always-interlocking nature of other inequality structures, inherent to additive intersectionality, becomes especially pronounced when the particular ontologies of those structures (namely sexism and cisgenderism) generate conflict, because they share key concepts and categories (namely gender/ 'woman').* Finally, I will look at lessons that emerge in terms of how intersectional political solidarity can be built, and the concepts of intersectionality that it requires; and what some of the limits to this are in these specific contexts.

I will argue that while coalition is a core part of intersectional practice, *which concept of intersectionality is employed by both coalitions themselves and participants in them determines how successful they are at building relationships of solidarity to further intersectional justice.*

Barriers to intersectional political solidarity

Siloed thinking

Siloed thinking is among the most significant barriers to operationalizing intersectionality generally, and to creating coalitions and networks characterized by intersectional solidarity more specifically. By siloed thinking I mean thinking about specific inequalities (and the equality sectors organized around them) in isolation from one another: in other words, lack of recognition of (or wilful blindness to (Hancock 2011)) the ways in which inequalities cross over or intersect.

Drivers

Siloed thinking is exacerbated by the broader context discussed in Chapter 3, though it is not determined by it. Equality work remains largely siloed across governments. Previously, much funding for equality work was also siloed (funds were earmarked for particular equality strands), which is one reason that the sectors have developed in siloed ways. In the context of the Equality Act, siloed funding is rarer. Nevertheless, the funding environment is important: I have observed differences in siloed thinking across cases, generated by particularities of the funding context. Siloed thinking is particularly prevalent when there are few overall sources of funding for equality organizations, compared with contexts where there is a greater diversity of funding sources (notably more private trusts and foundations), and thus less competition for the same few sources. The funding environment was felt by participants to engender conversations around who is 'more discriminated against', that is, whose work is more important and thus more deserving of funding. In other words, policy and public sector support for equality work in the absence of other funding sources can have the unintended effect of generating an atmosphere of greater competition, which drives siloed thinking and is an obstacle to working intersectionally. In all contexts, siloed thinking is exacerbated by diminishing resources in times of austerity, as Aziz, director of a funded racial justice organization in Scotland, explained: "The funders actually make people fight each other for that resource and that's where the resentment sometimes comes."

Beyond funding, siloed thinking is also related to the Equality Act. Some organizations and practitioners opposed the Act itself, favouring separate legislation for different inequalities. Some equality sectors opposed inclusion of certain other areas in the Act, and feel that their strand has been diluted since the Act (at times blamed on the inclusion of other areas per se). Many hoped that the Act would increase protections for all protected groups, but feel that these were lowered in some areas, for example Susan, director of a small, funded disabled people's organization in Scotland: "If you look at the Equality Act, putting everything together comes at a cost, it comes at the cost of diluting things. ... I think the approach of lumping everything together can be problematic when it's not done right." These sentiments have been exacerbated by diminished resourcing in the period of the Act and a concomitant perceived generic approach to equality (itself increasingly equated with intersectionality, as I identified in Chapter 4). Opposition to generic equality and 'generic intersectionality' can verge into espousing siloed thinking. Some participants, for example Yvonne, director of a small, funded women's organization in Scotland, viewed generic equality as a threat, and the organization's siloed thinking was exacerbated in response: "What happens is our specialisms get watered down." Here, silos are justified as separate bodies of expertise, which are at risk of being lost by generic policy approaches.

Manifestations

As part of this broader pattern of siloed thinking, at times participants had perceptions of other equality sectors as being better off than 'their' sector in various ways: in receipt of a disproportionate amount of available funding, or 'better organized'. This is particularly interesting because I found that often these perceptions were not reflective of available evidence showing, for example, where funding is allocated. In general, 'newer' sectors (those representing equality areas for which anti-discrimination legislation is more recent) were perceived to be better off by 'older' sectors, with the LGBTI sector often singled out: "Some strands are well-organized, some are not ... I meant LGBT that was never, I mean from legislation point of view; they just come new into it but they were well-organized. The disabilities came into the legislation very well-organized" (Aziz, director, racial justice organization, Scotland).

Underlying some of these juxtapositions is a view of other equality communities as being more homogeneous/having less complexity than one's 'own'; there were frequent assumptions made by participants that 'their' community is the one with the greatest diversity and complexity. This claim to greater complexity and diversity was made in different ways by participants from the disabled people's, racial justice, refugee and women's sectors; for example: "But because of the various, you know ... when you talk about race, you talk about 50 different people. How do you bring that together in the first place? The needs of Africans is different from Asians and Europeans. The needs are different" (attribution omitted).

At times, siloed attitudes extended to a seeming lack of awareness that strands cross over at all. This is the heart of the ontological challenge that intersectionality presents. This is illustrated by the following example.

At a network meeting, practitioners from a disabled people's organization presented on issues for disabled people that they had identified in the city and recommendations to address them, in an effort to engage equality organizations from other sectors present in these recommendations, and to identify overlapping constituencies among them. Amid a general lack of response to the presentation, a representative of another equality sector suggested that the presenters engage with *other disability organizations*, seeming not to get the point that there would likely be disabled people among her own constituents and those of others at the meeting, and thus opportunities for solidarity building. This opportunity to identify overlapping constituents and thus shared issues and concerns on which to work together in solidarity was therefore largely missed (fieldnotes, 2017).

Reflecting afterwards, Eilidh, a practitioner in a small, funded disabled people's organization felt:

> 'I was a bit surprised actually after that discussion that there wasn't more engagement with the actual content. I felt like there would have been a lot of parallels that a lot of the other organizations who were there may have identified ... you know, they may be working with people who face some of those issues. ... And actually I was quite surprised that the conversation, suddenly it seemed to turn a little bit towards people suggesting various other disability organizations that we could contact, which were really not necessary and I was a bit bamboozled by that, we know about [those organizations], we really don't need to go meet them to learn and I don't think there's a lot they can tell us that can improve our approaches. We know a lot about how to engage with disabled people, I think it was more the people you work with, that we're hoping to engage with. ... That was a bit frustrating.'

Siloed thinking, and the barrier it poses to coalition working and intersectional solidarity, is highlighted in the following example.

At another network meeting, participants from predominantly single-strand organizations discussed cuts to local mental health services. A director of an LGBTI organization told the group that "from an LGBT perspective", cuts would disproportionately affect "their" community, going on to say that they "did not know" about the other groups in the room. This inscribes a separation between groups and lack of awareness of crossover, as though no constituents of the other organizations present would also belong to the LGBTI community or vice versa, thereby pitting communities against one another: implicitly, it will affect the LGBTI community *more* than others. It also communicates a clear message that it is not his role to know about what the impacts on other equality communities might be: in other words, that there is little solidarity present (fieldnotes, 2016). This latter point is important because, in other contexts, participants identified lack of awareness of other inequalities as a significant barrier to working together in networks and coalitions; for example, Robin, from a small, funded trans organization in England:

> 'One of the things that we often face as marginalized groups is that general ignorance anyway, and coming into [an equalities space], and having to explain what the issues are can be exhausting to start with. ... Obviously, we work from there and we work together, but that initial can be exhausting to have yet another space where it's supposed to be an equalities space. It's supposed to be an intersectional or a diverse space, but it might be that other people still don't know about—and that you know.'

Meanings and uses of intersectionality

Siloed thinking is closely associated with diversity-within and multi-strand understandings of intersectionality; the examples shared here are from participants who articulate these understandings (sometimes among others). While siloed thinking is related to single-strand organizing, it is not determined by it; not all of those in single-strand organizations, or all practitioners within the same organization, were necessarily found to speak about inequalities in siloed ways.

The above example led into a conversation where the participant bemoaned the lack of public sector funding for LGBTI equality, at which point a representative of an intersectional (Black women's) organization pointed out that they were not the only sector not to receive funding. Siloed thinking, by necessity, compares single-strand organizations and sectors, and effaces intersectional marginalization, and intersectional organizing. For diversity-within and multi-strand concepts, intersectionality and siloed thinking are not inconsistent. These also efface intersectional organizing and intersectional marginalization.

Siloed thinking is also closely related to multi-strand intersectionality's demand that all strands be included and treated equivalently. Both diversity-within and multi-strand intersectionality engender resistance to work targeted at particular intersectionally marginalized communities, since this necessarily leaves out both some strands *and* those within strands who have relative privilege (for example, white women). Within siloed thinking, few practitioners are happy for 'their' strand to be put on the back burner: "When we're talking about equalities, we're talking about the whole intersectionality thing. There's the desire to just pick and choose certain groups. ... It shouldn't be either or ... you need to multi-task. When it comes to equality, you need to fucking multi-task, right?" (Yvonne, director, women's organization, Scotland).

Effects

Because of siloed thinking, there is substantial wariness about 'stepping on toes' of other sectors, which can work to prevent practitioners from raising concerns about intersectional disadvantage.

Moreover, siloed thinking ultimately can manifest in exclusion of intersectionally marginalized people from services and activities of organizations. Julie, director of a small, funded refugee organization in England provided an example of this.

> 'We still get a response after all these years [from some disability organizations], even now, we don't do refugees. So the fact they're disabled is irrelevant. All that matters is they're refugees. Either you work with disabled people or you don't. You can't just work with these ones and not with those ones, unless you say specifically, "We are a disability organization, for British-born [and] bred residents with nationality."... If you don't say that, and if you say you are a disability, equality, and rights organization, "We don't want to look after refugees." What are you doing?'

Siloed thinking also manifests in exclusion from policy agendas, as Emma, practitioner in a small, funded racial justice organization noted: "I know that [our organization] has not looked at many of the issues facing young people because we just assumed the children sector should be handling that but then there isn't anyone in the children sector that looks at predominantly BME issues."

Solutions

Siloed thinking is perhaps the most significant barrier to creating and maintaining coalitions with solidarity, and yet coalitions are also viewed as the solution to siloed thinking. Many participants, including those who espoused siloed thinking, recognized it as a major challenge for operationalizing intersectionality. Many view networks themselves, and network organizers in particular, as critical to moderate this. They often felt that relationship building, learning more about one another's areas, and working together on pan equality intersectionality offered a solution: "I think that's really valuable a role that [the network] has: bringing people together giving us all the opportunity to ... have solidarity together and to look at where there are overlaps I think" (Eilidh, practitioner, disabled people's organization).

Network organizers also reflected on this as their role to facilitate, as Elizabeth explained.

> 'Our role was to increase an understanding about intersectionality and to try and prevent things happening in silos ... and people not having

an understanding that if they were working with one particular group of people that the people they worked with were bringing in all kinds of experiences and identities with them that affected how they reported and what their experiences were.' (Elizabeth, network organizer)

Yet, as described here, siloed thinking at times persists in spite of these efforts. Later in this chapter I offer possible explanations for this.

For both pan equality intersectionality and 'intersections of equality strands' work, ultimately the challenge in relation to siloed thinking is to articulate needs to prioritize particular experiences and issues, without making the case in ways that reinscribe conceptual separation between groups: articulating that all issues are interrelated/any one community includes all others, rather than that all of these singular groups also experience the same issue.

Summary

In sum, siloed thinking presents a significant barrier to operationalizing intersectionality in the context of coalitions and networks. It is exacerbated by competitive funding environments, austerity and multi-strand policy focused on generic equality. It serves to reinscribe understandings of marginalized communities as mutually exclusive, foreclosing on identification of common issues on which to collaborate and build solidarity, and effacing notions of intersectional marginalization. Yet, networks and coalitions are viewed as the solution to siloed thinking.

Coalitions at work: operationalizing intersectionality

Having explored barriers *to* coalition and solidarity, I will now discuss coalitions at work, through analysis of network engagement in the development of local equality strategies. This analysis further explicates the applied concepts of intersectionality that I identified, and their implications for intersectional solidarity.

One concrete activity that each network engaged in collectively during the period of my fieldwork was attempting to influence local equality strategies. Under the Equality Act, public bodies are required to set equality objectives (England) and outcomes (Scotland) every four years. This activity was often identified as intersectional in various ways by participants, but this works differently in practice depending on which applied concept of intersectionality is employed. Moreover, the understandings of intersectionality used by both networks themselves and participants in them in this process have very different implications for intersectional solidarity.

These *processes* have been 'multi-strand' in that they have brought together distinct equality strand organizations (feminist, racial justice, disability and

LGBTI rights, refugee organizations, among others) into a conversation and collaboration to provide input into, and feedback on, draft equality strategies. Yet there are distinctions among the networks. The network most associated with a generic concept of intersectionality involved other kinds of organizations (not only equality organizations as I define them). The one in which multi-strand concepts of intersectionality were particularly prevalent is also the one that operated this process closest to the multi-strand model described earlier. The final network sought to take an 'intersections of equality strands' approach, alongside a pan equality one. I will discuss each of these in turn.

Operationalizing generic intersectionality

Networks engaged in contributing to local equality strategies through meetings, events and production of documents. In one city, the published equality strategy resulting from the network's processes of engagement rarely comments on issues affecting particular equality groups and intersectionally marginalized groups (AD 36–37).

At its consultative event, the network in the city organized discussion about what should go into the local equality strategy around policy areas rather than equality strands, which network organizers identified as key to their intersectional approach. However, discussions were framed around identifying key issues for 'people', rather than for marginalized (or intersectionally marginalized) people (AD 1). When specific issues of inequalities experienced by marginalized groups were highlighted in the discussions, at times the network took a deliberately generic approach to the write-up of these points, thereby obscuring them (AD 1, 30–35). Specific issues affecting intersectionally marginalized groups, if raised, were not recorded. This obfuscation of specific issues was exacerbated through the local government's translation of the resulting documents into strategy. Conceptualizing the network's specific approach to intersectionality as generic intersectionality helps to account for why, in this city, the 'equality' strategy scarcely discusses 'equalities' (in spite of this process being identified by network members as a good example of its intersectional work).

In the network's process of bringing equality organizations, among others, together to feed into the local equality strategy, little political solidarity was detectable, since no oppression or injustice was identified to engender any common commitment to opposing. In other words, solidarity was largely precluded. Power asymmetries between and within equality groups were not negotiated in any meaningful way since difference itself was flattened. The network organizer, in fact, commented that little in the way of conflict had emerged, which I interpret as being because: (i) discussion of identity-based inequalities was largely shelved in this process through dilution within discussion of a broad (socioeconomic, whitened) inequality, and (ii) because the conversation was so general with respect to how inequalities manifest across and within groups, and therefore vague. The network sought to operationalize intersectionality as issues that affect 'everybody', which failed to build any intersectional political solidarity.

Operationalizing multi-strand and diversity-within intersectionality

In another city, in contrast, the published equality strategy is centrally concerned with 'equalities', yet intersectional marginalization is effaced within it.

In the network's process of input into the local equality strategy, strands were largely considered in parallel, separately, simultaneously and equivalently. In its discussions and documents concerning the local equality strategy, the network frequently expressed a desire to see equality groups that had not been specifically named in relation to a given issue added onto various elements of the draft local strategy (AD 16–17), in a move concerned with equivalence. This evidences resistance to work that has a specific focus, when it is on another strand. This desire for equality groups to be treated equivalently is driven by a siloed view that work related to one strand is not at all relevant to other strands, as though they describe wholly separate communities. In contrast to pan equality intersectionality which seeks to identify issues common to marginalized groups, network members emphasized that issues themselves for different equality groups 'differ significantly' (AD 18); commonalities were thereby resisted, effacing intersectional marginalization in the process, since strands are considered to be separate with no crossover. At times, network members responded to strand-specific work (for example, relating to women), to point out/ask questions around diversity among women, but this was limited to consideration of one aspect of this/the strand speaking (AD 16–17). The overall implication is that network members were there to advocate for the interests of 'their' communities, and while they may at times have recognized that these communities overlap with particular others, the concern for 'intersections of equality strands' stopped there. Even the extent to which this was acknowledged in this network's documents and processes was very limited.

The multi-strand meaning given to intersectionality is perhaps most apparent in the following example: the network urged the local government to include the word 'intersectional' in the strategy (AD 16–17). Yet, in the same gesture to urge the council to include the term, the network also inscribed its multi-strand understanding of this term. It objected to the local government's draft wording underlining the importance of not viewing protected characteristics separately, and considering their connections and cumulative effects. Over two separate responses, the network urged that while intersectionality should be acknowledged, the protected characteristics should be considered separately; it constructed the local government's use of the *concept* of intersectionality (which was similar to an 'intersections of equality strands' meaning) as being opposed to recognition of the 'individual needs' of those with protected characteristics (AD 17). This can be understood primarily in relation to siloed attitudes inherent in multi-strand and diversity-within concepts of intersectionality, but also as part of resistance to what network members perceived as the local government's generic approach to equality. However, in this case, local government appears in the documents to look more committed to practising intersectionality than the local equality sector itself is.

This network almost solely discussed equality groups singularly in its written feedback (AD 16–17). Understanding the network's application of intersectionality as multi-strand intersectionality (and, to a lesser extent, diversity-within) helps to explain why multiple actors within the network identified this process as the best example of its intersectional work at the time, and why, in this city, the resultant equality strategy effaces intersectional marginalization.

In some instances, in addition to contributing to the multi-strand process, some strand-specific organizations with diversity-within understandings of intersectionality also contributed their own single-strand feedback, at times based on conversations among single-strand organizations in 'their' sectors (AD 18, 28). This further underlines an understanding of issues as separate, rather than shared; and evidences a lack of solidarity at the same time as it undermines solidarity. The single-strand organizations do not trust that the networks and other member organizations will advocate for 'their' issues; they do not feel that these issues are shared.

There was little in these processes that seemed to build intersectional solidarity. Issues were largely conceptualized singularly: each equality group has its own issues. Even where issues were recognized as being shared, the network demanded that all groups be specifically addressed within them, equivalently and separately: this is the most that can be achieved with this approach. Where it was acknowledged that the local government may need to prioritize certain protected characteristics, this was on the understanding that all will be considered equivalently in the longer term. The common commitment of network members was to *amplification of single-strand voices*, rather than opposing oppression or injustice. Power asymmetries were negotiated solely through treating equality groups equivalently. Intersectional marginalization was effaced. While intersectionally marginalized organizations and voices were present, they were in a minority, and concern for intersectional disadvantage was largely absent in the resulting documents (see also Bilge 2016).

Operationalizing 'intersections of equality strands' and pan equality intersectionality

In the third city, the published equality strategy does show some (albeit limited) recognition of intersectional marginalization.

In that city, the network sought representation of intersectionally marginalized communities and organizations representing them in these conversations. This network was also the only one to create dedicated space in events and sections of documents concerning the local equality strategy to talk specifically about intersectionality (AD 13). Where this space was not made in the processes of the other networks discussed, concerns about intersectional disadvantage were not included in the resulting documents. Like the network employing generic intersectionality, this network also largely organized discussion around issues rather than equality strands, but while difference and marginality were flattened using this approach by the former, here they came to the fore.

This network identified the specific experiences/effects of proposals on particular intersectionally marginalized groups, including potential *conflicting/contradicting needs* in relation to broad issues affecting equality groups (for example, provision of maternity services) along markers of intersectional marginalization (AD 13). This has the potential to create solidarity in identifying the broad issue, and to also pinpoint differences. Moreover, the network also pointed out where strand-specific work is inadequate and problematic because it *excludes* those who are intersectionally marginalized (AD 13). This network recommended to local government bodies ways that they could engage more intersectionally in the process of equality strategy development, including targeting specific intersectionally marginalized groups. The network raised issues of remuneration of equality organizations contributing expertise, and the value of specialist/experiential knowledge. It further recommended more explicit focus on intersectionality and particular intersectionally marginalized groups in the equality strategy (AD 13). Conceptualizing this network's employment of intersectionality as 'intersections of equality strands' and pan equality intersectionality helps to explain the differences between what these three networks did, and why (in contrast to the other two cities) the equality strategy does attempt to address issues of intersectional marginalization.

This network was also more effective in relation to building intersectional solidarity. From pan equality understandings of intersectionality, at times the network identified broad issues (for example, hate crime), perceived to affect all equality groups, without articulating differences for intersectionally marginalized equality groups within this. While this approach does not necessarily recognize the mutual constitution of inequalities, it is effective at building solidarity across different groups around the identified issue (AD 13).

Moreover, the network sought to negotiate power asymmetries between groups by including and centring intersectionally marginalized experiences, raising issues of intersectional marginalization, even when these were in perceived potential conflict with other equality groups, and by problematizing single-strand work. It took concrete steps to enable participation, including through remuneration of grassroots groups contributing expertise to these discussions. In contrast, the network operationalizing multi-strand and diversity-within intersectionality considers its members to be representative, and so did not seek to include other groups.

Summary

Comparison of three networks' processes of 'intersectional' work on local equality strategies accentuates their conflicting concepts of intersectionality, and the differences these make in practice. I have found that generic, multi-strand and diversity-within intersectionality do little to build intersectional solidarity between equality organizations, while employment of pan equality and 'intersections of equality strands' concepts together did draw attention to and underlie attempts to equalize power asymmetries, and produce common commitments around particular issues. Importantly, these concepts highlighted intersectional marginalization while others effaced it. Moreover, my analysis shows that, in fact, single-strand equality sector actors may serve as agents of *resistance* to policy maker attempts to consider intersectionality. Overall, competing concepts of intersectionality are very significant, since they have different implications for who is included in and who is excluded from processes of local equality strategy development, and on what terms. Furthermore, the resulting equality strategies are key documents that drive local resource allocation to equality, as well as wider policy making, for four years. Due in part to the (albeit limited) influence of equality networks, ultimately these strategies differ in the extent to which intersectional marginalization is effaced or prioritized, incurring material effects for intersectionally marginalized people and intersectional justice.

Having explored competing concepts of intersectionality at work in coalitions, I now turn to examine in greater detail the challenges and conflicts that emerged in these processes.

Challenges and conflicts: contesting intersectionality

A key challenge for intersectional political solidarity that research participants identified, across networks, was the opposition and resistance of some women's organizations to the expansion of rights of trans people in general and trans women in particular, in the context of proposed changes to the Gender Recognition Act (GRA) by Westminster and

Holyrood (Christoffersen and Emejulu 2023). This particular example of contested intersectionality demonstrates the ways that additive concepts of intersectionality (multi-strand and diversity-within) are unable to incorporate the idea that structures of inequality are always-interlocking; indeed, how they refuse this recognition. This refusal inherent to additive intersectionality in relation to *all* inequality structures is especially apparent in this example, because the particular ontologies of the inequality structures involved (sexism and cisgenderism) explicitly generate conflict around shared key concepts and categories (namely gender/'woman').[1]

In one network, a women's organization circulated a policy document concerning the local equality strategy on the email list of the inner governing circle of the network. The document, which had been submitted to a key local policy maker, asserted that trans rights were not 'real' rights, and constructed these rights as being in opposition to, and detrimental to, 'women's' rights (AD 28). The existence of trans women was effaced in putting these groups into opposition, constructing them as being mutually exclusive, thereby denying categorical intersection (Hancock 2011). Significantly, the same document later goes on to mention how important it is that equality policy considers intersectionality (a point I will return to). The circulation of this document signalled a breakdown of solidarity in the network, and a breakdown of the coalition in terms of coordination of claims. While a key aim of the network is for equality organizations to collaborate, to work in partnership to progress a vaguely defined 'equality', here one organization actively undermined the equality justice claims of some of its network partners; stating to a policy maker that it did not accept the human rights of whole constituencies of other coalition members. This was evidence of discriminatory attitudes within the network and among equality communities, which created a crisis in the network. The actions of the women's organization broke a relation of political solidarity, a duty of mutuality to others in the group (Scholz 2008).

There are various ways in which this is relevant to intersectionality, both in terms of its ontology and how intersectionality is operationalized in practice. Participants with 'intersections of equality strands' and pan equality concepts of intersectionality tended to view the proposed expansion of rights as a human rights issue affecting an intersectionally marginalized group. Moreover, in a wider theoretical and political context, intersectionality informs transfeminisms (Koyama 2003; Scott-Dixon 2006; Serano 2007, 2013; Stryker and Bettcher 2016) and trans inclusive feminisms. Both intersectionality theory and transfeminisms highlight privilege and oppression among women, that is, that individual experience is characterized simultaneously by oppression and privilege, relationally and along different axes of identity. Intersectionality theory and transfeminisms share a concern with intersectionally marginalized groups, particularly trans women of colour (Koyama 2003; simpkins 2016). However, the extent to which transfeminisms, in turn, inform intersectionality studies is a matter for debate (for divergences, see Bey 2023), since, in the latter, gender is often considered a binary category and solely relating to relations between women and men. Yet, an intersectional theoretical perspective informed by transfeminisms would see the structure of inequality that marginalizes trans people, that is, cisgenderism (which includes ideas of gender as binary, and fixed), as mutually constitutive with sexism and other inequality structures.

A trans exclusionary feminist position (see Hines 2019 for discussion), in contrast, generally differs ontologically from intersectionality theory. The former views sexism or 'patriarchy' as a totalizing structure, rather than as a mutually constituted and constituting structure, and often constructs sexism as being more fundamental than other inequality structures (similar to diversity-within intersectionality). It also relies on an essentialist view of individuals/individual experience as either wholly oppressed, or wholly privileged; in other words, it has an investment in victimhood at odds with engaging with privilege and thus complicity in the oppression of others. Trans exclusionary feminist positions are characterized by 'a lack of critical attention to the privilege of being stably gendered' (Heyes 2003, 1100). Yet, among my participants there are those I would consider as trans exclusionary, who nonetheless identified as working intersectionally. *This is enabled by employment of additive multi-strand and diversity-within concepts of intersectionality.* These concepts of intersectionality lack recognition of relationality and the simultaneity of privilege and oppression. For this reason, they enable juxtaposition of equality groups, which effaces those at the intersections of those groups. Multi-strand understandings, in particular, efface intersectional marginalization. Moreover, these understandings of intersectionality are not inconsistent with refusing ideas of privilege, refusal to recognize and locate ourselves in structures of inequality (as I explore further later).

Outright discrimination in the equality sector, such as that evidenced by this policy document, is a significant challenge for operationalizing intersectionality and building intersectional solidarity. A trans participant in my research shared this experience, which happened in the context of a major 'equality and diversity' sector event:

> 'So there were ten people to the table. There was a group of six people who, every time a trans person, trans woman, visible trans person almost, they would point and laugh ... we started doing small talk and they asked me, you know, why we're here ... so I ... said that ... I've been working with trans communities. So then they ask the inevitable, oh how did you get into that, oh personal experience, I'm trans and they were like, oh. And that conversation stopped there.' (Attribution omitted)

This was at an event of equality specialists. This is important because the breakdown of solidarity that I have described occurred in a wider context, where there is increasing organizing against the rights of trans and non-binary people. In the discourses that are circulating, we can detect a similar dual appropriation and rejection of (or 'non-performativity' of (Ahmed 2015; Nash 2019)) intersectionality as I have identified among participants employing multi-strand and diversity-within concepts of intersectionality. The Socialist Feminist Network, for example, which led campaigns against trans women's inclusion on all-women shortlists in the Labour Party, states 'austerity and the cuts to public services have a disproportionate impact on women and children and this is exacerbated by class and race' (Socialist Feminist Network 2019). A Woman's Place UK, the highest profile group organizing against the GRA reforms, similarly states 'we are very conscious of how sex, class and race intersect to oppress women' (Woman's Place UK 2019). Here, in line with diversity-within approaches, some limited attention is paid to other inequalities, but these are incorporated only as additional barriers among women rather than as mutually constituting structures of inequality. This dual rejection/appropriation of intersectionality among participants, as well as in wider discourses, involves policing of reified categories in which participants are heavily invested, and a refusal of the ontological idea of the simultaneity of privilege and oppression. In other words, there is much at stake in competing concepts of intersectionality.

Recognizing inequality structures

Intersectionality theory is fundamentally about recognition of the interrelation of structures of inequality (particularly white supremacy and sexism). Yet recognition of, and engagement with, the interrelationship of inequality structures, and thus building intersectional solidarity, requires a prior step of recognizing the ontology of the structures themselves. Those employing diversity-within understandings of intersectionality, a prevalent understanding among participants from the women's sector, view one strand (gender, always-already constituted as white) as primary. Therefore, they lack recognition of the interrelationship of other inequality structures and thus at times, of these structures themselves. Some do not recognize, or go to lengths to deny, a structure of inequality affecting trans people. Recognition of this structure of inequality is particularly problematic for the women's sector, since it offers fundamental challenges to some core beliefs and assumptions on which many organizations are premised (ideas of gender as a binary power relation between women and men, and of gender as fixed). In other words, there is a reification of categories inherent to diversity-within and multi-strand intersectionality. The structure of inequality affecting trans people has been variously theorized, but the emerging consensus in trans studies is that it is best theorized as cisgenderism, an ideology that 'denies, denigrates, or pathologizes ... [that] creates an inherent system of associated power and privilege' (Lennon and Mistler 2014, 63).

The related term 'cisgender' emerged from transfeminism (Serano 2007) and activism as an alternative to nontransgender, to disrupt the normativity of 'man' and 'woman' meaning nontransgender by default (Johnson 2013; Aultman 2014); though the term itself is neutral, simply meaning 'same' to connote the matching of gender identity and sex morphology, it has been used to be able to articulate cisgender privilege (Johnson 2013). The term 'cisgender' was rejected by another women's organization that I spoke with, in a different city.

> 'I [got really angry] at a meeting because somebody called me a cis woman. And I said, "You don't get to define me." I don't like the term cis because it's never been said to me as a description, it's been said to me as an accusation. I am not-You do not have the right. You have not earned the right to call me a cis woman just because that's your community as a trans community, as a trans woman because that's what you use.' (Attribution omitted)

In that city, relations between prominent women's sector organizations and the LGBTI sector had broken down. In this conversation, she is expressing discomfort with the idea of cisgender privilege. Because they are additive, multi-strand and diversity-within intersectionality lack recognition of relationality and the simultaneity of privilege and oppression. Instead of being viewed as fundamentally interrelated, structures of inequality are viewed additively, so that while it may be deemed preferable or desirable to work on other inequalities, it is not deemed essential. As a consequence, these concepts position people as solely oppressed (or wholly privileged) along one axis, and so consideration of how we are each located within always-interlocking equality structures is foreclosed upon. When other inequalities are considered, they can be incorporated as 'additional barriers' but less so as privileged social positions, since one inequality is viewed as primary and so other inequalities are viewed as being able to be subtracted at will. Any acknowledgement of privilege is then fleeting, not a permanent feature, and disappears once attention to that secondary inequality is put on the back burner. Therefore, these concepts foreclose meaningful consideration of privilege per se. Interrogating the interrelationships of inequality structures, and our own relationships to them, is also key to identifying convergences and shared political goals. Recognizing a structure of inequality in which we are all located would be an important initial step to acknowledging epistemological and social privileges, which is necessary for intersectional political solidarity (Scholz 2008).

A women's organization that others had told me was 'working on' trans inclusion had signed the policy document described earlier (AD 28). I suggest this may be indicative of the limits of diversity-within intersectionality, and its lack of attention to representation explored in Chapter 5: inclusion of trans women in services provided within cisgendered spaces, or simple inclusion of those previously excluded from service provision, does not necessarily signify any change in issue agendas that might facilitate coalition working, nor does it signify a lack of discriminatory attitudes, or a commitment to intersectional transformation. It may be that some organizations feel compelled to work toward inclusion by their equality sector peers, while others are compelled by equality and diversity funding requirements, against what they actually desire to do. Without representation of intersectionally marginalized people in decision-making, organizations practising intersectionality as diversity-within can oppose the expansion of rights of those they have sought to merely include in services, as multiply disadvantaged, 'hard to reach' people lacking agency. For these organizations, binary trans identity is incorporated merely as an additional barrier *among women*, but the relationship between sexism and cisgenderism is left uninterrogated.

The lack of recognition of the ontology of cisgenderism here goes beyond disagreement about what inequalities are *relevant*, argued to be a key part of defining contextual intersectional praxis (Townsend-Bell 2011), given the (growing) strength of mobilization of some women's organizations *against* such a recognition. Moreover, it also is a distinct point from divergent framings of gender (Cooper 2004; Verloo 2013) observed between women's and trans movements. Divergent framings of the 'problem' of gender between women's and trans organizations make visible how *additive intersectionality refuses the idea of always-interlocking inequality structures.* This is made visible through the rejection/refusal of a specific structure of inequality theorized by trans people by women's organizations employing diversity-within intersectionality. Cisgenderism is rejected on its own terms because to acknowledge it would require a reconceptualization of gender and the category woman, *and* it is rejected because to acknowledge its location in the always-interlocking intersectional matrix would necessitate meaningful engagement with the concept of cisgender privilege, and thus also a reconceptualization of gender.

Summary

Siloed thinking driven by diversity-within and multi-strand intersectionality can ultimately manifest in discrimination from some equality sectors and communities toward others, resulting in coalition breakdown. What those employing 'intersections of equality strands' and pan equality intersectionality tended to view as an issue of intersectional marginalization, was perceived as an issue of privilege by some employing diversity-within and multi-strand concepts of intersectionality. Those employing the latter concepts resist recognition of the interlocking nature of other inequality structures, and the acknowledgement of privilege and complicity on their parts, which this recognition would engender. This is because these concepts of intersectionality among those in the women's sector construct gender as a binary relation wherein other inequalities are considered only additively. This is important, because similar patterns can be seen in wider political discourses that have far reaching effects. Recognition of other inequality structures outside of sector silos is a prerequisite for intersectional solidarity. While diversity-within intersectionality may be able to address intersectional marginalization as 'acting for' those with 'compounded disadvantage', those employing it may concomitantly oppose the expansion of rights of those they seek to merely include.

Network responses to challenges and conflicts offer some insight into creating intersectional political solidarity.

Creating intersectional political solidarity

Responses to coalition breakdown can be analysed in relation to allyship and solidarity; addressing challenges; and dialogue and learning.

'Allyship' and solidarity

Competing concepts of intersectionality produce conflicting views on and approaches to allyship[2] and solidarity. Specifically, there are differing perspectives among participants about what role, if any, more privileged people have in intersectional practice concerning those in relation to whom they are privileged, hinging on competing understandings of intersectionality. I explored earlier the reasons that additive understandings of intersectionality cannot meaningfully engage with privilege. Because of this, they identify intersectionality as pertaining only to marginality, in individualized ways. These understandings of intersectionality prevent people with privileged aspects of identity relating intersectionality to themselves, and seeing roles and responsibilities for themselves as practising allyship (or as acting in political solidarity). As discussed in Chapter six, because they view inequality in terms of multiple barriers, these concepts lack recognition of agency and so facilitate 'acting for' in paternalistic ways. This acting for may be understood to be at odds with allyship and solidarity as political practices that strive for more equitable relationships (even, leadership of the marginalized (Kolers 2016)), while acknowledging the enduring power dynamic.

Some participants recognized this, and questioned the utility of multi-strand and diversity-within intersectionality for growing allyship. If conceptualized in an individualized way wherein intersectionality is only 'about' marginalized people, rather than the synthesis of inequality structures, privileged people have difficulty relating it to themselves.

> 'How do you get people like me to be allies if all you're talking about is an intersectionality between protected characteristics, which I'm not the bearer of any of those ... I'm not sure, with a name like intersectionality, with a word like intersectionality, I'm not sure it's a very good word for getting people who are allies, potentially, but who see this as being-this can be a, I suppose what I'm trying to say is if it's done badly, if it's seen as, that lot over there who are all otherable ... are all not the norm, then actually it lets us off the hook, people like me completely off. Then we just walk away, scot-free, we don't have to think about any of that stuff. That would be my worry, about how you build alliances beyond that, which good intersectionality is great at.' (Attribution omitted)

Yet allyship has been identified by other participants with non-additive concepts of intersectionality (pan equality and 'intersections of equality strands') as a key tool for creating intersectional political solidarity. Allyship is a problematic and problematized concept. It can be a source of comfortable identity affirmation, assuaging feelings of guilt associated with privilege; a reinscription of a power relation between 'allies' and those who are oppressed: a colonial relation. For these reasons, it has been argued that allyship is a verb, not a noun – that one can undertake acts of allyship but one cannot 'be' an ally (Garbasz 2015; Lyle 2015). This is how I use the term here: 'allyship asks us to act from the places where we have agent status in the interest of empowering those who are marginalized. This requires both an engagement with other "agents" around problematic dynamics of privilege and lifting up the voices, work, and efforts of marginalized people' (Beltrán and Mehrotra 2015, 114).

For those with 'intersections of equality strands' concepts of intersectionality, "[Intersectionality is] almost as much or more about helping me personally to realize the types of privilege I've got. Rather than the disadvantage or the intersectional disadvantage" (Eilidh, practitioner, disabled people's organization).

These participants are able to use intersectionality to locate themselves in interlocking structures of inequality, including recognizing types of privilege. They feel that being privileged in some respects creates a duty to act in allyship/solidarity on others' behalf, for example network organizer Catriona.

> 'For me, it's really important to know all those different parts of yourself and be prepared to state them and be prepared to, yes, stand

in solidarity with our brothers and sisters who might because of other intersections, might be in a less safe position to do that. ... I obviously have many more advantages than many other people that I work with or alongside. Even as [a marginalized person in some respects] I'm still in a much better position to open a door and hold it open for other people to get heard.'

Allyship has thus been identified by participants as a key tool for creating intersectional political solidarity, and coalitions can break down where the will for allyship among members is lacking. Yet, issues arise when coalitions are composed largely *of* allies, that is, when they lack representation of the relevant intersectionally marginalized group.

In the network where women's organization members had opposed the expansion of trans rights, a participant from an LGBTI organization felt that there were some allies in the network because of how they responded when they raised this opposition at a meeting. I also felt that there was solidarity in the room that day (fieldnotes, 2017). A number of those present had not been aware of the actions of the women's organizations and seemed genuinely shocked and to feel that this was not acceptable. To an extent, the LGBTI organization representative felt supported by responses of others in the meeting. On the other hand, they felt unsupported by the fact that it was left to them to raise it, making it seem to them that they were the only one to view it as problematic: "It just feels like ... it was left to the trans person or the [LGBTI] organization to highlight actually this isn't comfortable or acceptable. ... So I was left feeling whether well is this really important to people, do they really care?" (attribution omitted).

In terms of addressing the issue, and moving forwards to try to rebuild some intersectional solidarity, there was disagreement or lack of clarity around the role of 'allies' in doing so. The issue of how to address this and who addresses it was an important one to resolve to re-establish the network as a place of solidarity building, to achieve political goals. One network organizer was of the view that:

'Human rights are human rights ... we're a human rights network. A debate about trans women's rights will be led by trans women. ... If we say that the priority is for work to be directed by the people with lived experience of, then it kind of takes some of those politicized debates out of it, because this is the way that we work.' (Attribution omitted)

Here, in the interests of the coalition, they are trying to circumvent the politics of the issue (that is, long-running battles among self-proclaimed 'feminists' concerning trans rights). Intersectional justice is recognizable in the assertion that debates about trans women's rights should be led by trans women. Yet, returning to the definition of intersectional solidarity as being a process of negotiation of power asymmetries across social group differences (Tormos 2017), we might ask whether in this case it is sufficient to state that trans women will lead this debate. There were no trans women or trans women's organizations represented in the inner governing circle of the network; this is because the organizations represented are, for the most part, among the most powerful, resourced and influential in their respective sectors. There are also power differentials between organizations within the network. As discussed in Chapter 5, given that the network tends to employ 'intersections of equality strands' concepts of intersectionality, seeking representation of trans women in its absence would be important. However, there remained a key question of what to do in the meantime and who would be best positioned to do it. Moreover, there would be questions around both the political achievability and ethics of a predominantly cisgender network recruiting a trans woman/trans women's organization into the inner governing circle in this moment, where discriminatory attitudes have been laid bare, and the conflict is unresolved. Furthermore, relying on members of an intersectionally marginalized group to represent and lead the challenge to discrimination against that group, can also fall into essentialism. This is problematic because relying on essentialist representation can also be a way for supposed allies to avoid acting, if that representation is not present. The trans participant/LGBTI organization representative responded,

> 'There's also the danger of … saying, "Well that's your … thing." So [we need to make sure] to make it clear that we are also standing up. We're not making that person or those people speak on those things themselves, that we can be good supportive allies within those conversations as well. … It's about getting that balance between allowing those people the voice but, also, not relying on them to be the educators and to be the only people to speak.' (Attribution omitted)

Here, they are highlighting the need to balance seeking representation, enabling participation and 'voice', with responsibilities of allies to 'act' (Chan 2018), the need to avoid leaving it solely to those experiencing discrimination directly to challenge it; as well as the need to avoid putting people in a position where that is the case. This brings to the fore a key problem of representation in coalitions aiming at intersectional practice: in the absence of representation, how to practise solidarity while avoiding 'speaking for'. Here, the participant would have felt more solidarity, more supported if someone not directly affected, an 'ally', had spoken first.

However, people with privileged aspects of identity can struggle with how to practise allyship, how to act in solidarity. Relations of mutuality, seen as integral to political solidarity (Scholz 2008) are challenging to create in the context of unequal power. Others see privilege as a barrier, rather than a resource, for example:

> '[How do you try] to ally [yourself] with all of these oppressed groups and [do] it from a position of privilege. How do you sort of-surely that work is the work of somebody from one of those groups and you're nicking it. [laughs] … from my point of view anyway, there's a certain cautiousness about entering the debate from a privileged position. I'm worried that I'll say something, that's not-or that I can't possibly understand the experience of others and stuff like that.' (Christopher, network member)

Yet, as we have seen in the network, allyship and solidarity require action, including pointing out problematic practice, and seeking leadership from intersectionally marginalized groups. They also require reflective practice, as network organizer Catriona explains: "[Sometimes we are going to have to] put our hands up if we don't do it perfectly, and that we're all constantly trying to learn and improve that. I think, also, then, that requires you to tell people when they've got it wrong as well."

Addressing challenges

There was debate within the network as to how to approach this conflict. As a network committed to intersectionality, should it seek to balance opposing views (attempting to find a middle ground in which to 'represent' 'all' members), or take a principled position? Ultimately, lacking representation of the relevant intersectionally marginalized group (trans women) the actions of the network were ambiguous in this regard.

The initial response of network staff was not considered adequate by some members, with no clear response until it was raised in the meeting, although it had been flagged as a problem. The network committed to ultimately developing a statement but this had not yet happened by the time my fieldwork came to an end nine months later.

However, the network organized an externally facilitated session to discuss tensions between different equality areas for those on the inner governing circle and other members; revisited its terms of reference, code of conduct and associated policies around complaints and conflict resolution (AD 41); and committed to having ground rules at all of its events. The issue was taken seriously and formed an agenda item at subsequent meetings of the inner governing circle (AD 38–39).

The network ultimately took decisive action in the form of organizing a dedicated externally facilitated session to address this conflict as well as others that had arisen (AD 37). I observed similar tensions between strands around other issues in this and other networks, without these forms of action having been taken; and so, tensions remained unresolved and relationships fragile. However, the women's organization ultimately withdrew from the network, stating that it needed to focus on 'women's issues', singularly defined: siloed thinking at work. Diversity-within concepts of intersectionality can incorporate other inequalities only as secondary considerations; these are not considered core business, and so building relationships of solidarity is not necessarily a priority.

However, although there was discussion around it, no clear lines were drawn regarding what is and what is not up for debate, at the time. The network sought to be a space where difficult conversations could be had, and where the aim is not to reach consensus. Yet, it encouraged acknowledgement of biases and critical self-reflection.

Dialogue and learning

At a national level in Scotland, there was a different story of solidarity on this particular issue, one that was raised by several of my participants as a good example of intersectional practice.

Within the same policy context of proposed changes to the GRA, a coalition of women's organizations published a statement supporting the realization of rights of trans people (Close the Gap et al 2017).

In the statement and supporting documentation, the coalition describes the statement as being based on 'constructive dialogue' between the women's and LGBTI sectors, and importantly, 'deliberation on the interrelationship between trans equality and rights and women's equality and rights' (Close the Gap et al 2017). A key distinction between some of these women's organizations and many of those in my sample is the requirement for women's organizations in Scotland that are funded by the Scottish government to deliver violence against women and girls services, to have trans inclusion plans in place. Several years on from this requirement, it is not this requirement itself, but the learning, support and relationship building between sectors that it engendered, that participants identified as important. According to one of my participants who was party to these conversations, getting to a place where these women's organizations would hold, and make public, this current position as an act of solidarity was not easy, and moreover "didn't happen overnight ... there certainly was a job of building relationships and trust" (attribution omitted). Intersectional political solidarity requires members of the solidarity group to be open and attentive to learn about experiences of oppression that they do not share, as well as the social practices that produce them (Scholz 2008).

Yet, when organizations not subject to such funding requirements are not interested in dialogue and learning, nothing compels them to remain engaged in networks and coalitions or to practise solidarity, as the examples given here demonstrate. Which understanding of intersectionality is at play is an important factor to continued engagement. While the Scottish women's organizations' statement, in contrast, is an important act of solidarity, there are nevertheless impasses between these sectors due to the continuing prevalence of diversity-within concepts of intersectionality.

Summary

Creating intersectional political solidarity necessitates specific concepts of intersectionality that do not foreclose on meaningful allyship and solidarity (namely, 'intersections of equality strands' and pan equality intersectionality); addressing challenges; and dialogue and learning between equality sectors. Yet, additive concepts of intersectionality enable organizations to justify opting out of these processes, and without representation of the relevant intersectionally marginalized group, practitioners, organizations and networks struggle to do these effectively.

Intersectional justice and the limits of intersectional political solidarity

> 'Intersectional justice focuses on the mutual workings of structural privilege and disadvantage, i.e. that someone's disadvantage is someone else's privilege. For this reason, actions tend to be centered on people and groups of people who face the highest structural barriers in society – premised on the idea that if we reach the people at the greatest structural disadvantage, then we can reach everybody.' (Center for Intersectional Justice 2018)

The examples discussed in this chapter ultimately point to what some of the limits of intersectional political solidarity might be in these contexts. In the first example, the women's organization that understood intersectionality as diversity-within declined to continue engagement in the network, and in solidarity building among members. In the second example, women's organizations acted in solidarity at times in spite of these understandings. Yet at local level, several of my participants in the women's sector with diversity-within understandings of intersectionality have been able to incorporate *binary* trans identity *as another difference/'additional barrier' among women*, but they expressed their inability to incorporate *non-binary gender identity* into either their perspectives or their services. For example, following discussion of their efforts to be more (binary) trans inclusive, Helen, senior manager in a large, funded women's organization in England said:

> 'Hmmm I suppose the only thing for us is around ... gender neutrality ... it's important for us a woman-only organization to be able to emphasise the gendered nature of violence. So if there's a complete gender neutrality, which isn't really about trans women but just about the whole intersex [sic] or non-binary issues could impact on us being able to talk about women-only services and also perpetrators as being predominantly male. We want to be able to voice that.'

Some can additively recognize inequality that marginalizes trans people, and incorporate *binary female trans identity* as an 'additional barrier' among women; *but they cannot incorporate the always-interlocking nature of sexism and cisgenderism*. Because of this, they are left with no framework in which to recognize *non-binary gender* as a marginalized category. This identity presents a fundamental epistemological, ideological challenge to some of the bases on which these women's organizations are constructed (namely understandings of gender as a binary power relation). This can be understood as a parallel in equality practice to what has been observed about heteronormative assumptions of binary gender in the field of trans equality law and policy (Cowan 2004, 2005, 2009). Ultimately this exposes the limits of an intersectionality that reifies categories, which multi-strand and diversity-within approaches do in particular, but which even 'intersections of equality strands' understandings of intersectionality may be guilty of.

Moreover, while solidarity for intersectional justice necessitates reorienting agendas to issues affecting the most intersectionally disadvantaged groups (Tormos 2017), key questions remain about the extent to which other issues that disproportionately affect intersectionally marginalized trans women and non-binary people (Raha 2017) can be incorporated into much applied intersectionality at all, for instance sex work. On this issue there is largely an impasse between the LGBTI and women's sectors.

Ultimately, intersectionality challenges strand-specific work and single-strand organizations, when they are reliant on essential ideas about their constituents in relation to other groups constructed as 'other', fundamentally in particular their wholly oppressed status. It is difficult to absorb an idea of the simultaneity of privilege/oppression when a whole organization is based on a static view of its constituents as oppressed. Absorbing this idea would also necessitate a redirection of agendas away from benefitting those with relative privilege, which is both predicated on and requires a reconceptualization of what the issues are. The challenge for intersectionality is enacting this shift practically speaking without succumbing to generic intersectionality. Perhaps intersectionality can be absorbed (as diversity-within), until it necessitates the transformation that intersectionality demands.

Conclusions: coalition and the spectrum of intersectionality

Coalitions are key to operationalizing intersectionality. In this chapter, I explored how equality organizations operationalize intersectionality in networks and coalitions, and challenges and conflicts that emerge, driven by competing concepts of intersectionality. I first explored barriers *to* intersectional political solidarity, namely siloed thinking about equality communities as separate entities, which is driven in particular by additive multi-strand and diversity-within concepts of intersectionality. Siloed thinking effaces intersectional marginalization and works to materially exclude intersectionally marginalized people. Networks and coalitions are identified by participants as the solution to siloed thinking.

Each of the five applied concepts of intersectionality that I have identified has distinct implications for coalition.

Intersectionality as generic equality drives and is driven by all-encompassing structures and non-specific issues that affect 'everyone'. As discussed in Chapter 5, for those employing this concept it is either constructed as unimportant who representatives are, or, representation of dominant groups is favoured since these social positions are viewed as appropriately non-specific. Within this understanding in relation to coalition, more concretely it is unclear who would be in coalition with whom, and why. In other words, this concept is conducive to neither coalition building nor intersectional political solidarity. Networks at work using this concept failed to produce solidarity.

Intersectionality as pan equality favours campaigns and coalitions focused on broad issues that affect differently marginalized groups. Of the five concepts identified, this offers the broadest opportunities for coalition. On its own, this concept of intersectionality does not necessarily view representation and leadership of intersectionally marginalized people as essential, but it does in combination with an 'intersections of equality strands' concept. Similarly, it is conducive to building intersectional political solidarity in combination with an 'intersections of equality strands' concept of intersectionality.

Multi-strand intersectionality is often enacted in multi-strand networks, where each equality strand is represented. This representation is, in and of itself, conflated with intersectionality in essentializing ways. These are coalitions, and yet they may lack solidarity. When we look closely, strand actors align to further singular interests, united in the overall message that all strands need to be included and addressed separately. They align to further siloed, singular, non-intersectional understandings of equality, instrumentalizing multi-strand intersectionality to do so. Issues are highlighted, but these are not often felt to be common or shared across strands. When equality strands are conceptualized additively, the possibilities for more meaningful coalition and solidarity are very limited.

A diversity-within concept of intersectionality, in which one equality strand is viewed as more important than others, offers the fewest possibilities for coalition. Since one strand is constructed as more important than others, equitable relationships between strand-specific sectors are not viewed as essential to developing projects targeted at intersectionally marginalized groups, who are viewed as having 'additional barriers' and therefore lacking agency. Representation of these groups in decision-making may be viewed favourably, but not as essential. Similarly, participation in coalitions may be viewed favourably, but not as essential, as the example of the women's organization leaving the network to focus on 'women's issues' demonstrates.

An 'intersections of equality strands' concept of intersectionality values equitable partnership and representation, and is thus conducive to organizing intersectionally in organizations and coalitions. It is also conducive to solidarity since it views equalities as mutually constitutive. Yet this understanding of intersectionality in practice, at times, offers only narrow opportunities for coalition (restricted to the particular strands that are being considered), which I have called intersectional alliances. Nevertheless, networks employing 'intersections of equality strands' were able to operationalize intersectionality and to build intersectional solidarity in various ways.

In sum, the concept of intersectionality employed by coalitions and participants in them is a key determinant of how successful these are at building intersectional political solidarity. Moreover, competing concepts of intersectionality drive inclusion in and exclusion from important processes, including local equality strategy development. These strategies alternatively efface or prioritize intersectional marginalization, and have material effects for intersectionally marginalized people and intersectional justice. Some concepts of intersectionality are not inconsistent with discriminatory views of other equality communities.

Building on previous work on intersectional solidarity (Tormos 2017), empirical examples concerning trans rights reveal that intersectional political solidarity requires recognition of other structures of inequality, beyond those that practitioners are well versed in, as a precondition to recognizing the *interrelationship* of structures of inequality; as well as dialogue and relationship building, and addressing challenges that emerge. These practices are facilitated by some concepts of intersectionality and hampered by others, namely diversity-within and multi-strand ones. While additive concepts of intersectionality may be able to recognize other inequality structures as separate ontological entities that produce marginalization, they are inherently unable to incorporate the idea that these structures are always-interlocking, and are therefore *always* contingently at work producing marginalization *and* privilege. This inability is particularly highlighted in conflicts around trans rights, because they bring to the fore discomfort with acknowledging (cisgender) privilege, since meaningful engagement with this concept would explicitly call into question practitioner understandings of gender itself. Meaningfully practising allyship and solidarity is also prevented by additive concepts of intersectionality, since recognition of inequality structures and how we are each positioned within them is also a precondition for identification of roles and responsibilities in relation to those inequalities. Yet, more productive concepts of intersectionality do not necessarily provide the 'answers': those employing them struggle with how to practise solidarity while avoiding 'speaking for' marginalized others, when they are not represented. Finally, concepts of intersectionality that reify categories present a significant barrier to operationalizing intersectionality in the pursuit of intersectional justice. While coalitions remain an essential part of practising intersectionality, developing *shared*, constitutive, *understandings* of intersectionality is an integral and overlooked component of successful coalition building.

7

Conclusion: Intersectional Practice – Ideas, Politics and Policy

In this final chapter, I will explore the implications and contributions of my findings shared in the preceding four chapters. The chapter is in three sections. First, I will discuss ideas of intersectionality: the book's conceptual contributions. Second, I will discuss the politics of intersectionality, or the political implications of the research explored in this book. Third, I will reflect on recommendations arising for policy and practice. I will conclude with thoughts on directions for both empirical research and theory. Ultimately, I argue that the way in which 'intersectionality' is mobilized in competing and contradicting ways in policy and practice suggests that, in this context, new, more specific and more transformative concepts are required. I offer some thoughts arising from my findings on what intersectional practice for *intersectional justice* might involve.

Ideas of intersectionality

In Chapter 2, I noted several points of entry, or lines of rationale, for this project. First, intersectionality is often perceived as a theory on which more information is needed to understand how to apply it in practice; there is felt to be a gap between theory and practice (for example, Hankivsky and Cormier 2011). In other words, there is a 'dearth of principles for intersectional practice' (Luft and Ward 2009, 33). In the UK context, cross-sector coalitions had been called for in order to operationalize intersectionality (Hankivsky and Christoffersen 2011; Hankivsky et al 2019), but there had as of yet been no detailed research on what happens in existing networks and coalitions.

Somewhat conversely to perceiving a gap between the theory of intersectionality and its practice, intersectionality is also understood as a praxis in itself (Collins and Bilge 2016), with its application thought to be more evident to (intersectionally marginalized)[1] activist-practitioner subjects (or coalitional constellations of subjects).[2] My own experience as a practitioner, together with my scoping research, indicated that, at least among many NGO sector equality practitioners 'on the ground' in the UK context, this is not necessarily the case: many struggle with both how to understand and how to apply intersectionality, and not only those working in single-issue organizations. Nevertheless, there is a wealth of embodied and enacted knowledge (knowledge generated in action and interaction) (Freeman and Sturdy 2015) among practitioners that dedicated research could support in developing and sharing. On this basis, there is a small but growing number of empirical studies of intersectionality in practice, including this one.

Significantly, I found very few other published studies which specifically examined what activist-practitioners understand intersectionality *as*[3] – if we assume that activist-practitioners naturally know how to do intersectionality by virtue of their being (intersectionally marginalized) activist-practitioners, then we have little reason to interrogate their understandings. Available studies seem to either assume such a shared meaning between and among activists, practitioners and researchers (Chun et al 2013; Roberts and Jesudason 2013),[4] or to predefine what intersectionality means and operationalize it in particular ways (Luft and Ward 2009), and assess its presence more deductively (Strolovitch 2006, 2007; Cruells and García 2014; Marchetti 2014, 2015, 2019; English 2019). In so doing, these studies necessarily construct 'right' ways to do intersectionality. Those in the first category tend not to be very critical of movements, and rather to celebrate their intersectional knowledge. I read this as partly to do with a larger trend of academic romanticization of practitioners/activists/social movements and their knowledge. Moreover, in existing studies intersectionality may also be conflated with what I have described as 'pan equality' (Parken and Young 2008), 'multi-strand' (Parken 2010) or 'diversity-within' intersectionality (Townsend-Bell 2011)[5] more specifically. The lack of research exploring what activist-practitioners understand intersectionality *as* is both an important and a puzzling omission, given that so many commentators have noted that as 'travelling theory' (Knapp 2005, 250), meanings of intersectionality are at the least fluid, if it is not a completely empty signifier.[6] If we hold constant for a moment the role of intersectional marginalization in intersectional knowledge, the narrative of much of the literature is that activist-practitioners *really* know how to do intersectionality, academics know how in theory only, and neoliberal universities (and for some, policy makers) definitely *do not know* and corrupt intersectionality as a result. While it has been argued that the application of intersectionality matters more than its definition (Cho et al 2013), I contend that from the point of view of practitioners, these are inextricably interrelated and mutually constitutive.

My findings also indicate a particular relationship between theory and practice more generally. Rather than theory driving practice as with the literature identifying intersectionality as a theory which then needs to be applied in practice, I found that practitioners tended to articulate their understandings or theorizations of intersectionality by thinking through and describing how they apply it or would apply it in practice (rather than by reference to theory). In other words, their practice (or imagined practice) drove their understanding, and in turn, drove the theory or typology of intersectionality's operationalization that I develop in this book. Practitioners that I spoke with tended to think through doing or imagining doing, though sometimes what they actually do may be different from what they say they do or think that they do. Their knowledge is transactional (Sullivan 2017). However, this is not to say that practitioners by virtue of being practitioners have a privileged relationship to the 'truth' of how intersectionality should be applied: indeed, I found a plurality of five concepts to be meaningfully held among practitioners (while for some actors, some of these concepts act as strategic misunderstandings, as I discuss further later).

While existing literature has tended to be geographically focused elsewhere, predominantly in the US, and concerned with social movements and public policy, but less so the NGO sector, my research contributes to filling key gaps in knowledge of intersectionality's application in the NGO sector, and of intersectionality's application in the UK context (with implications and applicability elsewhere). Overall, my typology expands existing knowledge about the practicalities of grappling with intersectionality particularly in siloed contexts, whether these are equality strand silos or policy area silos, or most often, both; ultimately, there are only so many institutional configurations of intersectionality immediately possible in these contexts. Yet, identification of competing concepts and their institutional lives facilitates exploring the differences among them, revealing their conceptual and practical limits. Use of this typology also aids in accounting for problems that emerge when practitioners and organizations seek to operationalize intersectionality. Although I have focused empirically on the NGO sector, I believe this typology to be relevant to both the field of policy making and its implementation by public sector practitioners as well as NGOs. In all of these fields, equality has developed in siloed ways, and it is in this context that a range of actors currently struggle with how to organize their work more intersectionally. This typology is laid out in Table 7.1 at the end of this chapter, including how the concepts relate to both representation and coalition, and how these in turn relate to the parameters of intersectionality that I identified in Chapter 2.

This typology is comprised of five applied concepts of intersectionality. The first of these is 'generic intersectionality'. Generic intersectionality empties intersectionality of its attention to power and marginality. This concept is employed in the interests of maintaining white supremacy, gendered racism, racialized sexism and the status quo of inequalities, and to rationalize a lack of public sector investment in equality work (especially racial justice work) in the context of austerity politics. Yet, this is not to say that these effects and uses are always conscious or explicit. This concept is employed not only by policy makers, but by well-meaning practitioners seeking to avoid essentializing tendencies inherent to the current siloed context. This concept of intersectionality is highly significant because although intersectionality scholars may easily conclude that it is not intersectionality at all, it goes far beyond uses of intersectionality as institutionalization of diversity (Nash 2019) in further marginalizing social groups, particularly along racial lines; it propels equality as liberal sameness into the present and future under a new name (Christoffersen 2022). It is also highly significant because it is quietly achieving common sense status in some policy contexts, and on its own terms it is being operationalized with tremendous success. From the perspective of generic intersectionality, working on issues that affect only the most disadvantaged is successfully constructed as being *not intersectional*, and out of date in the era of intersectionality. Generic intersectionality is used to rationalize a wielding of power against the racial justice sector, in the form of material divestment and effacement per se (forcing organizations to change their missions entirely). This displacement serves to strengthen constructed associations of other inequalities, and the equality sectors working on them, with whiteness. Racial justice organizations are constructed as uniquely incapable of doing intersectionality, with real material consequences for those organizations, while white-led organizations benefit from this construction, since they are, by necessity, simultaneously constructed as *uniquely capable* of intersectionality (Christoffersen 2022).

Many practitioners recognize the threat of this understanding of intersectionality. In contexts where this meaning is dominant, not only is the viability of racial justice work under threat, but all work of intersectional organizations, and that employing an 'intersections of equality strands' concept of intersectionality by other organizations, is as well. This includes, in particular, organizations led by and for Black women and women of colour, which, like racial justice organizations, are constructed as incapable of doing intersectionality. Women of colour are constructed as niche, specific and non-credible knowers about intersectionality; a violent effacement that is both discursive and material (Christoffersen 2022).

The second practice-related concept in the typology is 'pan equality intersectionality', namely, identifying and tackling issues that are common to many marginalized groups. This concept of intersectionality, which I have found to be widely employed among equality practitioners, dovetails with some applications of intersectionality in policy making, and recommendations for how to apply it in policy literature (Parken and Young 2008; Parken 2010; Hankivsky and Cormier 2011; Walby et al 2012a). In some cases, as in the example shared in Chapter 4 wherein an organization considered marking an equality month by focusing on a common issue yet opted to continue to divide it up by strand, this amounts to conceptualizing issues as common to groups while the groups remain separately conceived (thereby effacing intersectional marginalization). Moreover, without a focus on intersectional marginalization, pan equality practice can reproduce the status quo of power dynamics within actual organizing.

Yet there are other empirical examples of work on hate crime, that includes *both* campaigning for parity in hate crime legislation across equality strands, identifying power imbalances as a common root, *and* highlighting the intersectional nature of hate crime (for instance that people may be particularly subject to hate crime because of their specific, mutually constitutive social location as disabled women of colour, and in particular ways). There are also examples of the use of strategic essentialism within wider pan equality campaigns, for example on mental health, to highlight the salience of particular markers of inequality (race), and at times how these intersect with gender. Therefore, while pan equality intersectionality *on its own* may at times efface intersectional marginalization, if efforts are made to highlight particular intersectional marginalizations within these wider issues (for example, mental health, hate crime) it can both build solidarity and inspire coalition around the common issue, as well as prioritize intersectional disadvantage (see Cohen 2005); yet this prioritization is a matter of constant negotiation, as network organizer Catriona described:

'I think sometimes there can be a feeling of a hierarchy of marginalization ... I'm thinking about [our hate crime coalition], there've been a couple of instances where people maybe felt that one intersection was being prioritized over their intersection or their community ... there are times when people might feel that ... an agenda is going off in a particular direction, and ... leaving them behind.'

A key strength of pan equality intersectionality is that it can avoid predetermining which issues affect which social groups; another is that in focusing on broader issues, it facilitates more structural understandings of intersectionality. A challenge is that it may flatten differences between inequalities. Perhaps most significantly, it precludes work on issues that are *not* necessarily perceived as common, as in the example of expanding trans rights[7] shared in the previous chapter.

During co-construction sessions, some participants were critical of intersectionality being conceptualized and applied in this way, because this concept does not necessarily focus on intersections of strands within wider issues. Yet I depart from some participants in advocating that this concept of intersectionality is needed *alongside* 'intersections of equality strands' ones, for the reason that most work labelled 'intersectional' in the equality NGO sector is purely individualized (this is explored further in the next section of this chapter).

The third practice-related concept is 'multi-strand intersectionality': where intersectionality is given the meaning of, or used to mask what is actually, addressing siloed inequalities simultaneously. This understanding of intersectionality is additive, and so among those who hold it, intersectionality is at times thought to be interchangeable with multiple discrimination and multiple identities. Multi-strand intersectionality resonates with what has been identified in the literature as the limited ways that intersectionality has been actually applied in policy making: 'additively organized diversity policies' (Townsend-Bell 2019, 735). It also resonates with not-quite-intersectional approaches to *research* on multiple inequalities (for example, Hancock's (2007) 'multiple' approaches). Multi-strand intersectionality reflects the collective vested interests that single-issue organizations have in maintaining a siloed context, and effaces intersectional marginalization. Yet, multi-strand institutions such as networks may be necessary spaces of challenge and learning to ultimately further intersectional practice.

Among the few published articles examining intersectionality's operationalization in policy in the UK is Walby et al (2012a). As discussed in Chapter 2, the authors put forward a 'mutual shaping' approach to intersectionality, in place of 'mutually constitutive'. I argued that this is in contradiction to Black feminist formulations of intersectionality; it seems to miss the point of intersectionality (Christoffersen and Emejulu 2023). Walby et al also offer a typology of approaches to intersectionality. My typology of intersectionality in practice departs from this, and not only because the one that I offer is in the language of practitioners. While Walby et al seek to expand typologies of the relationships between different inequalities developed to operationalize the study of these in *empirical research* (McCall 2005; Hancock 2007), to then *deductively* apply to policy analysis, I have *inductively* explored the meanings of intersectionality in use in policy and practice, and found that their typology does not match what I have identified in practice. In other words, I question the utility of typologies developed to operationalize intersectionality empirically in the study of policy and practice. The former concern variables while the latter are complex constellations of perceptions and practices (Christoffersen 2021a).

Together with diversity-within intersectionality, multi-strand intersectionality restricts intersectionality to the level of individual identity and experience, focusing work on the symptoms rather than the causes of inequality.

Multi-strand intersectionality has an interesting relationship to the predetermination of the relationship between social groups and social problems. On one hand, social groups are often thought to have separate issues. On the other hand, organizations somewhat childishly insist that 'their' strand be considered in relation to 'other' strands' issues. This may inadvertently pave the way for more useful applications of pan equality intersectionality.

The fourth concept of intersectionality is 'diversity-within', in which one inequality is considered primary or fundamental, and intersectionality is addressing differences within a predefined social group. These differences are, however, considered secondary, and so attention to them tends to be occasional rather than constant: ultimately, these secondary inequalities may be subsumed in the supposed interests of advancing equality for the social group (thereby advancing equality for privileged members of that group). Put bluntly, given its prevalence in the single-issue white-led women's sector, this concept of intersectionality can be read as how intersectionality is co-opted to align with the interests of white women, serving to reproduce structures of inequality that intersectionality was intended to address (Christoffersen and Emejulu 2023). Further research could critically interrogate whether and why this concept of intersectionality is particularly prevalent in the women's sector, as I found in my sample (see also McCabe 2023; Christoffersen and McCabe forthcoming). This understanding is often, though not always, correlated to multi-strand understandings: organizationally, practitioners practise diversity-within intersectionality, and in networks, multi-strand intersectionality. Those organizations with diversity-within understandings sometimes come reluctantly to the intersectionality table, compelled there by funder requirements of equality monitoring, highlighting the exclusive nature of their services and activities. Because like multi-strand intersectionality, diversity-within is additive, it is unable to incorporate the idea of always-interlocking inequality structures which produce both privilege and penalty; it cannot hold concepts of privilege constant.

Diversity-within intersectionality among practitioners bears striking similarity to additive intersectionality in the literature (for example, Walby et al 2012b). In exploring the limits of diversity-within in practice, I also reveal the theoretical limits of diversity-within: ultimately, it relies on some essential ideas about what a given social structure (gender) is and does, by refusing the idea that it becomes 'something totally different' (Walby et al 2012b, 235) at the point of intersection. In so doing, it reconstructs the social structure of gender, like the category 'woman' (Lewis 2017) as always-already white (Christoffersen and Emejulu 2023; see also Emejulu 2022).

Diversity-within intersectionality (like generic intersectionality), may readily be judged as not intersectionality at all. Academic arguments such as Walby et al (2012b) bolster practical applications of intersectionality as diversity-within, while I have demonstrated that this concept bears significant limitations, not least its implications for intersectionally marginalized groups.

It is in the interests of single-strand organizations to conflate intersectionality with multi-strand and diversity-within intersectionality. If intersectionality is conceptualized otherwise, then it becomes apparent that these organizations are not really doing intersectionality, though many are claiming to. Funders are also heavily complicit in this conflation and limiting use of intersectionality, since many recognize, encourage and expect diversity-within *as* intersectionality. This is, in and of itself, due to the influence of certain organizations and sectors (in particular, the white women's sector) on forming funder (including government) conceptualizations of intersectionality (particularly apparent in Scotland; see also McCabe 2023; Christoffersen and McCabe, forthcoming).

Diversity-within intersectionality characteristically predetermines which social group is affected by which social problems. Diversity-within views marginalized people as solely oppressed and 'intersectionalities' as 'additional barriers', so manifests in projects lacking meaningful representation of intersectionally marginalized people in decision-making. It poses a tremendous barrier to organizing in coalitions through being near synonymous with siloed thinking, which can manifest in discrimination.

Both diversity-within and multi-strand intersectionality are consistent with how I found intersectionality to be mobilized in national and UK level equality policy documents (Chapter 3).

During co-construction sessions, many participants felt that *both* diversity-within and 'intersections of equality strands' *were* intersectionality, while the three remaining concepts were not; initially some had difficulty distinguishing between these two. It is on this point that I diverge furthest from participant views, for all of the reasons elaborated above. Yet others recognized clear distinctions between this concept and 'intersections of equality strands', and between single-strand and intersectional organizations. It is perhaps not surprising that representatives of single-strand organizations felt diversity-within resonated, and that this was a valid way to conceptualize and apply intersectionality; yet as one pointed out, practitioners may work in organizations which apply diversity-within, but feel personally that 'intersections of equality strands' resonates more with their experience.

The fifth and final applied concept of intersectionality that I have elaborated in this book is 'intersections of (equality) strands': work of and with specific intersectionally marginalized groups, wherein no particular inequality bears primacy over the other(s). This concept is found within some practice of networks, within intersectional alliances characterized by relatively equitable relationships between single-strand organizations, and among intersectional organizations. This is a concept much closer to what we may readily recognize as intersectionality, and bears similarity to operationalizations of intersectionality/intersectional practice in the literature (for example, Cruells and García 2014). It is nearly opposite to generic intersectionality, within which focus on particular intersectionally marginalized groups is constructed as niche, not value for money, siloed and divisive, and *not actually intersectional*. Organizations employing this understanding may have undertaken 'intersectional' work for some time, without necessarily thinking about it as such, though they increasingly lay claim to the term in a sector characterized by competing concepts of intersectionality, and its increasing popularity. It is often less powerful actors (intersectionally marginalized people and organizations representing them, including organizations led by and for women of colour) who hold this understanding, compared with those holding all other concepts of intersectionality.

In intersectional alliances, practitioners who may otherwise or may have previously employed diversity-within approaches, are challenged to rethink their conceptualization of intersectionality and the nature of inequality; this challenge comes from the agency of those situated at the intersection, and/or those in the other single-issue area. A similar challenge is not present in diversity-within approaches (mainly, service provision targeted at intersectionally marginalized groups) because there is not space for agency in such projects: people are doubly or multiply disadvantaged, so need more things done *to* and *for* them.

However, given that I have studied NGOs characterized by all of the constraints and experiencing barriers discussed in Chapters 3 and 4 (including power relations with the state, and the effects of neoliberal austerity), this concept in practice often bears the significant limitation of individualization also common to multi-strand and diversity-within intersectionality. Intersectionality may be viewed in mutually constitutive ways, but it is frequently conceptualized exclusively at the level of individual identity and experience, with no explicit reference to inequality structures (at times in spite of my best efforts to bring these into the conversation). At most, structures were conceived as policies and political institutions. Moreover, these projects and organizations face challenges of accounting for *all* markers of inequality. Nevertheless, the model of mutual constitution facilitates this: once an organization or project engages in work on a particular inequality, understanding intersectionality as 'intersections of equality strands' makes it less likely and more difficult to subtract inequality areas at will. Empirically, the central involvement (representation) of women of colour has been essential to keeping race/gender in the picture when alliances are focused on other intersections.

Éléonore Lépinard identified four 'repertoires' that women's sector actors in Canada and France use to discuss differences among women: 'intersectional recognition'; 'gender first'; 'individual recognition'; and 'intersectional solidarity'[8] (Lépinard 2014, 2020). The repertoire of intersectional recognition shares similarities with what I have called 'intersections of equality strands'; Lépinard also associated this repertoire with 'dual axis' organizations (I use 'intersectional' instead since many are constituted around more than two axes of domination). The 'gender first' and 'individual recognition' repertoires share similarities with diversity-within. However, where Lépinard observed that within 'gender first', intersectional interests are subsumed into a more universal concept of 'women's interests', perhaps at the time of my research and in the UK context, this position is less tenable. Those women's organizations I associate with diversity-within would not necessarily explicitly argue that the interests of intersectionally marginalized women can be subsumed into a homogenizing 'women's interests'. While for diversity-within, specific interests may be recognized, the key distinction between this and 'intersections of equality strands' centres on whether intersectionally marginalized subjects are viewed as agential in a mutually constitutive model, or multiply oppressed in an additive one (similar to Lépinard's 'individual recognition') (Lépinard 2014).

In contrast to most research in the field, which focuses on gender (for example, Irvine, Lang, and Montoya 2019a) and feminist organizations (for example, Lépinard 2014, 2020; Evans 2015, 2016b; Laperriere and Lépinard 2016; Boucher 2018; English 2019), my research was with a range of equality organizations (also including racial justice, LGBTI, migrants' and disability rights and intersectional combinations). Thus I add to the growing literature expanding the study of intersectional practice to other social movements and sectors (for example, Tungohan 2015 on migrants' rights organizing; Terriquez et al 2018 on the undocumented youth movement; Beaman and Brown 2019 on racial justice movements; Evans and Lépinard 2020 on queer movements as well as feminist ones; Marchetti et al 2021 on women's labour movements; Evans 2022 on disability organizing) in response to calls for this broadening of intersectionality research (Irvine et al 2019b). Since it was conducted in the UK, my research also uniquely engaged with a unified equality policy, providing an opportunity to research across many types of organizations who work together in networks and coalitions. As I discuss above, my findings diverge from much of the literature focusing on gender and feminist movements, finding that the single-issue women's sector was particularly resistant to mutually constitutive understandings and applications of intersectionality (more so than the racial justice, disability rights, LGBTI, and migrants' rights sectors). Since my research was with a wide range of equality organizations and not exclusively women's organizations, and focused on participation in equality networks, it was able to build on previous research on feminist and other specific movements (for example, Lépinard 2014, 2020) to further identify cross-sector concepts of intersectionality (generic, pan equality and multi-strand).

Knowledge and representation

The social locations that people and organizations occupy influence the concept of intersectionality that they hold; and the concept of intersectionality that they hold influences how they interpret social locations: as being wholly, multiply oppressed and so lacking agency, or as being sites of oppression *and* privilege, agency, resistance and affirmation (Dhamoon 2023). Experience of intersectional marginalization is important to knowledge of intersectionality, though in complex ways. Such experience does not essentially produce a particular knowledge of intersectionality, though trends can be observed. This location/experience is always partial, and so even among organizations focused at the intersections of multiple inequalities, there are other inequalities that they do not meaningfully engage and identify as areas for learning (or, have problematic perspectives in relation to). These areas where they have relative privilege, and so are less visible, may be easier to grasp from the perspective of intersectional marginalization, but not necessarily: this is where the particular concept of intersectionality employed becomes highly relevant.

Additive multi-strand and diversity-within concepts are ultimately not able to incorporate the idea of mutually constituting inequality structures that produce privilege as well as oppression. Multiple inequalities are viewed as multiple barriers. In contrast, intersectionality theory moves beyond standpoint theory in positing the simultaneity of both privilege and oppression, incorporated in 'intersections of equality strands' concepts of intersectionality. This understanding facilitates those who are intersectionally marginalized in many respects to identify areas where they hold privilege. Those with mainly privileged aspects of identity may be less likely to hold 'intersections of equality strands' concepts of intersectionality, but for those that do, this concept enables them to position themselves within intersecting inequality structures, thereby relating intersectionality to themselves regardless of their privileged social positions. In contrast, those with multi-strand and diversity-within understandings tended to view themselves as wholly oppressed or wholly privileged along one particular axis, with other axes only amplifying this status in additive ways. They tended to associate intersectionality only with marginality, with intersectionality viewed near identically to multiple disadvantage. When other inequalities are brought into perspective, these are thought to create exceptional privilege, or exceptional marginality.

While not without exceptions, experience of intersectional marginalization is associated with 'intersections of equality strands' understandings, and experience of intersectional privilege is associated with generic intersectionality, and additive multi-strand and diversity-within intersectionality. However, knowledge of inequalities, including which concept of intersectionality is held, does not automatically flow from experience, identity or social position; participants narrate their 'specialisms' as additional expertise that does not neatly follow from their social positioning. Participants identify a range of sources of knowledge of intersectionality, and often express competing concepts of intersectionality themselves; their concepts are also at times easily amenable in the face of critique (as became apparent in some of my 'co-construction' sessions with participants). *This is precisely why identifying competing concepts of intersectionality and their limitations and effects is important.*

In Chapter 2, I reviewed literature on political representation, since representation (of particular social positions, in particular those occupied by Black women and women of colour) is a key issue in the practice of intersectionality (Collins 1990; Mügge et al 2018), which my findings confirm, and in light of the representative roles of equality organizations. I argued that intersectionality problematizes concepts of descriptive, substantive and group representation (Pitkin 1967; Young 1990), highlighting the impossibility of each due to (i) infinities of identity categories, and (ii) opposing interests within social groups, which existing literature does not account for adequately. Meanwhile, some existing intersectionality literature fails to adequately address issues of representation, by reducing intersectionality to its ontological project (for example, McCall 2005). I have argued that questions of representation (who is represented, and whether and how to represent) are central to operationalization of intersectionality.

To expand on this, in spite of the ways that they are interpellated as representatives by policy makers, some equality organizations (those in which 'intersections of equality strands' understandings are dominant) are less concerned to represent *at all*, that is, to act *for* others, and more concerned with self-representation, enabling participation and developing others to represent more authentically than they can. Therefore, in relation to equality NGOs, perhaps the question is less whether and how representatives can represent the substantive interests of the oppressed (Strolovitch 2006, 2007), and more about what they can do to limit the extent to which they represent these interests at all. For single-strand organizations, this means critically examining the concepts of intersectionality that they practise, and making space for self-organization of particular intersectionally marginalized groups.[9] In a broader context of epistemic injustice that constructs them as non-credible knowers, intersectionally marginalized people organize to represent *themselves*, rather than placing faith in single-strand or generic organizations to do so (which Lépinard terms 'intersectional recognition' (Lépinard 2014)). In other words, while much emphasis has been placed in the literature on how single-strand organizations can better represent intersectionally disadvantaged sub-groups (problematically conceptualized at times as 'voiceless' (Marchetti 2014, 116)), perhaps we need to more clearly ask the question of how those groups are organizing and representing themselves, and what single-issue organizations can do to *limit* the extent to which they are representing (acting for) those groups at all, and instead creating and facilitating meaningful opportunities for participation and influence. For policy makers, perhaps the lesson is not to view single-issue organizations as being representative (or even potentially representative) of intersectionally marginalized communities; even, not to desire that they become so. Single-issue organizations emerged because equality communities were not otherwise represented; intersectional organizations emerge because single-issue organizations do not represent them (and many employ particular concepts of intersectionality that mean that so long as they do, they *will not* represent intersectionally marginalized people in any meaningful way). The counter argument would be that this lets single-strand organizations off the hook; yet what they are accountable for can be looked on in a new light: not the extent to which they are representing the interests of intersectionally disadvantaged sub-groups, but rather, the extent to which they are facilitating self-organization of those groups (including in material terms). Moreover, they can also be accountable for the extent to which they are responsive to emergent claims, as explored in the previous chapter.

For this reason, *contra* Saward (2006), in equality organizing, *forms* of representation remain important, that is, the particular actors and not solely the *claims*; and legitimacy remains related to form and not merely content. This particular form (intersectional organization) combines different bases for representation, described as 'mirroring', 'self-representation', *and* 'specialist expertise' (Saward 2009). Authenticity is gained from these bases and from the relationship between social location, experience and knowledge. In other words, many of my participants view the claims made and claims-makers as closely interrelated, and remain deeply concerned with who is making claims, and for whom.

Summary

In this section, I have outlined this book's conceptual contributions to the literature: in particular, by uniquely exploring how policy makers and practitioners *themselves* understand intersectionality, I identify a typology of five applied concepts of intersectionality in circulation. This typology evidences a translational theory of knowledge and departs from those typologies of intersectionality developed to operationalize it in empirical research. The typology *specifies* intersectionality amid slippery uses in both literature and in practice, and facilitates understanding of the strengths and limitations of competing applications of intersectionality.

I highlighted that while experience of intersectional marginalization is important to knowledge of intersectionality, it does not determine it; which is precisely why identification of competing applied concepts and their effects is important. Similarly, representation of intersectional marginalization within organizations is important to the practice of intersectionality, while its complexity means it can never be perfectly achieved; in this light, not all equality organizations are concerned to represent 'intersectionally disadvantaged sub-groups', rather to enable their participation and self-representation instead. For this reason, the particular *form* of representation I have described as 'intersectional organizing' is key. I turn now to the political challenges associated with my findings.

The politics of intersectionality

Analysing attempts to operationalize concepts of intersectionality in practice reveals the messiness of the politics of intersectionality, enacted in interactions between distinct political actors. The typology of intersectionality that I have identified and elaborated is important because of the differing interests served by, and implications of, each of these concepts for intersectionally marginalized groups, including significant material implications – for example, who receives funding for 'intersectional' work, whom this work benefits and whom it disadvantages (or violently effaces).

Differently constituted equality organizations have vested interests in particular concepts of intersectionality. Generic organizations (those not organized around a particular equality strand/strands) have an interest in furthering generic concepts of intersectionality, and to a lesser extent, pan equality ones. Similarly, single-strand organizations have collective interests in furthering multi-strand concepts, and key singular interests in furthering diversity-within ones. Indeed, if diversity-within were to be reconceptualized as not really intersectionality at all, in contexts where intersectionality is gaining policy favour (in Scotland, for example), this would pose a huge threat to the viability of these organizations, many of whom rely entirely on Scottish government funding. Conversely, intersectional organizations and partnership projects between single-strand organizations have interests in furthering 'intersections of equality strands' understandings in order to gain funding for their organizations and projects. Equality networks and coalitions are more flexible: they have particular interests in furthering pan equality and multi-strand intersectionality, but are able to mobilize any concept of the typology except for diversity-within in their interests (the three networks that I have studied have successfully gained funding to operationalize variously, generic, pan equality, multi-strand and 'intersections of equality strands' concepts of intersectionality). Importantly, all non-Black-feminist organizations have an interest in dislodging intersectionality from this intersection, and all white-led organizations (that is, all other equality sectors except the racial justice and migrants' rights sectors) have an interest in dissociating intersectionality from race and race/gender, in contexts where intersectionality is becoming the current 'common sense' term to use in relation to in/equality, expected and desired by funders.

Jennifer Nash (2019) identified that intersectionality is both underdetermined and *overdetermined* in relation to Black women. The latter relationship is both absent and present in my findings from the NGO sector. Black women whom I interviewed were very aware of the origins of intersectionality in Black feminism, as were some other women of colour, others working in the racial justice sector and few others elsewhere. However, no participants expressed a view that intersectionality should be reserved to describing Black women, women of colour or the intersection of race/gender, though this was expressed to a white researcher in the context of this particular research project, and they may have related other views elsewhere. With this caveat then, the proprietariness and defensiveness highlighted by Nash in academic feminism, the 'intersectionality wars', was not prevalent in my data. Intersectionality has been embraced by cross-racial and predominantly white organizations working at other intersections of disability and gender, LGBTI and youth identity; this, in and of itself, was not problematized by other participants knowledgeable of its origins (though this does not mean that they would not see exclusion of race and race/gender from 'intersectional' work as highly problematic). These other sectors were described by those knowing of intersectionality's origins as 'slower to come on board' with it – so *resistance* to intersectionality was problematized, rather than its appropriation. This relative absence of the intersectionality wars in my sample might be read as being due to the ubiquity of intersectionality's lack of specificity in the wider policy environment (identified in Chapter 3), or to a form of the surrender advocated by Nash having already occurred in the sector, and most probably a combination of both.[10] The overall view among participants was that all equality organizations *should* be doing intersectionality across markers of inequality.

Several (predominantly white) participants were not aware of intersectionality's origins in Black feminism and to describe intersecting structures positioning Black women at all. From my perspective as researcher, there were quite a few clear examples where intersectionality was mobilized by white participants and white-led organizations without any meaningful attention to race, Black women or women of colour, consistent with my finding that in equality policy, meaningful engagement with race in the context of intersectionality is lacking. The latter finding is doubly echoed in more recent policy documents that mention intersectionality (for example, Women and Work All Party Parliamentary Group 2020). However, in the equality sector there were other examples where intersectionality was mobilized by those outwith the racial justice and women of colour sectors with sustained efforts to include race as an intersection, usually but not always correlated to representation of women of colour within the organization. One influential white-led organization in particular was perfectly aware of intersectionality's origins, but, frustrated with its continued association with them, purposefully, problematically (and seemingly successfully) sought to extend its meanings in policy and in the sector. Clearly, there is a pressing need to challenge white-led organizations and white practitioners and policy makers who do not recognize white supremacy or engage race and race/gender in their work that they describe as intersectional, but this need arguably does not arise solely because of intersectionality's origins. Rather, it arises from commitments to racial and intersectional justice and the empirical positions of race and race/gender as fundamental organizing logics of and social divisions producing inequality in the UK (Christoffersen 2022).

Policy makers have distinctive, contextual sets of interests in furthering particular concepts of intersectionality. I found that policy makers employ, and accept the validity of, whichever of these understandings of intersectionality suit their interests at particular junctures. In contexts of austerity, policy makers have clear interests in generic understandings of intersectionality, in which delivering little and the same to all is repackaged as being *innovative* by calling it 'intersectionality'. When difference is not collapsed entirely and some limited attention is given to marginality, policy makers have an interest in pan equality intersectionality, in which attention and resources are 'cost-effectively' focused on addressing issues perceived to be common to marginalized groups (putting aside those less cost-effective issues which are not). Multi-strand and diversity-within understandings are useful to maintain the status quo of the siloed sector, avoiding conflict with single-strand equality organizations, good relationships with whom some policy makers (and political parties) gain a great deal of legitimacy from. Indeed, the policy makers that I interviewed varied between these concepts of intersectionality in their narratives in relation to different objectives. Conversely, policy makers rarely have or express interest in 'intersections of equality strands' concepts of intersectionality, since from their perspective the implications of this would be funding a range of what they perceive as 'niche', 'small', 'statistically insignificant' communities, and a proliferation of projects and organizations focused on an ever expanding list of intersectionally marginalized groups (not, therefore, cost-effective). Like white-led equality organizations, they have an interest in dissociating intersectionality from race/gender, since the alternative would mean a complete reconceptualization of equality policy from the perspective of intersectional justice. While there are examples of policy makers applying pressure to sectors to be more inclusive, as has been the case in Scotland with women's organizations and trans women, I did not observe the same pressure applied to white-led organizations to meaningfully engage antiracism. Rather the opposite is true in that it has been racial justice organizations that have been pressured to engage other inequalities, and constructed as not intersectional since an assumption is already present that they will not or cannot: they are pressured to do something that they are already presumed to be incapable of doing or unwilling to do. At work here are implicit and familiar constructions of racial justice organizations (led by people of colour) as being *more* sexist, *more* homophobic, *more* ableist and *more* conservatively religious than white-led organizations (Christoffersen 2022).

I have shown that in the current, still largely siloed, context, the politics of intersectional practice – relations of power in which the applied meaning of *intersectionality* is contested, and interests compete – are expressed in the arenas of representation, and coalition – with and without solidarity. Operationalizing intersectionality is fundamentally about who is represented, and whether and how to represent, as well as coalition and solidarity building between organizations. Conflicts around and in these fields of representation and coalition are driven by competing concepts of intersectionality, at the same time that different representational arrangements and coalitional forms (or lack thereof) drive competing concepts: in other words, *representational arrangements and coalitional forms are mutually constitutive with competing concepts of intersectionality*. Competing concepts of intersectionality are the heart of conflicts around who 'does' it, and how; distinctions of who is doing it and how they are doing it coalesce in distinct applied concepts of intersectionality.

For equality organizations and networks employing 'intersections of equality strands' (sometimes in combination with pan equality) concepts of intersectionality, operationalizing intersectionality means self-organization of, and enabling participation of, intersectionally marginalized groups: seeking to equalize relationships of unequal power (insofar as possible). This resonates with intersectionality theory (Tormos 2017). These practices do not follow from other concepts of intersectionality (generic, multi-strand, diversity-within). Indeed, these latter understandings serve to maintain and further entrench inequitable power relationships: for generic understandings, this is accomplished through ostensibly treating everyone the same, but in practice privileging and extending whiteness; for multi-strand ones, through effacing intersectional marginalization, thereby continuing to centre those with relative privilege; and for diversity-within, through denying and effacing agency of those who are intersectionally marginalized, discursively and materially, and refusing to recognize and renounce privileges. Therefore, there is a pressing need to name, specify (Jordan-Zachery 2007) and ultimately to dissociate these concepts from 'intersectionality', and for *organizations, practitioners and policy makers to be much more specific about which particular concept of intersectionality they are employing when they mobilize the term* (Christoffersen 2021a).

Coalition is a core part of intersectional practice, as identified in the literature (Strolovitch 2007; Cole 2008; Roberts and Jesudason 2013; Bassel and Emejulu 2014; Collins and Bilge 2016; Irvine et al 2019b) and confirmed in my study. My contribution centres the importance of examining which particular concepts of intersectionality are employed by coalitions themselves as well as participants in them: I found this to be a key determinant of how successful coalitions are at building relationships of solidarity to further intersectional justice. Siloed thinking shapes and is shaped by additive concepts of intersectionality, and poses a barrier to coalition formation and success. Generic, multi-strand and diversity-within intersectionality empirically do little to build intersectional political solidarity, and those employing the latter justify opting out of coalitions. Building intersectional solidarity requires concepts of intersectionality ('intersections of equality strands') which recognize the mutually constitutive interrelationship of inequality structures as constant. This is a precondition for recognizing privilege; yet in the absence of representation, some coalition members struggle with whether and how to act from privileged positions. Beyond this, coalition building requires addressing challenges (see also Townsend-Bell 2011; Ishkanian and Peña Saavedra 2019) as well as dialogue and learning (see also Roberts and Jesudason 2013).

Intersectional organizations

I argued earlier that, though not in the perceived interests of policy makers, promising models of intersectional practice follow from 'intersections of equality strands' concepts of intersectionality, which are related to intersectional organizations (autonomous organizations constituted around multiple intersecting inequalities, comprising 20 per cent of my sample of network member organizations), and intersectional alliances. However, much existing literature specifically examining intersectionality's operationalization in public policy, the NGO sector and social movements, when considering identity-based equality organizations, has focused exclusively on single-strand organizations (Strolovitch 2007; Parken and Young 2008; Walby et al 2012a) (with notable exceptions including Chun et al 2013; Lépinard 2014; Tungohan 2015), thereby ignoring or effacing what I have called intersectional organizations. Concepts emerging from this literature such as 'affirmative advocacy' (Strolovitch 2007), 'intersectional praxis' (Townsend-Bell 2011) and 'mutual shaping' (Walby et al 2012a) are therefore largely developed for, and from the perspective of, single-strand organizations and movements: the first concerning how they can better represent disadvantaged sub-groups, the second concerning which inequalities to include in the rubric of 'intersectionality' (while intersectional organizations have already made these choices, and these are considered indivisible), and the third legitimizing single-strand diversity-within approaches as the correct way to organize and address inequality.

However, while the UK equality NGO sector may be predominantly composed of single-identity/strand organizations (working on one equality area), there are also many that have long been advancing intersectional justice claims, with the Black women's sector a key example; I have included such organizations in my sample insofar as possible given their underrepresentation in equality networks. Organizations focused around multiple identity axes are marginal to, and under-resourced compared with, the (already marginal) equality sub-sectors (Sudbury 1998; Kairos in Soho 2011, 2012; centred 2014). Intersectional organizations have been particularly hard hit by austerity; many intersectional organizations have closed in recent years, while many others are entirely voluntary (and would prefer to be funded). The loss of intersectional organizations has been identified by participants as a significant barrier to operationalizing intersectionality. Austerity also makes it more difficult for intersectionally marginalized people to participate in such organizations as volunteers and activists; at the same time, it propels grassroots activism within a politics of survival (Bassel and Emejulu 2017). Other research about the work of such organizations (Sudbury 1998; Bassel and Emejulu 2017), finds that, in the words of Leah Bassel and Akwugo Emejulu, 'minority women have distinctive patterns to their political behaviour that are often ignored, misrecognised or devalued in the wider political science literature and in the formal practice of politics' (Bassel and Emejulu 2017, 8).

An important implication of my research is the need to consider intersectional organizations as distinctive from single-strand organizations, rather than subsuming them as subcategories of the latter (Strolovitch 2007; English 2019; Marchetti 2019) where they are not omitted entirely. Indeed, future research on intersectionality's operationalization in both the NGO sector and social movements could usefully limit its scope solely to these organizations (those that continue to exist in times of austerity), as well as their grassroots counterparts. A key policy implication is the rationale for continuing to fund these organizations which I hope that I have helped to articulate. While Dara Strolovitch (2007)argues for single-issue advocacy organizations to adopt a principle of giving extra representation to intersectionally disadvantaged sub-groups, I argue that in the UK context, the definitions of intersectionality that many such groups adopt present barriers *in and of themselves* to be able to do this in a way that promotes intersectional justice and agency of those sub-groups. Therefore, I depart from this by advocating that rather than seek to simply incorporate intersectionally marginalized groups, these organizations support and make space for self-organization of these groups – not only or primarily *within* their organizations, but *outwith* them (see also D'Agostino 2021). Meanwhile, single-issue organizations could critically examine the concepts of intersectionality that they practise, and their limitations.

Intersectional organizations vs. diversity-within

Several of the concepts of intersectionality discussed here efface and threaten intersectional organizations: namely, all but the 'intersections of equality strands' understanding. Yet, my research indicates that in view of representation, these organizations present a model for intersectional practice. Though organizations rather than coalitions, they also provide a model for coalitional working, wherein one inequality is not subsumed to others, and wherein privilege can be meaningfully acknowledged in order for acts of allyship to proceed and intersectional political solidarity to be built (yet, research elsewhere has shown that these organizations have varying approaches to difference (see Luna 2016)). Although I identify intersectional organizations as providing models for intersectional practice, oddly (but reflective of certain privilege, and consistent with white supremacy and gendered racism), prominent policy makers in my sample (and some feminist academics, given that the vast majority of research on intersectionality in practice is confined to (predominantly white) feminist movements) seem to view the model of intersectional practice as the single-issue white women's sectors and movements (Christoffersen and Emejulu 2023). These organizations (many associated with diversity-within) lay claim to intersectionality; those who equate diversity-within to intersectionality can claim that they practise intersectionality, while others do not. For instance, Yvonne, director of a women's organization in Scotland: "we're not just focused on the gender issue, we're focused on the gender plus issues. Until very very recently, I think we were the only [equality organization in the city] that had that overarching equality work"; and Diane, practitioner in a women's organization in England: "successful services, sustainable services are built around that holistic approach, dealing with the whole woman, not just from a BME perspective or disabled perspective or an issue about class". In the latter quote, the women's sector is constructed as the only sector that does 'holistic' approaches, while the BME and disabled sectors are constructed as being inherently inattentive to gender/women. Autonomous organizing by and for women of colour is effaced (Christoffersen and Emejulu 2023).

In sharp contrast, an important implication of my research is that practising diversity-within, with all of the limitations it entails, is in fact a significant *barrier to*, rather than *model for*, operationalizing intersectionality for intersectional justice. Only for intersectional organizations and alliances is intersectionality the starting point, rather than something that comes later or not at all.

Structures of inequality

A significant political implication of my research is the need for better articulation and awareness raising of intersectionality as the fusion of structures of inequality (or, the impossibility of this articulation in the NGO sector as it stands, and the need to explore further what enables and inhibits it).

Elsewhere, other authors have analysed the neoliberalization of the NGO sector tracing back to Tony Blair's Labour government's new public managerialism and propelled by austerity, as organizations increasingly take on values of the private sector in order to remain competitive (Squires 2008b; Bassel and Emejulu 2017). A key component of this neoliberalization is individualization. In the NGO sector, this manifests in particular in service delivery wherein individualized, 'person centred' provision is a key value of health and social care, which forms part of contracts awarded to NGOs. Equality practitioners and organizations, particularly service providers, articulate applying intersectionality within the confines of this discourse: intersectionality is about being holistically responsive to each unique individual (see also Laperriere and Lépinard 2016). Yet it is not only in service provision where individualization penetrates: throughout the NGO sector, the bulk of funding is no longer core funding, but rather project funding on condition of achieving predefined outcomes, which are usually measured as changes in individuals.

Some concepts of intersectionality are better able to avoid individualization, and more conducive to conceptualizing it at the level of inequality structures, than others (namely, pan equality and 'intersections of equality strands' concepts). Even among those employing the latter concept however, I found understandings of intersectionality to be articulated largely at the individual level, with reference to identity and experience; although this concept does not reduce intersectional identity to 'multiple barriers/disadvantage' as diversity-within does. My observation of individualization resonates with what has been argued elsewhere to be the reduction of intersectionality to diversity (May 2015; Nash 2019); it also echoes my findings on the uses of intersectionality in equality policy documents shared in Chapter 3. Although intersectional organizations may take on discourses of individualization, in fact this is part of a wider discourse that works against their interests. Part of this neoliberalization is to see service delivery to 'hard to reach' intersectionally marginalized groups as 'new market share' (Bassel and Emejulu 2017, 59), fair game for generic organizations (as discussed in Chapter 5), thereby undermining not only intersectional organizations, but the principle of self-organization and therefore the equality sector itself more broadly.

Entwined with the neoliberal discourse of individualization is the discourse of evidence. Characteristic of the field of intersectionality's operationalization in the current context is measurement of outcomes in individuals, and their equality characteristics. This is a discourse taken on by participants; for example, Anya, practitioner in a racial justice organization: "when you're doing intersectional work you have to be … evidence-based … [intersectionality] would usually only arise where there was some evidence-based policy need."

The discourse of evidence serves to construct intersectionally marginalized communities as small, and on which there is little ('statistically significant') reliable evidence. This evidence discourse, particularly associated with additive multi-strand and diversity-within intersectionality but present in all concepts, further marginalizes self-organized intersectional organizations, as well as entrenching individualized understandings of intersectionality. Intersectionality is reduced to cross-tabulations of datasets wherein individuals are the unit of measurement, evidence is the basis of representation, and equality categories are both reified and subdivided. In quantifying intersectional work, it is actually 'un-intersectionalized' through disaggregation.

Moving forward, equality organizations could usefully learn from social movements to operationalize intersectionality 'prefiguratively' *within their organizations* (Ishkanian and Peña Saavedra 2019) as well as in their outward-facing work, in which they inevitably count and quantify service users and participants. This attention to internal practice could help to make structures of inequality, and their quiet operation *within* organizations and in the sector as well as outside of it, more visible. This would help to shed light on the *processes* by which intersecting inequalities manifest (Dhamoon 2011).

Category reification

As the example of conflicts around trans rights in the previous chapter demonstrates, and as discourses of evidence intertwined with and partially explaining the dominance of individualized intersectionality reinforce, category reification is a key political challenge for intersectionality's operationalization. Ultimately, many of the concepts of intersectionality identified here serve to both reify categories and proliferate new ones. This resonates with what has been identified as a risk associated with intersectionality's mainstreaming both in the literature: Rita Dhamoon (2011) argues that focus solely on identity categories leads to the reification of these categories; and in practice elsewhere (Luft and Ward 2009). To an extent, such reification may be a feature of intersectionality; Marquis Bey writes: 'the sentiment within work done through intersectionalist frameworks requires that one be this or that race or gender (among a variety, of course, of other identity vectors) and that everyone be subject to those frameworks. My gender abolitionist and transinsurgent politics simply cannot get behind such a project' (Bey 2023, 337).

Generic intersectionality may avoid category reification on one hand, but it reinforces an empty (and white) category of 'everyone', flattening difference, on the other. Pan equality intersectionality may also avoid reification, but the challenge is to focus on cross-cutting issues while retaining perspective on power: who is marginalized and who is privileged, and why. Multi-strand and diversity-within intersectionality have particular essentializing investments in equality categories: without them, single-strand sectors' whole *raison d'être* ceases to be. These understandings rely on constructions of whole social groups as being solely oppressed (or privileged); intersecting inequalities, conceptualized additively, only serve to augment this status. As such, there is real material resistance to the articulation of other inequality structures, as is the case with cisgenderism and some women's organizations. Recognition of other inequality structures would reveal the simultaneity of privilege and oppression, unseating the static dominance of the primary inequality. There is particular resistance to new categories that serve to dissolve the boundaries between old ones: 'queer'[11] and, especially at the time of writing, non-binary gender identity, being examples of this. New categories challenge the constituencies of organizations: who do they represent? On what basis do/can they exclude? And their bases: why do they exist?

I suggested in Chapter 2 that given the contingency of inequality, perhaps responsiveness to emerging identities and theorizations of inequality structures is a better measure of how 'intersectional' an organization is than inclusion of new statically conceived categories among those whom it seeks to represent. In very practical material terms, this is certainly a key challenge now among the equality networks that I have studied.

The challenge of reification is a political one because it may also be a necessary impulse, strategically necessary for marginalized communities, as Indigenous scholars have argued elsewhere (Coulthard 2014). To take again the example of non-binary gender identity that emerged empirically in the UK context, the naming of this category does not merely serve to deconstruct old categories; it itself is (strategically) mobilized as an identity under which to claim rights, and community; with all of the challenges for and of intersectionality that that entails: including struggles for visibility among non-binary Black people and people of colour (Alabanza 2020). For these reasons, I diverge from some other intersectionality scholars who argue that what is needed is a focus on issues and not identities (Verloo 2013): we need both (in other words, we need both pan equality and 'intersections of equality strands' concepts of intersectionality). The issue-only perspective seems to suggest that 'we' are finished with category development and proliferation, but there is little empirical indication that this is the case. Moreover, in the current political and economic context, if identities are put to one side, we are left with generic intersectionality.

Summary

In sum, my findings have significant political implications and highlight political challenges. Competing concepts in the spectrum of intersectionality serve distinct interests and are thus championed by particular actors, with varying positions in the field of power relations. This is evident in conflicts about and in the arenas of representation and coalition. While 'intersections of equality strands' concepts of intersectionality and intersectional organizations offer promising models of intersectional practice in view of equitable representation and coalitions with solidarity, this concept and these actors are effaced by much practice *and* empirical research on this topic. Because these are less powerful actors (intersectionally marginalized people and organizations representing them), those championing diversity-within (mainly white women's organizations) are able to claim intersectionality. Yet, through careful examination we can recognize this claim for what it is, and unseat the common sense academic (in some circles) and policy understanding that it is the single-strand women's sector we should be looking to for how to operationalize intersectionality (maybe it is anywhere but) (Christoffersen and Emejulu 2023).

There is a pressing political need for better articulation and awareness raising of intersectionality as the fusion of structures of inequality, yet equality NGOs are significantly constrained in their abilities to offer these by discourses of evidence and individualization that are constituent parts of neoliberal governance, and which serve to further marginalize both intersectional organizations and 'intersections of equality strands' concepts of intersectionality. Intersectional prefiguration may help to facilitate more useful understandings and applications of intersectionality in the sector (comprising both structures *and* identities, and the relationship between them).

Discourses of evidence, in turn, reinforce category reification, while new categories can serve to both disrupt and proliferate it. Nevertheless, claiming new disruptive identities is an important mobilizing strategy for rights claims, and so intersectional politics is about *both* issues *and* identities. Single-strand organizations with diversity-within concepts of intersectionality will continue to resist these new identity articulations together with theorizations of additional inequality structures, and this is a key way in which the politics of intersectionality are played out in this moment.

Policy and practice implications

Some concepts within the spectrum of intersectionality are complementary to one another (pan equality and 'intersections of equality strands'; multi-strand and diversity-within), while others are opposing (in particular, generic and 'intersections of equality strands'). Yet, all of these applied concepts are funded and delivered under the name of 'intersectionality' in the UK. At times, this confusion is instrumental, to further particular interests. Yet overall, this situation only serves to extend perceptions of intersectionality as 'difficult' if not impossible to apply in policy making and practice, bolstering lack of political will to apply it and contributing to inertia among those who seek to. Actually, if we are specific about which concept of intersectionality we are seeking to apply, then there are clear pathways in terms of what equality practitioners and organizations can do:

- Facilitate participation and self-organization of intersectionally marginalized people.
- Be responsive to emergent theorizations of identities and inequalities.
- Address perceived conflicts between strands which emerge.
- Facilitate dialogue and learning between equality sub-sectors.
- Work to balance practising solidarity with avoiding 'speaking for' marginalized others.
- Form intersectional alliances.
- Practise prefiguration within equality organizations.

Here I have argued that generic, multi-strand and diversity-within concepts do not serve to further intersectional justice; quite the contrary. Conversely, there are some clear means of operationalizing pan equality and 'intersections of equality strands' ones (see also Table 7.1). This specificity could be inscribed into policies, and it could be a requirement of funding to 'do' intersectionality. It could also form a basis of unity for more fruitful coalitions and partnerships.

Intersectionality needs to be the starting point, rather than being conceptualized as logically and temporally coming 'after' equality strands: the latter only leads to multi-strand and diversity-within intersectionality, which will fail to deliver greater equality for intersectionally marginalized groups because they efface intersectional marginalization. Placing intersectionality at the centre is accomplished in intersectional alliances and organizing.

This raises questions concerning the place (if any) of single-strand organizing/organizations, associated as they are with multi-strand and diversity-within intersectionality, where one inequality is considered paramount and others, if considered, are at best secondary and added and subtracted at will. I have argued that single-strand organizations should be held to account not for how they represent intersectionally marginalized groups, but for how they facilitate their meaningful participation and self-representation, and for their responsiveness to existing and emergent self-theorizations of inequalities that challenge established thinking.

Yet, in considering how to organize equality work in the interests of operationalizing intersectionality going forwards, there is a tension between focused work (including intersectional alliances and organizations) and more structural/pan equality work. Clearly there is still a place for strategic essentialism (as the examples of racial justice organizing by women of colour, and trans and non-binary organizing, highlight). Intersectional alliances and organizations can still be viewed as strategic essentialism, only of intersectionally marginalized groups rather than singular ones. This potentially leads down a road of there being a plethora of organizations and projects focused on particular points of intersectional marginalization, which may proliferate silos and which some view as both unsustainable in times of austerity, and fragmentary to the point that little in the way of structural change will be accomplished. For example, Anne, director of an equality network said:

> 'I think a lot of this might happen through merger and organizations falling over and closing. I just don't think there's the money around and there won't be in the future for so many different organizations looking at different things. It could be ... an unintended outcome of organizations losing funding might be that some of these silos get broken down.'

Moreover, silos may serve to make the equality sector fragile, according to Margaret, a policy maker: "The fact that ... organizations have their main focus on one thing means there's a vulnerability there that [if] ... funding got tight ... people tend to retrench."

There is a strong narrative in my data that a diversity of organizations is needed for 'personal choice' in a discourse of neoliberalism used as a rationale for siloing. Others argue that a diversity of single-strand and intersectional organizations is needed because people want to identify with whatever singular aspect(s) of their identity is the most important to them at the time. The latter point is highly questionable, and it is much more likely that often people have no option but to compartmentalize their identities given how siloed the sector is.

Is there a viable way to move to a less siloed sector (and perhaps even fewer organizations), overcoming the barrier of fear of 'stepping on toes', without becoming generic? Is it conceivable that we could see the emergence of more generalized political identities in the UK as observed elsewhere (Cruells and García 2014), which could *avoid* generic intersectionality? Marginalized communities/unpopular issues do not necessarily place any faith in organizations that are not of and by them to represent them, and nor should they. They organize to represent more authentically. The ongoing need for self-organization is why coalition and solidarity are so integral. Nevertheless, building coalitions across the multitude of self-organized intersecting identity-based organizations raises serious logistical challenges. A challenge of intersectionality is working to build greater unity while balancing these tensions: the impulse toward genericism propelled by austerity, as well as a willingness to act on issues which might not be our 'own'. This is ultimately about how to practise solidarity in ways that avoid the violence of speaking *for* others.

Pan equality work can be a starting point to identify common objectives, as well as differences and impasses. The challenge is to avoid it being 'lowest common denominator', thereby reinforcing inequalities. This is overcome through highlighting intersectional issues within broader campaigns. Employment of 'intersections of equality strands' concepts of intersectionality can overcome impasses (for example, the challenges that trans organizing poses to how practitioners think about gender explored in the preceding chapter), but not so diversity-within. Binary trans rights are controversial but can be incorporated into diversity-within; non-binary identity however, not so.

Summary

Broader policy and practice implications of this research include: (i) the need to specify applied concepts of intersectionality, to advocate for 'intersections of equality strands' and pan equality concepts to the exclusion of generic, multi-strand and diversity-within ones (whereas the latter two were found to coincide with the dominant uses of intersectionality in equality policy documents); (ii) the need to fund intersectional organizations and alliances; (iii) the need to hold single-strand organizations to account for facilitating meaningful participation and self-representation of intersectionally marginalized groups; (iv) seeking to build greater unity and coalition working around common issues and in solidarity, while highlighting and prioritizing intersectionally marginalized experiences among these, including emergent articulations; (v) respecting the principle of self-organization based on identity while avoiding neoliberal rationales resting on personal choice.

Toward intersectional justice

In this chapter, I have explicated the conceptual contributions of this book, particularly a typology of five competing applied concepts of intersectionality in policy and practice. I see as directions for future research, the interrogation of this typology in other national (La Barbera et al 2022) and supranational (Maes and Debusscher 2022) contexts and sectors (the fields of policy making and implementation in the public sector, and grassroots organizing).

While there are few ideal solutions to the problems of intersectionality's conceptualization and operationalization in siloed policy and practice, from the perspective of thinking through the implications for intersectionally marginalized groups, some compromises and imperfections may be deemed more acceptable than others. I have suggested that rather than seeking to represent intersectionally marginalized groups, single-strand organizations at this juncture could usefully focus on interrogating which concepts of intersectionality they use and their effects, and should be held to account for how they facilitate meaningful participation and self-representation of intersectionally marginalized groups (certain concepts of intersectionality being a precondition for this). The form of representation of intersectional organizing, effaced in much of the literature and in policy and practice, is essential to centre in the operationalization of intersectionality.

Competing applied concepts of intersectionality are employed by and serve distinctive interests. Models of intersectional practice are found among intersectional organizations and alliances, and not in the single-issue women's sector, among which actors nevertheless claim to be the only ones really doing intersectionality.

A key challenge for all applied concepts of intersectionality is balancing individualized descriptions of it with a focus on the inequality structures that produce these experiences and identities. I have suggested that practising intersectional prefiguration within equality organizations (often notably absent) may support this. I have argued that intersectionality's operationalization necessitates a twin focus on common issues and intersectionally marginalized identities, including emergent ones.

Policy makers and practitioners can specify their applied concepts of intersectionality and employ 'intersections of equality strands' and pan equality concepts. Policy makers can fund intersectional organizations and alliances. Equality organizations can build greater unity through ensuring shared understandings of intersectionality, and continue to balance acting in solidarity while prioritizing the agency of those who are intersectionally marginalized.

Given the range of meanings of intersectionality in UK equality practice, it is not sufficient to state that we are 'operationalizing intersectionality'. When it is used in three of the five ways that I have identified (generic, multi-strand and diversity-within), 'intersectionality' is mobilized in order to *not* do intersectionality: this is consistent with what Sara Ahmed names as 'non-performativity' (Ahmed 2006; see also Nash 2019). Intersectionality is so underdetermined, a 'floating signifier', that I suggest we need a new concept for use in NGO practice, and propose intersectional practice for *intersectional justice*. An explicit renaming and associating of 'intersectionality' with a concept of 'justice' may help to reinsert intersectionality's aim of social justice (Collins and Bilge 2016; Collins 2019b) and concern with inequality structures into its meanings and uses in practice. It may also offer something against which circulating applied concepts of intersectionality may be held to account, and expand conceptualization of intersectionality in NGO sector equality practice outside of the confines of equality policy (Cowan 2016). I aim not to define it once and for all, but to build on others' work (Luft and Ward 2009; Center for Intersectional Justice 2018) to further sketch what equality NGO work organized in the interests of intersectional justice might look like or need to include. In extant literature, the concept includes a principle that NGOs be accountable to the grassroots (Luft and Ward 2009), and that work be centred on those facing the greatest structural disadvantages (Center for Intersectional Justice 2018). I have argued that it also centrally and indivisibly involves self-representation and meaningful participation of intersectionally marginalized groups; a relational understanding of intersectionality which is open to integration of emergent articulations of identities and inequality structures (that may reveal some previously underexamined privileges which will prove challenging to many); and applications of intersectionality both *inside* organizations and in their outward-facing work. Further, it centrally concerns practising solidarity and willingness to act on both common and 'others" issues, while seeking and enabling leadership of intersectionally marginalized groups in pursuing structural transformation.

THE POLITICS OF INTERSECTIONAL PRACTICE

Table 7.1: The politics of intersectional practice: representation, coalition and competing concepts of intersectionality

Name	Meaning	Practice examples	Relationship to intersectionality as a theoretical framework				Representation	Coalition
			Additive vs. mutually constitutive	Individual vs. structural level of analysis	Relationality/ simultaneity of privilege and oppression	Focus on those who are most disadvantaged		
Generic	No focus or very little focus on any equality strand or strands in particular: the same work is delivered to benefit 'all'. Addressing issues that affect 'everybody' (that is, not only or even primarily marginalized equality groups).	Work is addressed at and intended to benefit 'everybody', so intersectionality is envisioned as being 'mainstreamed', or a general approach to the work. Since this concept treats everyone the same, work on specific inequalities is not consistent with this understanding of intersectionality.	Since this concept has no recognition of specific inequality structures, these are considered neither additively nor constitutively.	There is no recognition of inequality structures.	There is no recognition of inequality structures, which would need to be in place before recognizing how they relate to one another.	Does not focus on disadvantaged groups.	Preference for 'neutral', 'unspecific' and 'unbiased' representatives (that is, belonging to dominant social groups); constructed as the only ones capable of knowing about and doing intersectionality, and as representing all others. Intersectionally marginalized people (and organizations of them) constructed as non-credible knowers about and doers of intersectionality, unable to think beyond their own experience and identities.	All-encompassing structures and non-specific issues that affect 'everyone'. Within this understanding in relation to coalition, more concretely it is unclear who would be in coalition with whom, and why. In other words, this concept is conducive to neither coalition building nor intersectional political solidarity. Networks at work using this concept failed to produce solidarity.

Table 7.1: The politics of intersectional practice: representation, coalition and competing concepts of intersectionality (continued)

Name	Meaning	Practice examples	Relationship to intersectionality as a theoretical framework				Representation	Coalition
			Additive vs. mutually constitutive	Individual vs. structural level of analysis	Relationality/ simultaneity of privilege and oppression	Focus on those who are most disadvantaged		
Pan equality	Addressing issues that affect all/most marginalized equality groups.	Issues include mental health, hate crime.	Does not necessarily recognize mutual constitution. Issues may be viewed as though they happen to be common to distinct groups; or as being common because of the synthesis of structures of inequality, such that the groups overlap.	More structural view than other concepts.	Does not necessarily recognize the interrelationship of structures.	Some networks/ organizations seek to focus on those who are intersectionally marginalized within these wider issue campaigns, but not always.	Varying approaches; representation of intersectionally marginalized people not necessarily viewed as important. Some employing this concept justify acting for others.	Creates opportunities for campaigns and coalitions focused on broad issues that affect marginalized groups. Offers the broadest opportunities for coalition. Conducive to building intersectional political solidarity in combination with an 'intersections of equality strands' concept of intersectionality.

(continued)

Table 7.1: The politics of intersectional practice: representation, coalition and competing concepts of intersectionality (continued)

Name	Meaning	Practice examples	Relationship to intersectionality as a theoretical framework			Representation	Coalition
			Additive vs. mutually constitutive	Individual vs. structural level of analysis	Relationality/ simultaneity of privilege and oppression	Focus on those who are most disadvantaged		
Multi-strand	Addressing equality strands in parallel, separately, simultaneously and equivalently.	Some network collaboration and engagement on local equality strategies.	Additive.	Either, but structures would be conceptualized as separate. When conceptualized individually, multi-strand is synonymous with 'diversity'.	Does not recognize the interrelationship of structures, and consequently views people as solely oppressed or privileged.	No particular focus. Inclusive of an idea that all strands should be included and treated equally, that no strand is more important.	Intersectionality and singular representation are conflated: practising intersectionality stops at representation; effaces intersectional marginalization. Intersectional representation constructed as being the presence of all singular equality strands.	Coalitions, and yet they may lack solidarity. Strand actors align to further singular interests, united in the overall message that all strands need to be included and addressed separately. When equality strands are conceptualized additively, the possibilities for more meaningful coalition and solidarity are very limited.

Table 7.1: The politics of intersectional practice: representation, coalition and competing concepts of intersectionality (continued)

Name	Meaning	Practice examples	Relationship to intersectionality as a theoretical framework				Representation	Coalition
			Additive vs. mutually constitutive	Individual vs. structural level of analysis	Relationality/ simultaneity of privilege and oppression	Focus on those who are most disadvantaged		
Diversity-within	Addressing intersections within an equality strand, for example differences among women, and so on. One strand/ inequality viewed as primary and more important than others.	How intersectionality is often addressed within single-strand organizations: inclusion projects targeted at intersectionally marginalized groups.	Additive.	Mainly individual; neglects interactions of structures of inequality, since it views one inequality as fundamental.	Not recognized insofar as it is additive. Views groups as solely oppressed/ privileged along the primary axis. Belonging to other equality strands usually thought about as 'additional barriers'.	The primary inequality is predefined.	Acting *for* intersectionally marginalized others constructed as non-agential: 'inclusion without representation'. This is seeking representation of intersectionally marginalized people as service users or constituents, but not meaningfully in decision-making. Implicitly, therefore, constructs privileged sub-group members as ideal representatives.	Offers the fewest possibilities for coalition. Since one strand is constructed as more important than others, equitable relationships between strand-specific sectors are viewed as inessential to developing projects targeted at intersectionally marginalized groups. Participation in coalitions may be viewed favourably, but as inessential.

(continued)

Table 7.1: The politics of intersectional practice: representation, coalition and competing concepts of intersectionality (continued)

Name	Meaning	Practice examples	Relationship to intersectionality as a theoretical framework				Representation	Coalition
			Additive vs. mutually constitutive	Individual vs. structural level of analysis	Relationality/ simultaneity of privilege and oppression	Focus on those who are most disadvantaged		
'Intersections of equality strands'	Work of/with specific groups sharing intersecting identities, for example, women of colour, disabled women, and so on. No particular strand is primary or more in focus than the other(s).	Intersectional organizations; intersectional alliances (formal and informal partnership projects across equality strands; relatively equitable partnerships).	Tends to capture ideas of mutual constitution.	Multiple levels.	Recognized.	Does focus on issues of who is felt to be disadvantaged, though specific markers may be predefined.	Representation and enabling participation of intersectionally marginalized people viewed as important. Intersectionally marginalized people constituted as agents.	Values equitable partnership and representation, and is thus conducive to organizing intersectionally in organizations and coalitions. Conducive to solidarity since it views equalities as mutually constitutive.

APPENDIX 1

Participants

Table A1.1: Research participants

Pseudonym	Role	Equality sub-sector	Organization size	Organization funding	Country in which organization is based
Andrew	Director	LGBTI young people	...	Funded	...
Ange	Practitioner	Network	Small	Funded	Scotland
Anika	Director	Women of colour	Small	Funded	England
Anne	Director	Network	Small	Funded	....
Anya	Practitioner	Racial justice	Small	Funded	...
Aziz	Director	Racial justice	...	Funded	Scotland
Catherine	Practitioner	Disabled	Small	Funded	Scotland
Catriona	Network organizer	Network	Small	Funded	...
Charlie	Practitioner	LGBTI	Small	Funded	Scotland
Christopher	Network member	Network	Small	Funded	...
Claire	Director	Disabled women's	Small	Unfunded	...
David	Director	LGBTI	Small	Unfunded	England
Deborah	Senior practitioner	Women's	Small	Funded	England
Diane	Practitioner	Women's	Small	Funded	England

(continued)

Table A1.1: Research participants (continued)

Pseudonym	Role	Equality sub-sector	Organization size	Organization funding	Country in which organization is based
Eilidh	Practitioner	Disabled	Small	Funded	…
Elizabeth	Network organizer	Network	Small	Funded	…
Emma	Practitioner	Racial justice	Small	Funded	…
Fiona	Director	Women's	Small	Unfunded	Scotland
Helen	Senior manager	Women's	Large	Funded	England
Jacqueline	Practitioner	Disabled	Small	Funded	England
John	Practitioner	Racial justice	…	Funded	Scotland
Julie	Director	Refugee	Small	Funded	England
Karen	Practitioner	Faith	Medium	Funded	Scotland
Kya	Practitioner	LGBTI refugee	Small	Funded	England
Leanne	Network organizer	Network	Small	Funded	…
Linda	Director	Disabled	Small	Funded	England
Margaret	Policy maker	N/A	N/A	N/A	…
Myra	Director	Women's	Small	Unfunded	Scotland
Nia	Senior practitioner	Refugee	Large	Funded	…
Nicola	Network organizer	Network	Small	Funded	…
Olivia	Director	Racially minoritized women of faith	…	Funded	…
Peter	Policy maker	N/A	N/A	N/A	…
Raka	Director	Racially minoritized women of faith	Small	Funded	…
Robin	Practitioner	Trans	Small	Funded	England
Stephen	Director	Racial justice	Small	Funded	England

APPENDIX 1

Table A1.1: Research participants (continued)

Pseudonym	Role	Equality sub-sector	Organization size	Organization funding	Country in which organization is based
Susan	Director	Disabled	Small	Funded	Scotland
Tracey	Practitioner	Deaf	Small	Funded	England
Yvonne	Director	Women's	Small	Funded	Scotland

Table A1.2: Research participant equality characteristics

In/equality marker		Number of participants	Percentage*
Age	35–39	3	33.3
	40–44	1	11.1
	45–49	1	11.1
	50–54	1	11.1
	55–59	1	11.1
	60–64	2	22.2
	Unknown	29	
Disability status	Disabled	11	64.7
	Non-disabled	6	35.3
	Unknown	21	
Racially minoritized/white identity	Racially minoritized	9	36.0
	White	16	64.0
	Unknown	13	
Faith	Of a minority faith	5	45.5
	Not of a minority faith	6	54.5
	Unknown	27	
Gender	Female	25	86.2
	Male	4	13.8
	Unknown	9	
Gender and racial identity	Racially minoritized female	6	27.3
	Racially minoritized male	...	...
	White female	12	54.5

(continued)

Table A1.2: Research participant equality characteristics (continued)

In/equality marker		Number of participants	Percentage*
	White male	...	...
	Unknown	13	
Gender and disability status	Disabled female	9	52.9
	Disabled male	...	...
	Non-disabled female	5	29.4
	Non-disabled male	...	...
	Unknown	21	
Sexual orientation	LGBQ	13	65.0
	Straight	7	35.0
	Unknown	18	
Sexual orientation and gender	LGBQ female	9	50.0
	LGBQ male	...	...
	Straight female	5	27.8
	Straight male	...	...
	Unknown	18	
Trans status	Cisgender	...	90.0
	Trans	...	10.0
	Unknown	...	

Note: This table reports on the equality characteristics of 38 research participants. This is predominantly done in aggregate (in acknowledgement that this has numerous limitations from an intersectional perspective) because to report these alongside one another may enable identification of individuals: I report cross tabulations of the characteristics only where more than one combination corresponds to at least five participants, in order to ensure anonymity.

This information is based on that provided in an equality monitoring questionnaire. This was limited by a relatively low return rate (21.0 per cent).[1] I have supplemented this through data provided during interview or readily publically available but I have not assumed equality characteristics of any participants where this information could not be determined by these sources, so the data are incomplete. All data are based on self-reporting. While I collected detailed data on age, impairment type, ethnicity, faith and sexual orientation, here I report these as marker variables that I created based on detailed data. Where numbers are small, these are omitted for anonymity indicated above by '...'.

*Percentages are based on known data.

APPENDIX 1

Table A1.3: Research participant job role

Role	Description	Number of participants	Percentage
Director	Includes CEOs, chairs etc.; includes unpaid roles in unfunded organizations	15	39.5
Network organizer	Staff of the equality network	4	10.5
Policy maker	Civil servant or local government officer	2	5.3
Practitioner	Includes project officers, policy officers, development workers	9	23.7
Senior manager	Senior manager in a large organization	2	5.3
Senior practitioner	Senior officers and workers or managers in small and medium organizations	5	13.2
Volunteer	Unpaid role which is not a director	1	2.6
Total		*38*	*100.0*

Note: This table describes job roles of participants, grouped into broad categories. Except for policy makers, all participants worked in the NGO sector. All were paid roles unless otherwise stated.

Table A1.4: NGO characteristics

Characteristic		Number of organizations	Percentage
Country in which organization is based	England	14	48.3
	Scotland	15	51.7
Funding	Funded	24	82.8
	Unfunded	5	17.2
Type	Community development	2	6.9
	Network	3	10.3
	Policy/campaigning	11	37.9
	Service provider	7	24.1
	Mixed policy/campaigning/ service provider	6	20.7
Equality sub-sector	Racially minoritized women of faith	2	6.9
	Women of colour	1	3.4

(continued)

Table A1.4: NGO characteristics (continued)

Characteristic		Number of organizations	Percentage
	Deaf	1	3.4
	Disabled	3	10.3
	Disabled women's	1	3.4
	Faith	1	3.4
	LGBTI	2	6.9
	LGBTI refugee	1	3.4
	LGBTI young people	1	3.4
	Network (all strands)	3	10.3
	Racial justice	4	13.8
	Refugee	2	6.9
	Trans	1	3.4
	Women's	6	20.7
Single-strand vs. intersectional	Intersectional	6	20.7
	Single-strand	23	79.3
Size	Small (10 staff or less)	22	75.9
	Medium (11–29 staff)	3	10.3
	Large (30 staff or more)	4	13.8

Note: This table describes NGOs that 29 participants represented (policy makers working in government are excluded). Unfunded organizations are nevertheless considered as NGOs since they are formally constituted and/or seeking funding. In some cases (4), I interviewed more than one representative of an organization or network. Therefore, the number of participants is not aligned to the number of organizations. I report these characteristics in aggregate in order to preserve organization anonymity.

I have assigned organizations to one of five types based on my knowledge of the organization gathered through fieldwork. Organizations classified as 'mixed' have a roughly equal split to their function; while most organizations cross these functions, they can in contrast be classified according to one primary type.

Similarly, I have assigned organizations to an equality sub-sector. In the interests of grouping organizations, these labels may not match precisely with how the organization self-defines (notably, some but not all women's organizations would define as 'feminist' rather than 'women's' organizations; not all of what I have classified as 'intersectional' organizations (meaning constituted around multiple equality strands) would necessarily define themselves as such).

Organization size is based on number of staff (some of the classifications are estimates due to availability of information). Most organizations (75.9 per cent) have ten staff or fewer (including a small number with no staff), and a few 'large' organizations have 30 staff or more. Generally speaking, many (perhaps most) staff are part time.

APPENDIX 2

Selection and Methods

Selection and recruitment

I conducted a mapping of equality networks in England and Scotland, using desk research and informants through my prior professional and academic networks. Based on the results of this mapping, I employed a purposive approach to select networks where cross-strand dialogue generating intersectional understandings and practices, and operationalization of intersectionality was in evidence, at least in name. Additionally, I selected urban networks, because cities have higher concentrations of equality NGOs, which work in more racially and ethnically diverse communities.

Selection criteria

Specific selection criteria for the equality networks were, therefore:

- is explicitly multi-strand: Formed in part or in whole of single-strand organizations representing different equality strands;
- is based in a city;
- explicitly takes an intersectional approach;
- has participation of a range of organizations across single-issue area;
- has policy intermediary and representative roles;
- is formally constituted and/or has members of staff.

Overall, the selected networks represent a balanced (across countries and cities, more established and newer networks, larger and smaller networks, those applying intersectionality for some time and those newer to it) and varied selection, including those found to have the greatest attention to intersectionality.

My practitioner background aided in recruitment of networks: not only did this mean that I had some connection with some participants prior, but my having worked in and so being seen to some extent to be part of the equality sector was, I believe, a key factor in many participants agreeing to participate.

A decision to participate in the research was taken by each network within its particular decision-making structure. During recruitment of individuals within and across networks, attention was paid to representation of differently situated marginalized and intersectionally marginalized identities across the research participants in terms of their own identities, as well as the strands that they work within.

Methods

I employed four methods. I conducted in-depth, semi-structured interviews (41 in total: 39 with representatives of organizations from 13 equality sub-sectors/intersectional combinations and network staff, and two with policy makers); focus groups (1 in total); participant observation; and documentary analysis of two sets of documents: national and UK level equality policy documents (24 in total) and documents pertaining to the equality networks (42 in total).

I used several specific methods in order to address all research questions in their multidimensionality (Mason 2006). The use of methods is broadly consistent across each network: interviews, documentary analysis and participant observation were conducted within each (with the exception of focus groups, which were conducted only in one). Equality organizations that are members of networks are considered to be included if I have conducted an interview with a representative of them, and representatives of most included organizations were also present during at least one instance of participant observation. While interview data form the majority of the data that I quote from in the book, data from other methods, particularly participant observation and documentary analysis have also been important. Ethnographic data collected through participant observation have been particularly important to understand the interactions of representatives of different equality sub-sectors and the tensions therein.

Interviews

I conducted 41 in-depth, semi-structured interviews with representatives of equality networks and equality NGOs, and equality policy makers. Interviews within equality networks (37) were aimed at understanding more about: the participant, their organization and their organization's relationship to the network; the origins of their knowledge of the term and idea of intersectionality; the origins of their organization's engagement with it; their perception of its relationship to the equality network; their perception of intersectionality's meaning, and whether this was shared in the organization and in the network; how intersectionality had been taken up and addressed in their organization and in the network; and finally their perceptions of the challenges involved.

Two interview participants from equality NGOs were selected not because of their connection to networks, but for context. One was conducted during my pilot phase, and the other due to the significance of meaning accorded them through other methods during the research (for contextual interviews slightly different questions were posed). In three instances I interviewed the same participant twice (two network organizers and one network member organization).

One policy maker was selected due to their connection to networks, and one was selected due to the significance of meaning accorded them through other methods during the research. These interviews aimed to establish the policy context of work in the equality NGO sector, and to better understand the relationship between equality policy and equality practice. Interviews were interactional conversations and collaborative processes of sharing and reflecting on experience (and at times the relationship between experience and positionality). Most interviews were conducted in person, while six were conducted over the phone and one over email. All interviews were conducted in English except one which I conducted in British Sign Language. Each interview conducted in English was audio recorded.

Focus group

I conducted one focus group with the inner governing circle of one network during my observation at their meeting. The portion of the meeting that I facilitated and describe as a focus group was audio recorded.

Both the focus group and the participant observation (described below) were particularly aimed at understanding the interaction of participants/network members representing different 'strands', having divergent histories and movements that have constructed them, and different interests: the possibilities for solidarity and the challenges and conflict involved; as well as whether and how concepts of intersectionality are built in cross-strand dialogue; and whether and how these concepts are collectively operationalized. In the focus group, I was additionally interested in whether, through dedicated facilitated discussion, concepts and thinking on intersectional practice can be further developed. The focus group was conducted face to face and audio recorded.

Observation/participant observation

Conducting ethnography of networks is quite different from conducting ethnography of organizations, wherein a researcher may attend the workplace of the organization regularly for a long period of time. For this research project, this was not practical or possible: all network staff worked part time and were hosted within the office spaces of other organizations.

Like policy and politics (Freeman 2019), ultimately, much NGO sector practice, and in particular of networks, consists of meetings. I participated in/observed nine network meetings and events. I observed meetings of each network (two in one case; two in another; and three in the third). I also participated in/observed one open event organized by a network, and a meeting about a specific project described as intersectional organized by a network for invited members and non-members; the latter two observations sought to understand specifically how intersectionality is *operationalized*. The extent to which I participated in (as opposed to just observed) these events varied; according to the typology offered by Bryman (2012), my role ranged from 'non-participating observer' to 'participating observer'.

Documentary analysis

I analysed two distinct sets of documents using different methods.

UK and national equality policy documents

While much previous research on intersectionality and UK policy has employed interviews (Hankivsky and Christoffersen 2011; Hankivsky et al 2019), the analysis that I present in Chapter 3 complements this, focusing on 'inscribed' (Freeman and Sturdy 2015) understandings and applications of intersectionality. UK and national equality policy documents were analysed to better understand the relationship between equality policy and NGO sector equality practice, that is, how intersectionality's conceptualization and application in the latter is influenced by the former. These were found through advanced searching of English and Scottish national government websites (gov.uk, gov.scot), the website of the Equality and Human Rights Commission, the Great Britain-wide equality body charged with enforcing the Equality Act (equalityhumanrights.com), and finally the parliament websites (parliament.uk, parliament.scot), for documents containing 'intersectionality'. Documents found were analysed with respect to how they define intersectionality, that is, the language employed, and how it is used: I identified broad uses across the set of documents. I have placed the documents in as much context as this method allows, and provide some comment on the relative power of specific documents analysed. Documents analysed are cited in Chapter 3.

Equality network documents

I analysed 42 documents pertaining to the three equality networks that I studied. Documents analysed comprise a small fraction of all documents that I collected and read during the course of my fieldwork. From these I selected documents for analysis based on emerging themes and theory generated from other methods.

Documentary analysis was primarily interested in explicit and implicit 'inscribed' (Freeman and Sturdy 2015) network understandings and applications of intersectionality, as well as in tracing the process of equality network formation, including the involvement of policy actors. In other words, this method allowed for the study of the understandings of intersectionality constructed as authoritative through their inscription into documents. A minority of documents concern practice identified by participants as intersectional within network member organizations. Network meeting minutes were also analysed with a view to interactions between members, like the aims of the focus group described above. Specifically, documents have been analysed with respect to how they define intersectionality, explicitly and implicitly, and what influenced work and knowledge in this area; and how intersectionality was being operationalized in the context of specific activities to which the documents pertain (identified by participants as 'intersectional' work).

Understandings of intersectionality inscribed in documents may, of course, diverge from those reflected in data generated by other methods; they also themselves influence these other data including participant narratives: 'documents are important for the vocabularies and ways of thinking they generate, reproduce, translate, and set in motion. But they are also material objects or tools, part of the essential technology of politics and government' (Freeman 2006, 52), as well as NGOs.

The documents were analysed using techniques of constructivism and discourse analysis (Prior 2003; Atkinson and Coffey 2004; Cheek 2004; Stanley 2016). Specifically, I considered: the context in which the document was produced; the immediate pretext to the document; and its use, circulation and impact. In relation to the document itself, I considered: its purpose; how it was produced and by whom; assumptions and implicit meanings within it; omissions and exclusions; and framing. Finally, I was interested in the relations between documents ('intertextuality'). In other words, following Freeman and Maybin (2011), I combined attention to the context in which documents are produced, the language/discourse of documents, as well as their power and impact. The four methods that I employed, together, captured intersectional knowledge that is embodied, inscribed and enacted (Freeman and Sturdy 2015). I rarely quote directly from documents, in order to maintain the anonymity of organizations and networks. Each document analysed was listed in a database and renamed as 'Anonymous Document [number]', which is how it is cited in the book (for example, AD 1).

Notes

Chapter 1

1. There are varying ways of measuring 'led by/for' in the NGO sector. Here I mean that the organization developed purposefully to be Black majority-led among its trustees during my time there, which is distinct from a 'Black LGBTQ organization' since permanent staff were usually majority white and our work was directed more widely: our priority target communities were the overlapping groups of Black, Deaf, disabled and female LGBTQ people. Nevertheless, this is an important distinction from an 'LGBTQ organization' since at least at the time in London these were heavily white-led and served predominantly white people, according to my sector research (Kairos in Soho 2011, 2012; centred 2014).
2. Led by and for lesbian, gay, bisexual, trans and queer people.
3. Infrastructure organizations (also called umbrella organizations in Scotland) support front-line organizations and liaise with policy makers. These have been hit particularly hard by cuts associated with austerity in England.
4. Led by and for disabled LGBTQ people.
5. While not without their problems, I use the terms 'people of colour' and 'women of colour' commonly used in intersectionality scholarship (albeit much of which is US based), as well as 'racially minoritized'. In the UK policy context, 'Black and minority ethnic' (BME) or 'Black, Asian and minority ethnic' (BAME) were commonly used at the time the research was conducted, so many of my participants employ these terms.
6. Throughout, I do *not* use the term 'Black' in a political sense unless otherwise stated; used to mean 'Black, Black Scottish or Black British – African' or 'Black, Black Scottish or Black British – Caribbean' or 'any other Black background'.
7. Members of the British Sign Language-using Deaf community tend to capitalize 'D' and tend not to consider themselves as having an impairment, but rather as belonging to a cultural and linguistic minority.
8. Not led by and for disabled people.
9. We were a small team of around six at the time, who all worked to deliver the event.
10. 'Q' is bracketed because, while my organization included this letter/identity 'queer' in our self-description, many LGBT and LGBTI organizations do not (a point which I return to in Chapter 7).
11. 'Strand' is common terminology among policy makers and practitioners meaning equality area, for example, race equality, gender, disability, and so on. 'Single-strand' or 'strand-specific' is used to mean single-issue. I also use 'equality group' or 'equality community', by which I mean, marginal groups pertaining to the strand, that is, women, disabled people, and so on.
12. In this book, I use 'NGO sector' in place of the more common, in the UK, language of 'third sector'.

13 For instance, the term 'activist' is at times problematically applied to those who are *employed* and *paid* by equality organizations, and the term 'movement' is used to encompass both NGOs and grassroots organizations, thereby obscuring conflicting interests of each (see, for example, Evans 2016a).
14 While I take the 'equality sector' as the subject of my research, there are vital distinctions of sub-sectors within it along lines of experience of intersectional privilege and marginalization, which I discuss throughout the book.
15 However not all equality organizations have all of these features.
16 Used to mean 'doings and sayings' (Schatzki, 2001, 48ff cited in Freeman 2019).
17 This was when my final interview took place.

Chapter 2
1 Used 'as an umbrella term that includes a range of gender identities that fall across, between or beyond the categories of male and female as defined at birth' (Hines et al 2018, 1).

Chapter 3
1 This chapter is adapted from Christoffersen (2020a) by permission of Oxford University Press, and Christoffersen (2019) with permission of the Licensor through PLSclear.
2 In Scotland, 'poverty and inequality'.
3 The 'Fairer Scotland duty' is a separate duty to the PSED, but also within the Equality Act, and came into force in April 2018.
4 Led by and for the target group; self-organization is explored in full in Chapter 5.
5 In wider civil society the trade union movements are self-organized.
6 And regionalized, with all those experiencing socioeconomic disadvantage in England often constructed as residing in the (predominantly white) North. Concern with regional disparities (conceptualized singularly and to the exclusion of racial ones) is currently driving the 'Levelling Up' agenda.
7 There is, however, a range of equality organizing that happens within the trade union movements, often somewhat separately from and in parallel to their foremost priorities.
8 As distinct from 'multiple discrimination', additive and combined (Solanke 2021).
9 All participant names used in this book are pseudonyms.
10 There are, however, important legal differences between England and Scotland in this regard.
11 Duties to consult exist in Scotland but not England.
12 Called the Equal Representation Coalition.

Chapter 4
1 This chapter is adapted from Christoffersen (2021a) (reproduced with permission).
2 I would like to caveat that some of these (notably pan equality and multi-strand) are terms which are already in use in the sector, and sometimes assume competing meanings to those that I will give them here. In particular, what I describe as pan equality, while it corresponds to uses in some contexts, is by some practitioners in other contexts referred to as multi-strand, and vice versa (there are differences between England and Scotland in this regard).
3 Here used as a political identity encompassing Black, Asian and other racially minoritized women, following the organization's own self-description.
4 I do not wish to romanticize the affected racial justice organizations as beacons of intersectional thought and practice. To do so would be to perpetuate the erasure of Black women and women of colour that intersectionality responds to. By and large, this has been a male-dominated sector (this is oft-repeated among participants, yet I question

whether this sector really is or has been *more* male-dominated than other sectors, and what else might be at work in these pronouncements). Therefore, self-organized, autonomous organizations led by and for Black women and women of colour have long existed.

5   Each document analysed was listed in a database and renamed as anonymous document (AD) [number]. Documents are generally not quoted from directly since they are anonymized.

6   This is not to at all imply that disability justice work is *actually* easy.

7   There are, however, racially minoritized disabled people's organizations who work at this intersection, though these have been hit particularly badly by austerity. Also, some disabled people's organizations do make substantial effort to engage racially minoritized disabled people.

8   These are: academic; diverse staff and personal experience; equality organizing; the internet; organization constituencies; equality networks; policy and the Equality Act; professional learning; and the NGO sector.

9   This is also the case for the diversity-within concept of intersectionality.

10   'Evidence based funding' is one component of wider neoliberal 'evidence based policy' discourse; for implications for feminist policy work see Squires (2008b).

11   My observation that meanings of intersectionality are usually articulated at the level of individual identity and experience among research participants is fully supported by my observations of articulations of meanings among my gender studies students.

Chapter 5

1   In this chapter, I use 'constituents' broadly to include both service users of service-providing organizations, and communities of identity in relation to community development and policy/campaigning organizations.

2   Particularly in Scotland where intersectionality is nominally popular in equality policy, this is not necessarily the case any longer.

Chapter 6

1   Meaningfully engaging with white supremacy would *also* call gender/'woman' into question, but perhaps less explicitly.

2   There is debate about the utility of 'allyship' vs. 'solidarity' for social justice (for example, Black Girl Dangerous 2015), although there is no agreed clear-cut delineation between the two. My participants used both of these terms so I include both here. In general, in spite of the important differences outlined by various authors, my analysis is that my participants used these terms in similar ways, provided that 'ally' is used in the way I use it here, which is an action rather than a state of being/identity.

Chapter 7

1   This is bracketed because in Collins and Bilge (2016) while this may be implied, it is not specified.

2   Conversely, Luft and Ward (2009) argue that practitioners often focus on how intersectionality can be used in the interests of *institutions*, rather than intersectional justice.

3   Ishkanian and Peña Saavedra (2019) examined understandings of intersectionality among activists within one UK organization; at the time of writing these results have yet to be published. Lépinard (2014, 2020) examined understandings of difference among women's organizations in France and Canada. La Barbera et al (2022) examined meanings among policy makers.

⁴ This is likely related to the fact that these studies were co-produced by academics and activist-practitioners.
⁵ This study is based on perspectives within women's organizations as to what other categories are relevant to include in intersectional praxis, among whom the importance of gender is predetermined.
⁶ Nash (2019) notes that intersectionality is simultaneously overdetermined in its relationship to Black women.
⁷ Though expanding trans rights may be constructed as an issue affecting only trans people, and even one that competes with rights of other groups (for example, 'women'), in fact 'constraining heteronormative assumptions and ideologies about sex and gender that underpin the dominant medico-legal and social discourses about trangenderism, also constrain the sexed/gendered lives of non-trans people. It is important that we all remain alert to this and, in recognising the unique specificity of trans experience, do not compartmentalise trans issues as single issue politics' (Cowan 2013, 4–5).
⁸ These are used to mean, respectively: interests conceived as specific to an intersectional group; intersectional interests can be subsumed to 'women's interests'; interests are individual and self-defined; intersectional group interests included on mainstream agendas (Lépinard 2014).
⁹ Provision of a space for self-representation does not, however, solve all problems of representation: 'deciding not to speak for others and letting others speak can lead to imposing a burden on others by demanding a simplified, essentialized (re)presentation' (de Jong 2017, 126); this remains reflective of a power dynamic in favour of those doing the provisioning.
¹⁰ My findings are limited to the organizations/networks/cities that I have studied; these debates are certainly in evidence among grassroots actors and in popular media in the UK.
¹¹ Although a feature elsewhere, the 'Q' in 'LGBTQI' (among other variations) is conspicuously absent for many organizations in the UK LGBTI sector, particularly in Scotland. The organization that I used to work for in England debated for years about the addition of this category before it was added to our mission, precisely because it was viewed to undermine the boundaries of the other categories.

Appendix 1

¹ In interview, several participants were highly critical of equality monitoring, so this may have impacted on the return rate.

References

Afridi, Asif, and Joy Warmington. 2009. *The Pied Piper*. Birmingham: brap.

Ahmed, Sara. 2006. 'The Nonperformativity of Antiracism.' *Meridians* 7 (1): 104–126.

Ahmed, Sara. 2012. *On Being Included: Racism and Diversity in Institutional Life*. Durham, NC: Duke University Press.

Ahmed, Sara. 2015. 'Women of Colour as Diversity Workers.' *Feministkilljoys* (blog), 26 November. https://feministkilljoys.com/2015/11/26/women-of-colour-as-diversity-workers/

Alabanza, Travis. 2020. 'Janelle Monae Reminds Us That Non-Binary Does Not Equal White.' *Metro News*. 18 January. https://metro.co.uk/2020/01/18/janelle-monae-reminds-us-that-non-binary-does-not-equal-white-12077252/

Alcoff, Linda Martín. 1992. 'The Problem of Speaking for Others.' *Cultural Critique* 20: 5–32.

Alexander-Floyd, Nikol G. 2012. 'Disappearing Acts: Reclaiming Intersectionality in the Social Sciences in a Post-Black Feminist Era.' *Feminist Formations* 24 (1): 1–25.

Amos, Valerie, Gail Lewis, Amina Mama, and Pratibha Parmar. 1984. 'Editorial.' *Feminist Review* 17: 1–2.

Anthias, Floya. 1993. *Racialized Boundaries: Race, Nation, Gender, Colour and Class and the Anti-Racist Struggle*. London: Routledge.

Atkinson, Paul, and Amanda Coffey. 2004. 'Analysing Documentary Realities.' In *Qualitative Research: Theory, Method and Practice*, edited by David Silverman, second edition, 56–75. London: SAGE.

Aultman, B. Lee. 2014. 'Cisgender.' *TSQ: Transgender Studies Quarterly* 1 (1–2): 61–62.

Babouri, Electra. 2014. 'An Introduction to How Intersectionality Relates to Equality and Human Rights.' In Intersections Research Project, HEAR Network. London: London Voluntary Service Council.

Bassel, Leah, and Akwugo Emejulu. 2010. 'Struggles for Institutional Space in France and the United Kingdom: Intersectionality and the Politics of Policy.' *Politics & Gender* 6 (4): 517–544.

Bassel, Leah, and Akwugo Emejulu. 2014. 'Solidarity under Austerity: Intersectionality in France and the United Kingdom.' *Politics & Gender* 10 (1): 130–136.

Bassel, Leah, and Akwugo Emejulu. 2017. *Minority Women and Austerity: Survival and Resistance in France and Britain.* Bristol: Policy Press.

Beaman, Jean, and Nadia E. Brown. 2019. 'Sistas Doing it for Themselves: Black Women's Activism and Black Lives Matter in the U.S. and France.' In *Gendered Mobilizations and Intersectional Challenges: Contemporary Social Movements in Europe and North America*, edited by Jill A. Irvine, Sabine Lang, and Celeste Montoya, 226–243. London: ECPR Press.

Beltrán, Ramona, and Gita Mehrotra. 2015. 'Honoring Our Intellectual Ancestors: A Feminist of Color Treaty for Creating Allied Collaboration.' *Affilia* 30 (1): 106–116.

Benhabib, Seyla. 2002. *The Claims of Culture: Equality and Diversity in the Global Era.* Princeton, NJ: Princeton University Press.

Bey, Marquis. 2023. 'Insurgent Trans Study: Radical Trans Feminism Meets Intersectionality.' In *The Routledge Companion to Intersectionalities*, edited by Jennifer C. Nash and Samantha Pinto, 335–344. London: Routledge.

Bhambra, Gurminder K. 2017. 'Brexit, Trump, and "Methodological Whiteness": On the Misrecognition of Race and Class.' *The British Journal of Sociology* 68 (S1): S214–232.

Bhavnani, Reena. 2005. *Tackling the Roots of Racism: Lessons for Success.* Bristol: Policy Press.

Bilge, Sirma. 2013. 'Intersectionality Undone: Saving Intersectionality from Feminist Studies.' *Du Bois Review* 10 (2): 405–424.

Bilge, Sirma. 2016. 'Theoretical Coalitions and Multi-Issue Activism.' In *Decolonizing Sexualities: Transnational Perspectives Critical Interventions*, edited by Sandeep Bakshi, Suhraiya Jivraj, and Silvia Posocco, 102–117. Oxford: Counterpress.

Bishwakarma, Ramu, Valerie H. Hunt, and Anna Zajicek. 2008. 'Beyond One-Dimensional Policy Frameworks: A Practical Guide for an Intersectional Policy Analysis.' *Himalaya Research Bulletin* 27 (1–2): 19–30.

Black Girl Dangerous. 2015. 'How to Tell the Difference Between Real Solidarity and "Ally Theater".' November. www.bgdblog.org/2015/11/the-difference-between-real-solidarity-and-ally-theatre/

Boucher, Lisa. 2018. 'Radical Visions, Structural Constraints: Challenges to Anti-oppressive Practice in Feminist Organizations.' *Affilia – Journal of Women and Social Work* 33 (1): 24–38.

Bowes, Lindsey, James Evans, Tej Nathwani, Guy Birkin, Andy Boyd, Craig Holmes, Liz Thomas, and Stephen Jones. 2015. *Understanding Progression into Higher Education for Disadvantaged and Under-Represented Groups*, BIS Research Paper Number 229. London: Department for Business, Innovation and Skills.

Bowleg, Lisa. 2008. 'When Black + lesbian + woman ≠ Black lesbian woman: The Methodological Challenges of Qualitative and Quantitative Intersectionality Research.' *Sex Roles* 59: 312–325.

Bowleg, Lisa. 2020. 'We're Not All in This Together: On COVID-19, Intersectionality, and Structural Inequality.' *American Journal of Public Health* 110 (7): 917.

Bowleg, Lisa. 2021. 'Evolving Intersectionality within Public Health: From Analysis to Action.' *American Journal of Public Health* 111 (1): 88–90.

Brewer, Rose M. 2011. 'Black Women's Studies: From Theory to Transformative Practice.' *Socialism and Democracy* 25 (1): 146–156.

Broad-Wright, Kendal. 2017. 'Social Movement Intersectionality and Re-centring Intersectional Activism.' *Atlantis: Critical Studies in Gender, Culture & Social Justice* 38 (1): 41–53.

Bryman, Alan. 2012. *Social Research Methods*, fourth edition. Oxford: Oxford University Press.

Byrne, Bridget, Claire Alexander, Omar Khan, James Nazro, and William Shankley, eds. 2020. *Ethnicity and Race in the UK: State of the Nation*, first edition. Bristol: Bristol University Press.

Cabinet Office. 2007. *Fairness and Freedom: The Final Report of the Equalities Review*. London: Cabinet Office.

Cabinet Office. 2015. 'Equalities.' https://web.archive.org/web/2015091 7024836/http://www.redtapechallenge.cabinetoffice.gov.uk/themehome/ equalities-act/

Campbell, Fiona. 2014. 'The Anti-Racism "Industry": A Case Study of the Perspectives of Those Working in the "Race" Sector in Scotland.' PhD thesis. ProQuest Dissertations Publishing.

Cantle, Ted. 2001. *Community Cohesion: A Report of the Independent Review Team*. London: Home Office.

Carastathis, Anna. 2016. *Intersectionality: Origins, Contestations, Horizons*. Lincoln: University of Nebraska Press.

Carbado, Devon W. 2013. 'Colorblind Intersectionality.' *Signs: Journal of Women and Culture in Society* 38 (4): 811–845.

Case, Kim. 2017. *Intersectional Pedagogy: Complicating Identity and Social Justice*. New York: Routledge.

CEMVO (Council for Ethnic Minority Voluntary Organisations). 2010. *The Impact of the Economic Downturn on BME VCOs*. London: CEMVO.

Center for Intersectional Justice. 2018. 'FAQ.' www.intersectionaljustice. org/faq

centred. 2014. *The London Lesbian, Gay, Bisexual, Transgender and Queer Voluntary and Community Sector Almanac*, third edition. London: centred.

Chan, Christian D. 2018. 'Families as Transformative Allies to Trans Youth of Color: Positioning Intersectionality as Analysis to Demarginalize Political Systems of Oppression.' *Journal of GLBT Family Studies*, February, 43–60.

Chaney, Paul. 2012a. 'New Legislative Settings and the Application of the Participative-Democratic Model of Mainstreaming Equality in Public Policy Making: Evidence from the UK's Devolution Programme.' *Policy Studies* 33 (5): 455–476.

Chaney, Paul. 2012b. 'Quasi-Federalism and the Administration of Equality and Human Rights: Recent Developments and Future Prospects – a Preliminary Analysis from the UK's Devolution Programme.' *Public Policy and Administration* 27 (1): 69–88.

Cheek, Julianne. 2004. 'At the Margins? Discourse Analysis and Qualitative Research.' *Qualitative Health Research* 14 (8): 1140–1150.

Childs, Sarah. 2004. 'A Feminised Style of Politics? Women MPs in the House of Commons.' *The British Journal of Politics and International Relations* 6 (1): 3–19.

Childs, Sarah. 2008. *Women and British Party Politics: Descriptive, Substantive and Symbolic Representation*. London: Routledge.

Cho, Sumi, Kimberlé Williams Crenshaw, and Leslie McCall. 2013. 'Toward a Field of Intersectionality Studies: Theory, Applications, and Praxis.' *Signs* 38 (4): 785–810.

Choo, Hae Yeon, and Myra Marx Ferree. 2010. 'Practicing Intersectionality in Sociological Research: A Critical Analysis of Inclusions, Interactions, and Institutions in the Study of Inequalities.' *Sociological Theory* 28 (2): 129–149.

Christoffersen, Ashlee. 2017. *Intersectional Approaches to Equality Research and Data*. London: Equality Challenge Unit.

Christoffersen, Ashlee. 2018a. *Intersectional Approaches to Equality and Diversity in Higher Education*. London: Equality Challenge Unit.

Christoffersen, Ashlee. 2018b. 'Researching Intersectionality: Ethical Issues.' *Ethics and Social Welfare* 12 (4): 414–21.

Christoffersen, Ashlee. 2019. 'Are We All "Baskets of Characteristics?" Intersectional Slippages and the Displacement of Race in English and Scottish Equality Policy.' In *The Palgrave Handbook of Intersectionality in Public Policy*, edited by Olena Hankivsky and Julia S. Jordan-Zachery, 705–732. Basingstoke: Palgrave Macmillan.

Christoffersen, Ashlee. 2020a. 'Barriers to Operationalizing Intersectionality in Equality Third Sector Community Development Practice: Power, Austerity, and in/Equality.' *Community Development Journal* 55 (1): 139–158.

Christoffersen, Ashlee. 2020b. 'Race, Intersectionality and Covid-19,' Discover Society (blog), 15 May. https://discoversociety.org/2020/05/15/race-intersectionality-and-covid-19/

Christoffersen, Ashlee. 2021a. 'The Politics of Intersectional Practice: Competing Concepts of Intersectionality.' *Policy & Politics* 49 (4): 573–593.

Christoffersen, Ashlee. 2021b. 'Operationalising Intersectionality in COVID-19 Recovery.' The International Public Policy Observatory (IPPO) (blog), 11 August. https://covidandsociety.com/operationalising-intersectionality-covid-19-recovery/

Christoffersen, Ashlee. 2022. 'Is Intersectional Racial Justice Organizing Possible? Confronting Generic Intersectionality.' *Ethnic and Racial Studies* 45 (3): 407–430.

Christoffersen, Ashlee. 2024. 'The Whiteness of "Sex Discrimination": Theorising White Feminist Ideology in Politics.' *European Journal of Politics and Gender*. https://doi.org/10.1332/25151088Y2023D000000010

Christoffersen, Ashlee, and Annette Behrens. 2014. *Intersectionality Literature Review*. London: centred.

Christoffersen, Ashlee, and Akwugo Emejulu. 2023. '"Diversity Within": The Problems with "Intersectional" White Feminism in Practice.' *Social Politics: International Studies in Gender, State & Society* 30 (2): 630–653.

Christoffersen, Ashlee and McCabe, Leah. Forthcoming, in press. 'Operationalising Intersectionality in Equality and Domestic Abuse Policy in Scotland: Contradictions, Contestations and Erasure.' *Critical Social Policy*.

Chun, Jennifer Jihye, George Lipsitz, and Shin Young. 2013. 'Intersectionality as a Social Movement Strategy: Asian Immigrant Women Advocates.' *Signs: Journal of Women in Culture and Society* 38 (4): 917–940.

Ciccia, Rossella, and Conny Roggeband. 2021. 'Unpacking Intersectional Solidarity: Dimensions of Power in Coalitions.' *European Journal of Politics and Gender* 4 (2): 181–198.

Close the Gap. 2010. *Close the Gap Single Equality Duty Consultation*. Edinburgh: Scottish Government.

Close the Gap. n.d. *Still Not Visible: Research on Black and Minority Ethnic Women's Experiences of Employment in Scotland*. Scotland: Close the Gap.

Close the Gap, Engender, Equate Scotland, Rape Crisis Scotland, Scottish Women's Aid, Women 50:50, and Zero Tolerance. 2017. 'Statement in Support of the Equal Recognition Campaign.' Zero Tolerance. www.zerotolerance.org.uk/news/statement-support-equal-recognition-campaign

Cohen, Cathy J. 2005. 'Punks, Bulldaggers, and Welfare Queens: The Radical Potential of Queer Politics?' In *Black Queer Studies: A Critical Anthology*, edited by E. Patrick Johnson and Mae G. Henderson, 21–51. New York: Duke University Press.

Cole, Elizabeth. 2008. 'Coalitions as a Model for Intersectionality: From Practice to Theory.' *Sex Roles* 59 (5): 443–453.

Colgan, Fiona, Chrissy Hunter, and Aidan McKearney. 2014. *Staying Alive: The Impact of 'Austerity Cuts' on the LGBT Voluntary and Community Sector (VCS) in England and Wales*. London: TUC.

Collins, Patricia Hill. 1990. *Black Feminist Thought: Knowledge, Consciousness and the Politics of Empowerment*. New York: Routledge.

Collins, Patricia Hill. 2014. 'Black Feminist Epistemology.' In *Black Feminist Thought: Knowledge, Consciousness, and the Politics of Empowerment*, second edition, 251–271. New York: Routledge.

Collins, Patricia Hill. 2015. 'Intersectionality's Definitional Dilemmas.' *Annual Review of Sociology* 41: 1–20.

Collins, Patricia Hill. 2019a. 'The Difference that Power Makes: Intersectionality and Participatory Democracy.' In *The Palgrave Handbook of Intersectionality in Public Policy*, edited by Olena Hankivsky and Julia S. Jordan-Zachery, 167–192. Basingstoke: Palgrave Macmillan.

Collins, Patricia Hill. 2019b. *Intersectionality as Critical Social Theory*. Durham, NC: Duke University Press.

Collins, Patricia Hill, and Sirma Bilge. 2016. *Intersectionality*, first edition. Cambridge: Polity.

Combahee River Collective. 1977. *Combahee River Collective Statement*. US: Combahee River Collective.

Committee on the Rights of Persons with Disabilities. 2017. *Concluding Observations*. Geneva: Committee on the Rights of Persons with Disabilities.

Cooper, Anna Julia. 1892. *A Voice from the South*. Xenia, OH: The Aldine Printing House.

Cooper, Davina. 2004. *Challenging Diversity: Rethinking Equality and the Value of Difference*. Cambridge: Cambridge University Press.

Coulthard, Glen Sean. 2014. *Red Skin, White Masks: Rejecting the Colonial Politics of Recognition*. Minneapolis: University of Minnesota Press.

Cowan, Sharon. 2004. '"That Woman Is a Woman!" the Case of *Bellinger v. Bellinger* and the Mysterious (Dis)Appearance of Sex: Bellinger v. Bellinger [2003] 2 All E.R. 593; [2003] F.C.R. 1; [2003] 2 W.L.R. 1174; [2003] UKHL 21.' *Feminist Legal Studies* 12 (1): 79–92.

Cowan, Sharon. 2005. '"Gender Is No Substitute for Sex": A Comparative Human Rights Analysis of the Legal Regulation of Sexual Identity.' *Feminist Legal Studies* 13 (1): 67–96.

Cowan, Sharon. 2009. 'Looking Back (To)Wards the Body: Medicalization and the GRA.' *Social & Legal Studies* 18 (2): 247–252.

Cowan, Sharon. 2013. '"We Walk Among You": Trans Identity Politics Goes to the Movies.' *Canadian Journal of Women and the Law* 21 (1): 91–117.

Cowan, Sharon. 2016. 'Sex/Gender Equality: Taking a Break from the Legal to Transform the Social.' In *Exploring the 'Legal' in Socio-Legal Studies*, edited by David Cowan and Daniel Wincott, 115–134. London: Palgrave Macmillan UK.

Cowan, Sharon, and Gillian Calder. 2013. 'Re-Imagining Equality: Meaning and Movement.' University of Edinburgh, School of Law, Working Papers.

Craig, Gary. 2011. 'Forward to the Past: Can the UK Black and Minority Ethnic Third Sector Survive?' *Voluntary Sector Review* 2 (3): 367–389.

Crenshaw, Kimberlé Williams. 1989. 'Demarginalizing the Intersection of Race and Sex: A Black Feminist Critique of Antidiscrimination Doctrine, Feminist Theory and Antiracist Politics.' *University of Chicago Legal Forum* Vol. 1989, Article 8: 139–168.

Crenshaw, Kimberlé Williams. 1991. 'Mapping the Margins: Intersectionality, Identity Politics, and Violence against Women of Colour.' *Stanford Law Review* 43 (6): 1241–1299.

Crenshaw, Kimberlé Williams. 2011. 'Postscript.' In *Framing Intersectionality: Debates on a Multi-Faceted Concept in Gender Studies*, edited by Helma Lutz, Maria Teresa Herrera Vivar and Linda Supik, 221–233. Burlington, VT: Ashgate.

Crenshaw, Kimberlé Williams. 2015. 'Why Intersectionality Can't Wait.' *Washington Post*, 24 September. www.washingtonpost.com/news/in-theory/wp/2015/09/24/why-intersectionality-cant-wait/

Crowder, Chaya. 2022. 'Doing More Than Thanking Black Women: The Influence of Intersectional Solidarity on Public Support for Policies.' *Journal of Women, Politics & Policy* 44 (2): 186–205.

Cruells, Marta López, and Sonia Ruiz García. 2014. 'Political Intersectionality within the Spanish Indignados Social Movement.' *Research in Social Movements, Conflicts and Change* 37: 3–25.

Curry, Tommy J. 2017. *The Man-Not: Race, Class, Genre, and the Dilemmas of Black Manhood*. Philadelphia: Temple University Press.

D'Agostino, Serena. 2021. '(In)visible Mobilizations: Romani Women's Intersectional Activisms in Romania and Bulgaria.' *Politics, Groups, and Identities* 9 (1): 170–189.

de Jong, Sara. 2017. *Complicit Sisters Gender and Women's Issues across North-South Divides*. Oxford: Oxford University Press.

Department for Work and Pensions. 2012. *Equality Impact Assessment of the Innovation Fund*. London: DWP.

Dhamoon, Rita Kaur. 2011. 'Considerations on Mainstreaming Intersectionality.' *Political Research Quarterly* 64 (1): 230–243.

Dhamoon, Rita Kaur. 2023. 'Journeys of Intersectionality: Contingency and Collision.' In *The Routledge Companion to Intersectionalities*, edited by Jennifer C. Nash and Samantha Pinto, 161–173. London: Routledge.

Dovi, Suzanne. 2002. 'Preferable Descriptive Representatives: Will Just Any Woman, Black, or Latino Do?' *American Political Science Review* 96 (4): 729–743.

DRILL. 2020. 'Services for Who? The experiences of disabled people with other characteristics when accessing services.' DRILL. www.drilluk.org.uk/wp-content/uploads/2020/06/Services-for-who-final-report-1.pdf

Dursun, Ayşe. 2022. *Organized Muslim Women in Turkey: An Intersectional Approach to Building Women's Coalitions*. Basingstoke: Palgrave.

Dwidar, Maraam A. 2022. 'Coalitional Lobbying and Intersectional Representation in American Rulemaking.' *American Political Science Review* 116 (1): 301–321.

Edwards, Rosalind. 1990. 'Connecting Method and Epistemology: A White Women Interviewing Black Women.' *Women's Studies International Forum* 13 (5): 477–490.

Emejulu, Akwugo. 2011. 'Re-theorizing Feminist Community Development: Towards a Radical Democratic Citizenship.' *Community Development Journal* 46 (3): 378–390.

Emejulu, Akwugo. 2014. 'Institutionalizing Intersectionality: The Changing Nature of European Equality Regimes Book Review.' *Ethnic and Racial Studies* 37 (10): 1922–1923.

Emejulu, Akwugo. 2015. *Community Development as Micropolitics: Comparing Theories, Policies and Politics in America and Britain*. Bristol: Policy Press.

Emejulu, Akwugo. 2022. *Fugitive Feminism*. London: Silver Press.

Emejulu, Akwugo, and Edward Scanlon. 2016. 'Community Development and the Politics for Social Welfare: Rethinking Redistribution and Recognition Struggles in the United States.' *Community Development Journal* 51 (1): 42–59.

Emejulu, Akwugo, and Leah Bassel. 2018. 'Austerity and the Politics of Becoming.' *Journal of Common Market Studies Annual Review* 56 (S1): 109–119.

Emejulu, Akwugo, and Leah Bassel. 2020. 'The Politics of Exhaustion.' *CITY: Analysis of Urban Trends, Culture and Theory* 24 (1–2): 400–406.

Emejulu, Akwugo, and Inez van der Scheer. 2021. 'Refusing Politics as Usual: Mapping Women of Colour's Radical Praxis in London and Amsterdam.' *Identities* 29 (1): 9–26.

Engender. 2014. *Gender Equality and Scotland's Constitutional Futures*. Edinburgh: Engender.

English, Ashley E. 2019. 'She Who Shall Not be Named: The Women that Women's Organizations Do (and Do Not) Represent in the Rulemaking Process.' *Politics and Gender* 15 (3): 574–598.

Equal Rights Trust. 2016. 'Interview: Kimberlé Crenshaw and Patricia Schulz on Intersectionality.' 19 April. www.equalrightstrust.org/news/interview-kimberl%C3%A9-crenshaw-and-patricia-schulz-intersectionality

Equality and Human Rights Commission. 2009a. *Disabled People's Experiences of Targeted Violence and Hostility*. Manchester: EHRC.

Equality and Human Rights Commission. 2009b. *Trans Research Review*. Manchester: EHRC.

Equality and Human Rights Commission. 2010. *Refugees and Asylum Seekers: A Review from an Equality and Human Rights Perspective*. Manchester: EHRC.

Equality and Human Rights Commission. 2012a. *Attitudes Measurement Framework Series Briefing Paper No. 1*. Manchester: EHRC.

Equality and Human Rights Commission. 2012b. *Individual, Family and Social Life Measurement Framework Series Briefing Paper No. 2*. Manchester: EHRC.

Equality and Human Rights Commission. 2012c. *Publishing Equality Information: Commitment, Engagement and Transparency*. Manchester: EHRC.

Equality and Human Rights Commission. 2013. *Assessment of the Publication of Equality Objectives by English Public Authorities*. Manchester: EHRC.

Equality and Human Rights Commission. 2015a. *Is Britain Fairer?* Manchester: EHRC.

Equality and Human Rights Commission. 2015b. *Is Britain Fairer Evidence Paper Series: Methodology Paper*. Manchester: EHRC.

Equality and Human Rights Commission. 2016a. *Equality Measurement Framework*. Manchester: EHRC.

Equality and Human Rights Commission. 2017. *Public Authorities' Performance in Meeting the Scottish Specific Equality Duties 2017: Measuring Up? Report 7*. Manchester: EHRC.

Equality and Human Rights Commission. 2018a. *Effectiveness of the PSED Specific Duties in Scotland*. Manchester: EHRC.

Equality and Human Rights Commission. 2018b. *Pressing for Progress: Women's Rights and Gender Equality in 2018*. Manchester: EHRC.

Equality and Human Rights Commission. 2018c. *Reviewing the Aims and Effectiveness of the Public Sector Equality Duty (PSED) in Great Britain*. Manchester: EHRC.

Equality and Human Rights Commission Scotland. 2013. *Measuring Up? Monitoring Public Authorities Performance against the Scottish Specific Equality Duties*. Edinburgh: EHRC Scotland.

Equality Network. 2016. *Including Intersectional Identities: Guidance on Including Intersectional LGBTI People in Services*. Edinburgh: Equality Network.

Evans, Elizabeth. 2015. *The Politics of Third Wave Feminisms: Neoliberalism, Intersectionality, and the State in Britain and the US*. Basingstoke: Palgrave.

Evans, Elizabeth. 2016a. 'Feminist Allies and Strategic Partners: Exploring the Relationship between the Women's Movement and Political Parties.' *Party Politics* 22 (5): 631–640.

Evans, Elizabeth. 2016b. 'Intersectionality as Feminist Praxis in the UK.' *Women's Studies International Forum* 59: 67–75.

Evans, Elizabeth. 2022. 'Political Intersectionality and Disability Activism: Approaching and Understanding Difference and Unity.' *The Sociological Review* 70 (5): 986–1004.

Evans, Elizabeth and Éléonore Lépinard, E. eds. 2020. *Intersectionality in Feminist and Queer Movements: Confronting Privileges*. Abingdon: Routledge.

Fraser, Nancy. 1997. *Justice Interruptus: Critical Reflections on the 'Postsocialist' Condition* . New York: Routledge.

Freeman, Richard. 2006. 'The Work the Document Does: Research, Policy, and Equity in Health.' *Journal of Health Politics, Policy and Law* 31 (1): 51.

Freeman, Richard. 2019. 'Meeting, Talk and Text: Policy and Politics in Practice.' *Policy & Politics* 47 (2): 371–388.

Freeman, Richard, and Jo Maybin. 2011. 'Documents, Practices and Policy.' *Evidence & Policy* 7 (2): 155–170.

Freeman, Richard, and Steven Sturdy. 2015. 'Knowledge and Policy in Research and Practice.' In *Knowledge in Policy: Embodied, Inscribed, Enacted*, edited by Richard Freeman and Steven Sturdy, 201–218. Bristol: Policy Press.

Freeman, Richard, Steven Griggs, and Annette Boaz. 2011. 'The Practice of Policy Making.' *Evidence and Policy* 7 (2): 127–136.

Garbasz, Yishay. 2015. "We Have to Think Intersectionally": Yishay Garbasz on the Politics of Allyship and Solidarity.' Versobooks.com. www.versobooks.com/blogs/2309-we-have-to-think-intersectionally-yishay-garbasz-on-the-politics-of-allyship-and-solidarity

Gedalof, Irene. 2013. 'Sameness and Difference in Government Equality Talk.' *Ethnic and Racial Studies* 36 (1): 117–135.

Glasius, Marlies, and Armine Ishkanian. 2015. 'Surreptitious Symbiosis: Engagement between Activists and NGOs.' *VOLUNTAS: International Journal of Voluntary and Nonprofit Organizations* 26 (6): 2620–2644.

Government Equalities Office. 2018. *National LGBT Survey: Research Report*. Manchester: Government Equalities Office.

Government Equalities Office. 2019. *Gender Equality Monitor*. London: HM Government.

Hancock, Ange-Marie Alfaro. 2007. 'When Multiplication Doesn't Equal Quick Addition: Examining Intersectionality as a Research Paradigm.' *Perspectives on Politics* 5 (1): 63–78.

Hancock, Ange-Marie Alfaro. 2011. *Solidarity Politics for Millennials: A Guide to Ending the Oppression Olympics*. New York: Palgrave Macmillan.

Hancock, Ange-Marie Alfaro. 2013. 'Empirical Intersectionality: A Tale of Two Approaches.' *UC Irvine Law Review* 3: 259–296.

Hancock, Ange-Marie Alfaro. 2014. 'Intersectional Representation or Representing Intersectionality?: Reshaping Empirical Analysis of Intersectionality.' In *Representation: The Case of Women*, edited by Maria C. Escobar-Lemmon and Michelle M. Taylor-Robinson, 41–57. New York: Oxford University Press.

Hancock, Ange-Marie Alfaro. 2016. *Intersectionality: An Intellectual History*. Oxford: Oxford University Press.

Hankivsky, Olena. 2005. 'Gender Mainstreaming vs. Diversity Mainstreaming: A Preliminary Examination of the Role and Transformative Potential of Feminist Theory.' *Canadian Journal of Political Science* 38 (4): 977–1001.

Hankivsky, Olena. 2011. *Health Inequities in Canada: Intersectional Frameworks and Practices*. Vancouver: UBC Press.

Hankivsky, Olena, ed. 2012. *An Intersectionality Based Policy Analysis Framework*. Vancouver: Institute for Intersectionality Research and Policy.

Hankivsky, Olena, and Ashlee Christoffersen. 2008. 'Intersectionality and the Determinants of Health: A Canadian Perspective.' *Critical Public Health* 18 (3): 271–283.

Hankivsky, Olena, and Ashlee Christoffersen. 2011. 'Gender Mainstreaming in the United Kingdom: Current Issues and Future Challenges.' *British Politics* 6: 30–51.

Hankivsky, Olena, and Renée Cormier. 2011. 'Intersectionality and Public Policy: Some Lessons from Existing Models.' *Political Research Quarterly* 64 (1): 217–229.

Hankivsky, Olena, and Julia S. Jordan-Zachery. 2019a. 'Introduction: Bringing Intersectionality to Public Policy.' In *The Palgrave Handbook of Intersectionality in Public Policy*, edited by Olena Hankivsky and Julia S. Jordan-Zachery, 1–28. Basingstoke: Palgrave Macmillan.

Hankivsky, Olena, and Julia S. Jordan-Zachery, eds. 2019b. *The Palgrave Handbook of Intersectionality in Public Policy*, first edition. Basingstoke: Palgrave Macmillan.

Hankivsky, Olena, and Anuj Kapilashrami. 2020a. 'Intersectionality Offers a Radical Rethinking of Covid-19.' The British Medical Journal (blog), 15 May. https://blogs.bmj.com/bmj/2020/05/15/intersectionality-offers-a-radical-rethinking-of-covid-19/

Hankivsky, Olena, and Anuj Kapilashrami. 2020b. 'Beyond Sex and Gender Analysis: An Intersectional View of the COVID-19 Pandemic Outbreak and Response.' Melbourne School of Population and Global Health, 31 March. https://mspgh.unimelb.edu.au/news-and-events/beyond-sex-and-gender-analysis-an-intersectional-view-of-the-covid-19-pandemic-outbreak-and-response

Hankivsky, Olena, Daniel Grace, Gemma Hunting, Melissa Giesbrecht, Alycia Fridkin, Sarah Rudrum, Olivier Ferlatte, and Natalie Clark. 2014. 'An Intersectionality-Based Policy Analysis Framework: Critical Reflections on a Methodology for Advancing Equity.' *International Journal for Equity in Health* 13: 119.

Hankivsky, Olena, Diego de Merich, and Ashlee Christoffersen. 2019. 'Equalities "Devolved": Experiences in Mainstreaming across the UK Devolved Powers Post-Equality Act 2010.' *British Politics* 14 (2): 141–161.

Hartman, Saidiya. 2008. *Lose Your Mother: A Journey Along the Atlantic Slave Route*, reprint edition. New York: Farrar Straus Giroux.

Hemmings, Clare. 2012. 'Affective Solidarity: Feminist Reflexivity and Political Transformation.' *Feminist Theory* 13 (2): 147–161.

Hepple, Bob. 2010. 'The New Single Equality Act.' *Equal Rights Review* 5: 11–24.

Hermanin, Costanza, and Judith Squires. 2012. 'Institutionalizing Intersectionality in the "Big Three": The Changing Equality Framework in France, Germany and Britain.' In *Institutionalizing Intersectionality: The Changing Nature of European Equality Regimes*, edited by Andrea Krizsan, Hege Skjeie, and Judith Squires, 89–118. Basingstoke: Palgrave Macmillan.

Heyes, Cressida J. 2003. 'Feminist Solidarity after Queer Theory: The Case of Transgender.' *Signs* 28 (4): 1093–1120.

Hines, Sally. 2019. 'The Feminist Frontier: On Trans and Feminism.' *Journal of Gender Studies* 28 (2): 145–157.

Hines, Sally, Zowie Davy, Surya Monro, Joz Motmans, Ana Cristina Santos, and Janneke Van Der Ros. 2018. 'Introduction to the Themed Issue: Trans★ Policy, Practice and Lived Experience within a European Context.' *Critical Social Policy* 38 (1): 5–12.

HM Government. 2023. Equality Hub. www.gov.uk/government/organisations/the-equality-hub

Hoggett, Paul. 2008. *The Dilemmas of Development Work: Ethical Challenges in Regeneration*. Bristol: Policy Press.

Howard, Jo, and Violeta Vajda. 2017. *Navigating Power and Intersectionality to Address Inequality*. Vol. 2017. IDS Working Paper 504. Sussex: IDS.

Inclusion Scotland, Engender, Close the Gap, CRER, Equality Network, LGBT Youth Scotland, Scottish Women's Aid, Scottish Women's Convention, Stonewall Scotland, and Health and Social Care Alliance. 2017. *The Socio-Economic Duty: A Consultation Equality Sector Response*. Scotland.

Irvine, Jill A., Sabine Lang, and Celeste Montoya. 2019a. *Gendered Mobilizations and Intersectional Challenges: Contemporary Social Movements in Europe and North America*. London: ECPR Press.

Irvine, Jill A., Sabine Lang, and Celeste Montoya. 2019b. 'Introduction'. In *Gendered Mobilizations and Intersectional Challenges: Contemporary Social Movements in Europe and North America*, 1–22. London: ECPR Press.

Ishkanian, Armine, and Irum S. Ali. 2018. 'From Consensus to Dissensus: The Politics of Anti-austerity Activism in London and Its Relationship to Voluntary Organizations.' *Journal of Civil Society* 14 (1): 1–19.

Ishkanian, Armine, and Anita Peña Saavedra. 2019. 'The Politics and Practices of Intersectional Prefiguration in Social Movements: The Case of Sisters Uncut.' *The Sociological Review* 67 (5): 985–1001.

Johnson, Julia R. 2013. 'Cisgender Privilege, Intersectionality, and the Criminalization of CeCe McDonald: Why Intercultural Communication Needs Transgender Studies.' *Journal of International and Intercultural Communication* 6 (2): 135–144.

Jones, Stephen H., Therese O' Toole, Daniel Nilsson Dehanas, Tariq Modood, and Nasar Meer. 2015. 'A "System of Self-appointed Leaders"? Examining Modes of Muslim Representation in Governance in Britain.' *British Journal of Politics & International Relations* 17 (2): 207–223.

Jordan-Zachery, Julia S. 2007. 'Am I a Black Woman or a Woman Who Is Black? A Few Thoughts on the Meaning of Intersectionality.' *Politics & Gender* 3 (2): 254–263.

Jordan-Zachery, Julia S. 2013. 'Now You See Me, Now You Don't: My Political Fight against the Invisibility/Erasure of Black Women in Intersectionality Research.' *Politics, Groups, and Identities* 1 (1): 101–109.

Jordan-Zachery, Julia S. 2017. *Shadow Bodies: Black Women, Ideology, Representation, and Politics*. New Brunswick, NJ: Rutgers University Press.

Kairos in Soho. 2011. *The London Lesbian, Gay, Bisexual and Transgender Voluntary and Community Sector Almanac 1st Edition*. London: Kairos in Soho.

Kairos in Soho. 2012. *The London Lesbian, Gay, Bisexual and Transgender Voluntary and Community Sector Almanac 2nd Edition*. Edited by Ashlee Christoffersen. London: Kairos in Soho.

Kantola, Johanna, and Kevät Nousiainen. 2012. 'The European Union: Initiator of a New European Anti-Discrimination Regime?' In *Institutionalizing Intersectionality: The Changing Nature of European Equality Regimes*, edited by Andrea Krizsan, Hege Skjeie, and Judith Squires, 33–58. Basingstoke: Palgrave Macmillan.

Kapilashrami, Anuj, Sarah Hill, and Nasar Meer. 2015. 'What Can Health Inequalities Researchers Learn from an Intersectionality Perspective? Understanding Social Dynamics with an Inter-Categorical Approach.' *Social Theory & Health* 13 (3/4): 288–307.

Kelliher, Diarmaid. 2018. 'Historicising Geographies of Solidarity.' *Geography Compass* 12 (9): e12399.

Knapp, Gudrun-Axeli. 2005. 'Race, Class, Gender: Reclaiming Baggage in Fast Travelling Theories.' *European Journal of Women's Studies* 12 (3): 249–265.

Kolers, Avery. 2016. *A Moral Theory of Solidarity*. Oxford: Oxford University Press.

Koyama, Emi. 2003. 'The Transfeminist Manifesto.' In *Catching a Wave: Reclaiming Feminism for the 21st Century*, edited by Rory Cooke Dicker and Alison Piepmeier, 244–259. Boston, MA: Northeastern University Press.

Krizsan, Andrea, Hege Skjeie, and Judith Squires. 2012a. 'European Equality Regimes: Institutional Change and Political Intersectionality.' In *Institutionalizing Intersectionality: The Changing Nature of European Equality Regimes*, edited by Andrea Krizsan, Hege Skjeie, and Judith Squires, 209–239. Basingstoke: Palgrave Macmillan.

Krizsan, Andrea, Hege Skjeie, and Judith Squires. 2012b. 'Institutionalizing Intersectionality: A Theoretical Framework.' In *Institutionalizing Intersectionality: The Changing Nature of European Equality Regimes*, edited by Andrea Krizsan, Hege Skjeie, and Judith Squires, 1–32. Basingstoke: Palgrave Macmillan.

Krizsan, Andrea, Hege Skjeie, and Judith Squires, eds. 2012c. *Institutionalizing Intersectionality: The Changing Nature of European Equality Regimes*. Basingstoke: Palgrave Macmillan.

La Barbera, MariaCaterina, Julia Espinosa-Fajardo, and Paloma Caravantes. 2022. 'Implementing Intersectionality in Public Policies: Key Factors in the Madrid City Council, Spain.' *Politics & Gender*, 1–28. https://doi.org/10.1017/S1743923X22000241

Laperriere, Marie, and Éléonore Lépinard. 2016. 'Intersectionality as a Tool for Social Movements: Strategies of Inclusion and Representation in the Quebecois Women's Movement.' *Politics* 36 (4): 374–382.

Larasi, Marai. 2011. 'Policy: Silence Is Not an Option.' *Race on the Agenda Supplement*. www.rota.org.uk/sites/default/files/webfm/supplement/supplement_issue2_011_all_web.pdf

Lennon, Erica, and Brian J. Mistler. 2014. 'Cisgenderism.' *TSQ: Transgender Studies Quarterly* 1 (1–2): 63–64.

Lépinard, Éléonore. 2014. 'Doing Intersectionality: Repertoires of Feminist Practices in France and Canada.' *Gender and Society* 28 (6): 877–903.

Lépinard, Éléonore. 2020. *Feminist Trouble: Intersectional Politics in Post-Secular Times*. Oxford: Oxford University Press.

Lewis, Gail. 2005. 'Welcome to the Margins: Diversity, Tolerance, and Policies of Exclusion.' *Ethnic and Racial Studies* 28 (3): 536–558.

Lewis, Gail. 2013. 'Unsafe Travel: Experiencing Intersectionality and Feminist Displacements.' *Signs* 38 (4): 869–892.

Lewis, Gail. 2017. 'Questions of Presence.' *Feminist Review* 117 (1): 1–19.

Lovenduski, Joni. 2005. *Feminizing Politics*. Cambridge: Polity.

Luft, Rachel E., and Jane Ward. 2009. 'Toward an Intersectionality Just Out of Reach: Confronting Challenges to Intersectional Practice.' In *Perceiving Gender Locally, Globally, and Intersectionally*, edited by Vasilikie Demos and Marcia Texler Segal, 9–37. Bingley: Emerald Group Publishing Limited.

Luna, Zakiya. 2016. '"Truly a Women of Color Organization": Negotiating Sameness and Difference in Pursuit of Intersectionality.' *Gender & Society* 30 (5): 769–790.

Lutz, Helma. 2015. 'Intersectionality as Method.' *DiGeSt. Journal of Diversity and Gender Studies* 2 (1–2): 39–44.

Lyle, Timothy S. 2015. 'An Interview with Janet Mock.' *Callaloo* 38 (3): 502–508.

Macpherson, William. 1999. *The Stephen Lawrence Inquiry Report of an Inquiry by Sir William Macpherson of Cluny*. London: Home Office.

Maes, Eva Luna, and Petra Debusscher. 2022. 'The EU as a Global Gender Actor: Tracing Intersectionality in the European Gender Action Plans for External Relations 2010–2025.' *Social Politics: International Studies in Gender, State & Society*: jxac046. https://doi.org/10.1093/sp/jxac046

Manuel, Tiffany. 2006. 'Exploring the Possibilities for a Good Life: Exploring the Public Policy Implications of Intersectionality Theory.' In *Intersectionality and Politics: Recent Research on Gender, Race and Political Representation in the United States*, edited by Carol Hardy-Fontana, 173–203. USA: The Haworth Press.

Marchetti, Kathleen. 2014. 'Crossing the Intersection: The Representation of Disadvantaged Identities in Advocacy.' *Politics, Groups, and Identities* 2 (1): 1–16.

Marchetti, Kathleen. 2015. 'Consider the Context: How State Policy Environments Shape Interest Group Advocacy.' *State and Local Government Review* 47 (3): 155–169.

Marchetti, Kathleen. 2019. 'Intersectional Advocacy and Policy making Across US States'. In *The Palgrave Handbook of Intersectionality in Public Policy*, edited by Olena Hankivsky and Julia S. Jordan-Zachery, 451–470. Basingstoke: Palgrave Macmillan.

Marchetti, Sabrina, Daniela Cherubini, and Giulia Garofalo Geymonat. 2021. *Global Domestic Workers: Intersectional Inequalities and Struggles for Rights*. Bristol: Bristol University Press.

Mason, Jennifer. 2006. *Six Strategies for Mixing Methods and Linking Data in Social Science Research ESRC National Centre for Research Methods NCRM Working Paper Series 4/06*. Manchester: ESRC National Centre for Research Methods.

May, Vivian M. 2015. *Pursuing Intersectionality, Unsettling Dominant Imaginaries*. New York: Routledge.

Mayblin, Lucy, and Andri Soteri-Proctor. 2011. 'The Black Minority Ethnic Third Sector: A Resource Paper.' June. http://tsrc.ac.uk/LinkClick.aspx?fileticket=LQmEkNIkNtQ%3d&tabid=500

McCabe, Angus, Jenny Phillimore, and Lucy Mayblin. 2010. '"Below the Radar" Activities and Organisations in the Third Sector: A Summary Review of the Literature.' http://epapers.bham.ac.uk/796/

McCabe, Leah. 2023. 'An Intersectional Analysis of Contestations within Women's Movements: The Case of Scottish Domestic Abuse Policy making.' *Policy & Politics* (published online ahead of print). https://doi.org/10.1332/03055736Y2023D000000021

McCall, Leslie. 2005. 'The Complexity of Intersectionality.' *Signs* 30 (3): 1771–1800.

McConkey, Jane. 2004. 'Knowledge and Acknowledgement: "Epistemic Injustice" as a Problem of Recognition.' *Politics* 24 (3): 198–205.

McIntosh, Peggy. 1998. 'White Privilege: Unpacking the Invisible Knapsack.' In *Re-Visioning Family Therapy: Race, Culture, and Gender in Clinical Practice*, edited by Monica McGoldrick, 147–152. New York: Guilford Press.

McKinnon, Rachel, and Adam Sennet. 2017. 'Survey Article: On the Nature of the Political Concept of Privilege.' *Journal of Political Philosophy* 25 (4): 487–507.

Meer, Nasar. 2017. 'What Will Happen to Race Equality Policy on the Brexit Archipelago? Multi-Level Governance, "Sunk Costs" and the "Mischief of Faction".' *Journal of Social Policy* 46 (4): 657–674.

Meer, Nasar. 2019. 'Race Equality Policy Making in a Devolved Context: Assessing the Opportunities and Obstacles for a "Scottish Approach".' *Journal of Social Policy* 49 (2): 233–250.

Meer, Nasar. 2022. *The Cruel Optimism of Racial Justice*. Bristol: Policy Press.

Meer, Nasar, and Tariq Modood. 2014. 'Cosmopolitanism and Integrationism: Is British Multiculturalism a "Zombie Category"?' *Identities* 21 (6): 658–674.

Mendez, Matthew S. 2018. 'Towards an Ethical Representation of Undocumented Latinos.' *PS: Political Science & Politics* 51 (2): 335–339.

Menon, Nivedita. 2015. 'Is Feminism about "Women"? A Critical View on Intersectionality from India.' *Economic and Political Weekly* 50 (17): 37–44.

Mills, Charles W. 2017a. *Black Rights/White Wrongs: The Critique of Racial Liberalism*. Oxford. Oxford University Press.

Mills, Charles W. 2017b. 'Racial Exploitation.' In *Black Rights/White Wrongs: The Critique of Racial Liberalism*, 114–136. Oxford: Oxford University Press.

Mills, Helen. 2009. *Policy, Purpose and Pragmatism*. London: Centre for Crime and Justice Studies, King's College.

Mirza, Heidi Safia. 1997. *Black British Feminism: A Reader*. London: Routledge.

Mohanty, Chandra Talpade. 2003. *Feminism without Borders: Decolonizing Theory, Practicing Solidarity*. Durham, NC: Duke University Press.

Mohanty, Chandra Talpade. 2013. 'Transnational Feminist Crossings: On Neoliberalism and Radical Critique.' *Signs: Journal of Women in Culture and Society* 38 (4): 967–991.

Moraga, Cherríe, and Gloria Anzaldúa, eds. 1983. *This Bridge Called My Back: Writings by Radical Women of Colour*, second edition. New York: Kitchen Table Press.

Mügge, Liza, Celeste Montoya, Akwugo Emejulu, and S. Laurel Weldon. 2018. 'Intersectionality and the Politics of Knowledge Production.' *European Journal of Politics and Gender* 1 (1–2): 17–36.

Nash, Jennifer C. 2019. *Black Feminism Reimagined: After Intersectionality*. Durham, NC: Duke University Press.

Nash, Jennifer C., and Samantha Pinto. 2023. 'Introduction: Accompanying Intersectionality.' In *The Routledge Companion to Intersectionalities*, edited by Jennifer C. Nash and Samantha Pinto, 1–10. London: Routledge.

National Equality Partnership. 2008. *Supporting Equality Groups: An Overview of Support to the Diverse Third Sector in England*. London: Women's Resource Centre.

Northamptonshire Rights and Equality Council. 2012. *Equality Duties Audit: Public Authorities in Northamptonshire Relating to the Publication of Information and Setting Equality Objectives*. Northamptonshire: Northamptonshire Rights & Equality Council.

Opportunity Agenda, The. 2017. *Ten Tips for Putting Intersectionality into Practice*. New York: The Opportunity Agenda. https://opportunityagenda.org/sites/default/files/2017-06/Intersectionality-into-Practice-Edits05.30.17.pdf

O'Thomson, Jess. 2023. 'The EHRC Wants to Redefine Sex. Here's What it Means for Trans People.' *Open Democracy*. www.opendemocracy.net/en/5050/ehrc-equality-act-trans-rights-sex-definition-legal-biological/

Parken, Alison. 2010. 'A Multi-Strand Approach to Promoting Equalities and Human Rights in Policy Making.' *Policy & Politics* 38 (1): 79–99.

Parken, Alison, and Hannah Young. 2008. *Facilitating Cross Strand Working*. Wales: Equality and Human Rights Commission and Welsh Assembly Government.

Phillips, Anne. 1995. *The Politics of Presence*. Oxford: Oxford University Press.

Phipps, Alison. 2016. 'Whose Personal Is More Political? Experience in Contemporary Feminist Politics.' *Feminist Theory* 17 (3): 303–321.

Pitkin, Hanna Fenichel. 1967. *The Concept of Representation*. Berkeley: University of California Press.

Prior, Lindsay. 2003. *Using Documents in Social Research*. London: SAGE.

Puar, Jasbir. 2013. '"I Would Rather Be a Cyborg than a Goddess": Intersectionality, Assemblage, and Affective Politics.' *Meritum, Revista de Direito Da Universidade FUMEC* 8 (2).

Raha, Nat. 2017. 'Transfeminine Brokenness, Radical Transfeminism.' *South Atlantic Quarterly* 116 (3): 632–646.

Refugee Action. 2023. 'Facts About Refugees'. London: Refugee Action. www.refugee-action.org.uk/about/facts-about-refugees/

Resolution Foundation. 2023. 'Costly Differences: Living Standards for Working-age People with Disabilities.' London: Resolution Foundation. www.resolutionfoundation.org/publications/costly-differences/

Roberts, Dorothy, and Sujatha Jesudason. 2013. 'Movement Intersectionality: The Case of Race, Gender, Disability, and Genetic Technologies.' *Du Bois Review* 10 (2): 313–328.

Rodriguez, Jenny K., Evangelina Holvino, Joyce K. Fletcher, and Stella M. Nkomo. 2016. 'The Theory and Praxis of Intersectionality in Work and Organisations: Where Do We Go from Here?' *Du Bois Review: Social Science Research on Race* 23 (3): 201–222.

Saward, Michael. 2006. 'The Representative Claim.' *Contemporary Political Theory* 5 (3): 297–318.

Saward, Michael. 2009. 'Authorisation and Authenticity: Representation and the Unelected.' *Journal of Political Philosophy* 17 (1): 1–22.

Schatzki, Theodore. 2001. 'Practice Mind-ed Orders.' In *The Practice Turn in Contemporary Theory*, edited by Karin Knorr Cetina, Theodore R. Schatzki, and Eike von Savigny. London: Routledge.

Scholz, Sally J. 2008. *Political Solidarity*. University Park: Penn State University Press.

Scott, James C. 1990. *Domination and the Arts of Resistance: Hidden Transcripts*. New Haven, CT: Yale University Press.

Scott-Dixon, Krista. 2006. *Trans/Forming Feminisms: Trans/Feminist Voices Speak Out*. Canada: Sumach Press.

Scottish Government. 2003. 'Equality Proofing Budget Seminar.' Minutes. 10 February. www.gov.scot/Publications/2003/02/16316

Scottish Government. 2010. 'Equality Statement Scotland's Budget 2011–12.' 17 November. www.gov.scot/Publications/2010/11/17115419/0

Scottish Government. 2011. 'Equality Statement Scottish Spending Review 2011 and Draft Budget 2012–13.' 21 September. www.gov.scot/Publications/2011/09/26110945/26

Scottish Government. 2013a. 'Scottish Government Equality Outcomes.' 7 March. www.gov.scot/Topics/People/Equality/EqualityOutcomes

Scottish Government. 2013b. 'Rights to Reality: A Framework of Action for Independent Living in Scotland 2013 to 2015.' 15 October. www.gov.scot/Publications/2013/10/1226

Scottish Government. 2014. 'Equality Evidence Strategy 2014.' 13 February. www.gov.scot/Topics/People/Equality/Equalities/EqualFramework/equalityevstrategy2014

Scottish Government. 2016a. *CEMVO Consultation Response Public Sector Equality Duty Amendment Regulations 2016*. Edinburgh: Scottish Government.

Scottish Government. 2016b. 'Race Equality Framework for Scotland 2016–2030.' 21 March. www.gov.scot/Publications/2016/03/4084

Scottish Government. 2016c. 'EQIA Public Sector Equality Duty Amendment Regulations 2016.' 23 March. www.gov.scot/Publications/2016/03/9832/1

Scottish Government. 2017a. 'Race Equality Framework Implementation Approach.' 23 February. www.gov.scot/Publications/2017/02/7935

Scottish Government. 2017b. 'Equality Outcomes and Mainstreaming Report 2017.' 30 April. www.gov.scot/Publications/2017/04/4384

Scottish Government. 2018. 'Fairer Scotland Duty – Interim Guidance for Public Bodies.' 27 March. www.gov.scot/Publications/2018/03/6918

Sen, Gita, Aditi Iyer, and Chandan Mukherjee. 2009. 'A Methodology to Analyse the Intersections of Social Inequalities in Health.' *Journal of Human Development and Capabilities* 10 (3): 397–415.

Serano, Julia. 2007. *Whipping Girl: A Transsexual Woman on Sexism and the Scapegoating of Femininity*. Emeryville, CA: Seal Press.

Serano, Julia. 2013. *Excluded: Making Feminist and Queer Movements More Inclusive*. Berkeley, CA: Seal Press.

Shakespeare, Tom, Lisa I. Iezzoni, and Nora E. Groce. 2009. 'Disability and the Training of Health Professionals.' *The Lancet* 374 (9704): 1815–1816.

Sharpe, Christina Elizabeth. 2014. 'Black Studies: In the Wake.' *The Black Scholar* 44 (2): 59–69.

Sharpe, Christina Elizabeth. 2016. *In the Wake: On Blackness and Being*. Durham, NC: Duke University Press.

Siddique, Haroon. 2023. 'NGOs, MPs and Academics Call for Withdrawal of UK's Illegal Migration Bill.' *The Guardian*, 28 March. www.theguardian.com/uk-news/2023/mar/28/ngos-mps-and-academics-call-for-withdrawal-of-uks-migration-bill

simpkins, reese. 2016. 'Trans★feminist Intersections.' *TSQ: Transgender Studies Quarterly* 3 (1–2): 228–234.

Siow, Orly. 2023. 'What Constitutes Substantive Representation, and Where Should We Evaluate It?' *Political Studies Review* 21 (3): 532–538.

Small, Sika Valery. 1994. *From Arts to Welfare*. London: Sia.

Smith, Valerie. 1998. *Not Just Race, Not Just Gender: Black Feminist Readings*. New York: Routledge.

Smooth, W. 2006. 'Intersectionality in Electoral Politics: A Mess Worth Making.' *Politics & Gender*, 2 (3): 400–414.

Socialist Feminist Network. 2019. 'Socialfeminist.network: A Network of Social Feminists.' https://web.archive.org/web/20190506203903/https://www.SocFem.Net/

Solanke, Iyiola. 2011. 'Infusing the Silos in the Equality Act 2010 with Synergy.' *The Industrial Law Journal* 40 (4): 336–358.

Solanke, Iyiola. 2021. 'The EU Approach to Intersectional Discrimination in Law.' In *The Routledge Handbook of Gender and EU Politics*, edited by Gabriele Abels, Andrea Krizsán, Heather MacRae, and Anna van der Vleuten, 93–104. London: Routledge.

Spillers, Hortense J. 1987. 'Mama's Baby, Papa's Maybe: An American Grammar Book.' *Diacritics* 17 (2): 65–81.

Spivak, Gayatri Chakravorty. 2003. 'Can the Subaltern Speak?' *Die Philosophin* 14 (27): 42–58.

Squires, Judith. 2008a. 'Intersecting Inequalities: Reflecting on the Subjects and Objects of Equality.' *Political Quarterly* 79 (1): 53–61.

Squires, Judith. 2008b. 'The Constitutive Representation of Gender: Extra-Parliamentary Re-Presentations of Gender Relations.' *Representation* 44 (2): 187–204.

Squires, Judith. 2009. 'Intersecting Inequalities: Britain's Equality Review.' *International Feminist Journal of Politics* 11 (4): 496–512.

Stanley, Liz. 2016. 'Archival Methodology inside the Black Box.' In *The Archive Project: Archival Research in the Social Sciences*, edited by Niamh Moore, Andrea Salter, Liz Stanley, and Maria Tamboukou, 33–68. London: Routledge.

Strolovitch, Dara Z. 2006. 'Do Interest Groups Represent the Disadvantaged? Advocacy at the Intersections of Race, Class, and Gender.' *Journal of Politics* 68 (4): 894–910.

Strolovitch, Dara Z. 2007. *Affirmative Advocacy: Race, Class, and Gender in Interest Group Politics*. Chicago, IL: University of Chicago Press.

Stryker, Susan, and Talia M. Bettcher. 2016. 'Introduction Trans/Feminisms.' *TSQ: Transgender Studies Quarterly* 3 (1–2): 5–14.

Sudbury, Julia. 1998. *'Other Kinds of Dreams': Black Women's Organisations and the Politics of Transformation*, first edition. London: Routledge.

Sullivan, Shannon. 2017. 'On the Harms of Epistemic Injustice: Pragmatism and Transactional Epistemology.' In *The Routledge Handbook of Epistemic Injustice*, edited by Ian James Kidd, José Medina, and Gaile Pohlhaus Jr, first edition, 205–212. London: Routledge.

Terriquez, Veronica, Tizoc Brenes, and Abdiel Lopez. 2018. 'Intersectionality as a Multipurpose Collective Action Frame: The Case of the Undocumented Youth Movement.' *Ethnicities* 18 (2): 260–276.

Tilly, Charles, and Sidney G. Tarrow. 2007. *Contentious Politics*. London: Paradigm Publishers.

Tomlinson, Barbara. 2013a. 'Colonizing Intersectionality: Replicating Racial Hierarchy in Feminist Academic Arguments.' *Social Identities* 19 (2): 254–272.

Tomlinson, Barbara. 2013b. 'To Tell the Truth and Not Get Trapped: Desire, Distance and Intersectionality at the Scene of Argument.' *Signs: Journal of Women in Culture and Society* 38 (4): 993–1017.

Tormos, Fernando. 2017. 'Intersectional Solidarity.' *Politics, Groups, and Identities* 5 (4): 707–720.

Townsend-Bell, Erica. 2011. 'What Is Relevance? Defining Intersectional Praxis in Uruguay.' *Political Research Quarterly* 64 (1): 187–199.

Townsend-Bell, Erica. 2019. 'Timid Imposition: Intersectional Travel and Affirmative Action in Uruguay.' In *The Palgrave Handbook of Intersectionality in Public Policy*, edited by Olena Hankivsky and Julia S. Jordan-Zachery, 733–748. Basingstoke: Palgrave Macmillan.

Trades Union Congress. 2012. 'Two Steps Forward, One Step Back.' 14 September. www.tuc.org.uk/equality-issues/two-steps-forward-one-step-back

TransActual. 2021. *Trans Lives Survey 2021: Enduring the UK's Hostile Environment*. UK: TransActual.

Truth, Sojourner. 1851. *Ain't I a Woman*. Akron, OH: Speech delivered at Women's Convention 28–29 May.

Tungohan, Ethel. 2015. 'Intersectionality and Social Justice: Assessing Activists' Use of Intersectionality through Grassroots Migrants' Organizations in Canada.' *Politics, Groups, and Identities* 4 (3): 347–362.

United Nations CEDAW Committee. 2013. *Concluding Observations and Recommendations*. Geneva: United Nations.

Vacchelli, Elena, Preeti Kathrecha, and Natalie Gyte. 2015. 'Is It Really Just the Cuts? Neo-Liberal Tales from the Women's Voluntary and Community Sector in London.' *Feminist Review* 109: 180–189.

Verloo, Mieke. 2013. 'Intersectional and Cross-Movement Politics and Policies: Reflections on Current Practices and Debates.' *Signs: Journal of Women in Culture and Society* 38 (4): 893–915.

Walby, Sylvia, Jo Armstrong, and Sofia Strid. 2012a. 'Intersectionality and the Quality of the Gender Equality Architecture.' *Social Politics* 19 (4): 446–481.

Walby, Sylvia, Jo Armstrong, and Sofia Strid. 2012b. 'Intersectionality: Multiple Inequalities in Social Theory.' *Sociology* 46 (2): 224–240.

Ward, Jane. 2004. '"Not All Differences Are Created Equal": Multiple Jeopardy in a Gendered Organization.' *Gender and Society* 18 (1): 82–102.

Ward, Jane. 2008. *Respectably Queer: Diversity Culture in LGBT Activist Organizations*. Nashville, TN: Vanderbilt University Press.

Weber, Lynn, and M. Elizabeth Fore. 2007. 'Race Ethnicity and Health: An Intersectional Approach.' In *Handbook of the Sociology of Racial and Ethnic Relations*, edited by Joe R. Vera and Hernán Vera, 191–218. New York: Springer.

Wells, Ida B. 1892. *Lynch Law in All Its Phases*. New York: The New York Age Print.

Williams, Fiona. 2021. *Social Policy: A Critical and Intersectional Analysis*. Cambridge: Polity.

Woman's Place UK. 2019. 'Woman's Place UK – Violence against Women and Sex Discrimination Still Exist: Women Need Reserved Places, Separate Spaces and Distinct Services.' https://web.archive.org/web/20191223123914/https://womansplaceuk.org/

Women and Work All Party Parliamentary Group. 2020. *Inclusivity and Intersectionality: Toolkit and Annual Report 2019*. London: Women and Work All Party Parliamentary Group.

Women's Budget Group, Runnymede Trust, RECLAIM and Coventry Women's Voices. 2017. 'Intersecting Inequalities: The Impact of Austerity on Black and Minority Ethnic Women in the UK.' https://wbg.org.uk/wp-content/uploads/2018/08/Intersecting-Inequalities-October-2017-Full-Report.pdf

Young, Iris Marion. 1990. *Justice and the Politics of Difference*. Princeton, NJ: Princeton University Press.

Yuval-Davis, Nira. 2006. 'Intersectionality and Feminist Politics.' *The European Journal of Women's Studies* 13 (3): 193–209.

Yuval-Davis, Nira. 2013. 'A Situated Intersectional Everyday Approach to the Study of Bordering: Working paper 2.' Brussels: European Commission EU Borderscapes.

Yuval-Davis, Nira. 2015. 'Situated Intersectionality: A Reflection on Ange-Marie Hancock's Forthcoming Book: Intersectionality—an Intellectual History.' *New Political Science* 37 (4): 637–642.

Index

References to tables appear in **bold** type.

A

ableism 3, 25, 99
  see also disability sector
activist organizations 10
advocacy, restrictions on 74
affirmative advocacy 29, 43, 194
age 5, 26
Ahmed, Sara 204
AIWA (Asian Immigrant Women Advocates) 38–39
Alcoff, Linda 46
allyship 166–170, 176
antiBlackness 2, 25, 31
anti-discrimination legislation 4–5
  see also Equality Act 2010
applied concepts of intersectionality 11, 15, 17, 79–81, 105–110, 179, 189, 190, 203, 204
  diversity-within intersectionality 17, 80, **83**, 97–102, 104, 107, 108, 109, 110, 178, 182, 183–184, 185, 186, 187, 190, 192, 193, 194, 197, 198, 199, 200, 201, 203, 204, **209**
    coalition 147, 149, 153, 157–158, 160, 162, 163, 164, 165, 166, 171, 172, 173, 174, 175, **206–210**
    vs intersectional organizations 195–196
    representation 114, 126, 131, 133–134, **144**
  generic intersectionality 17, 80, 81, **82**, 85–92, 102, 106, 108–109, 179–180, 184, 185, 190, 193, 194, 198, 200, 201, 202, 203, 204, **206**
    coalition 151, 156–157, 159, 160, 174
    representation 114, 115, 133, 135–139, 140, 142–143, **144**
  and intersectionality theory 106–107
  'intersections of equality strands' 17, 80, **84**, 97–98, 102–105, 107, 108, 109, 110, 184–185, 186, 187–188, 190, 192, 193, 194, 197, 199, 200, 201, 203, 204, **210**
    coalition 147, 155, 156, 157, 159–160, 161, 165, 166, 169, 173, 174, 175
    representation 114, 115, 126, 131, 134–135, 142, **144**
  multi-strand intersectionality 17, 80, **83**, 95–97, 106–107, 107–108, 109–110, 178, 182–183, 185, 187, 190, 192, 193, 194, 198–199, 200, 201, 203, 204, **208**
    coalition 147, 149, 153, 155–156, 157–158, 160, 162, 163, 164, 166, 173, 174–175
    representation 114, 132–133, 136, 137, 138, 142, **144**
  pan equality intersectionality 17, 80, **82**, 93–95, 106, 107, 109, 178, 180–182, 185, 190, 192, 193, 197, 198, 199, 200, 201, 203, 204, **207**
    coalition 147, 155, 157, 159–160, 165, 166, 174
    representation 133, **144**
Asian Immigrant Women Advocates (AIWA) 38–39
assimilation 86
austerity 8, 10, 16, 57, 58, 59, 70–71, 72–73, 76, 89, 150, 192, 195, 197

B

Bassel, Leah 49, 71, 107, 195
Beltrán, Ramona 167
Bey, Marquis 198
Bilge, Sirma 28, 30, 40, 47, 48, 51, 77
Bishwakarma, Ramu 34
Black feminism 27, 31, 191
Black Power 24
Black women 1, 9, 10, 23, 24, 26, 30–31, 51, 108, 180, 188, 190–191, 194
  representation 136, 140–141
Blair, Tony 4, 197
Brexit 6, 70

C

Cabinet Office 62, 65
Cameron, David 6

campaigning, restrictions on 74
Canada, migrants' rights sector 39
capitalism 25
Caravantes, Paloma 35
Carbado, Devon W. 29
categories, reification of 198–199, 200
CEMVO Scotland 64
Center for Intersectional Justice 172
Chun, Jennifer Jihye 38–39
cisgenderism 25, 161, 162, 164, 165, 173, 199
civil rights 24
claims-making 44, 45
class 25, 26
Close the Gap 10, 63, 171
coalition and solidarity 11, 16, 146–149, 155–160, 174–176, 177, 190, 193–194, 196, 200, 202, 203, **206–210**
 and allyship 166–170, 176
 barriers to 150–155
 challenges and conflicts 160–166, 174
 creating intersectional political solidarity 166–172, 175
 diversity-within intersectionality 147, 149, 153, 157–158, 160, 162, 163, 164, 165, 166, 171, 172, 173, 174, 175, **209**
 generic intersectionality 151, 156–157, 159, 160, 174, **206**
 'intersection of equality strands' 147, 155, 156, 157, 159–160, 161, 165, 166, 169, 173, 174, 175, **210**
 intersectional political solidarity, and intersectional justice 172–174
 intersectional solidarity 147–148, 149, 158, 159–160, 193–194
 multi-strand intersectionality 147, 149, 153, 155–156, 157–158, 160, 162, 163, 164, 166, 173, 174–175, **208**
 operationalization of intersectionality 11, 16, 23, 44, 47–49, 49–50, 52, 155–160, 174
 pan equality intersectionality 147, 155, 157, 159–160, 165, 166, 174, **207**
 political solidarity 147–148
 siloed thinking 18, 34, 89, 97, 136, 149, 150–155, 165, 171, 174, 194
coalition government 6, 61
Cole, Elizabeth 47
Collins, Patricia Hill 24–25, 28, 40, 47, 50, 51, 77
Commission for Racial Equality (CRE) 87
community organizations 8
 see also NGO sector
Conservative governments 6, 61
Cooper, Anna Julia 23
Cormier, Renée 33, 34, 37, 39–40, 64
COVID-19 pandemic 6, 33
Cowan, Sharon 9
CRE (Commission for Racial Equality) 87

Crenshaw, Kimberlé 23, 24, 25, 28, 29, 40–41, 47
'crip' terminology 23
culture wars 6

D

D/deafness 26, 125
Denham, John 86–87
Department for Levelling Up, Housing and Communities 5
Department for Works and Pensions 5
descriptive representation 43–45, 113, 114, 143, 188
 see also representation
Dhamoon, Rita 28, 198
disability
 Department for Works and Pensions responsibility for 5
 equality policy, Scotland 7
 medical model of 99
 as a 'protected characteristic' 5
 violence against disabled women 133–134
disability sector 1, 4, 8, 26, 186
 disabled LGBTQ organizations, London 2–3
 disabled people of colour 99–100
 disabled women's sector 92, 134–135
 networks of organizations 12
 'nothing about us without us' 116
 self-organization 116–117
 siloed thinking 151, 152
Disability Unit 62
diversity 35, 107
diversity-within intersectionality 17, 80, **83**, 97–102, 104, 107, 108, 109, 110, 178, 182, 183–184, 185, 186, 187, 190, 192, 193, 194, 197, 198, 199, 200, 201, 203, 204, **209**
 coalition 147, 149, 153, 157–158, 160, 162, 163, 164, 165, 166, 171, 172, 173, 174, 175
 vs intersectional organizations 195–196
 representation 114, 126, 131, 133–134, **144**
Dovi, Suzanne 44
DRILL 10
'dual discrimination' 61

E

EDF (Equality and Diversity Forum) 12
EHRC (Equality and Human Rights Commission) 5, 6, 36, 62, 63, 65–66, 69, 70, 87
EIA (equality impact assessment) 6
Emejulu, Akwugo 40, 49, 52, 71, 107, 195
Engender 63
England
 diversity-within intersectionality 101
 equality networks 12
 equality NGO sector 2, 8–11

INDEX

equality policy 5, 65, 68–70, 184
generic intersectionality 90–91
intersections of equality strands 104
pan equality intersectionality 94
PSED (public sector equality duty) 5–6
see also UK
Equalities Review (Cabinet Office) 65
Equality Act 2010 4, 5–6, 7–8, 13, 36, 40, 58, 59, 60–62, 63, 65, 66, 69, 70, 75, 77, 87, 89, 90, 96, 97, 100, 108, 155
and siloed thinking 150–151
Equality and Diversity Forum (EDF) 12
Equality and Human Rights Commission (EHRC) 5, 6, 36, 62, 63, 65–66, 69, 70, 87
equality 'communities' 17, 115
equality, definition of 9
Equality Evidence Strategy 2014 (Scottish Government) 66
Equality Hub, Cabinet Office 62
equality impact assessment (EIA) 6
Equality, Inclusion and Human Rights Directorate, Scotland 7
equality mainstreaming 7, 33, 64, 70, 90
Equality Network 10
equality networks 12–14, 190
coalition and solidarity 146–149, 174–176, 190
barriers to 149, 150–155
challenges and conflicts 149, 160–166
creating intersectional political solidarity 149, 166–172
intersectional justice and the limits of intersectional political solidarity 172–174
operationalizing intersectionality 155–160, 193
generic intersectionality 135–139
governance 118–119
representation 119–120
siloed thinking 18, 34, 89, 97, 136, 149, 150–155, 165, 171, 174
equality NGO sector 2, 3–4, 7, 8–11, 108
impact of austerity on 70–73
networks of organizations 12–14
regulation of campaigning activities 74
relationship with the state 6, 10, 16, 57, 58, 59, 73–76
representation and intersectionality 120–132
Scotland 74
equality policy 16, 57, 108, 184
England 5, 65, 68–70, 184
and intersectionality 16, 57–59, 60–70, 76–77
research objectives 11
Scotland 7–8, 59, 63–64, 65, 66–70, 77
UK 4–6, 36, 39, 40, 51, 59, 69
Equality Unit, Scotland 7, 101
Equally Ours 12

Espinoza-Fajardo, Julia 35
Ethnicity Pay Gap, Scotland 63
European Union Directives 5
European Union, UK exit from 6, 70
evidence, discourse of 197–198, 200

F

feminist sector 4, 8, 30
and intersectionality 48
networks of organizations 12
self-organization 116
and substantive representation 45
trans exclusionary 162
trans inclusive feminisms 161
transfeminisms 161–162, 164
white feminism 24, 26–27
see also women's sector
flexible solidarity 50
funding
equality networks 148
impact of austerity on 72–73
siloed 150

G

gender 1, 5, 26, 31
'gender first' 185, 186
gender mainstreaming 33, 63
gender pay gap 63–64
gendered racism 1, 30, 99
non-binary identity 163, 172–173, 199, 203
Scottish equality policy 63–64
see also trans sector
see also feminist sector; women's sector
gender/woman 149, 161, 196
generic intersectionality 17, 80, 81, **82**, 85–92, 102, 106, 108–109, 179–180, 184, 185, 190, 193, 194, 198, 200, 201, 202, 203, 204, **206**
coalition 151, 156–157, 159, 160, 174
representation 114, 115, 133, 135–139, 140, 142–143, **144**
GEO (Government Equalities Office) 5, 62
GRA (Gender Recognition Act) 160–161, 163, 165, 171
grassroots organizations 8, 10, 37
group representation 44, 188
see also representation

H

Hancock, Ange-Marie 30–31, 66
Hankivsky, Olena 26, 33, 34, 37, 39–40, 53, 64
hate crime 181
health policy 33, 34
heterosexism 25
Heyes, Cressida J. 162
human rights 5
and trans rights 161, 168

see also EHRC (Equality and Human Rights Commission)
Hunt, Valerie H. 34

I

IBPA (intersectionality-based policy analysis) 34
'identity politics' 59
immigration policies 6
Indigeneity 26
Indigenous women 1, 23
'individual recognition' 185–186
individualization 197, 200
inequality/inequalities
   and equality policy 59–60
   structures of 196–197, 204
'integration' 86
'intersectional advocacy' 43
intersectional alliances 103, 104, 105, 175, 184, 185, 194, 201–202
intersectional justice 8, 11, 17, 29, 149, 168–169, 177, 201, 203–205
   and intersectional political solidarity 172–174
intersectional organizations 10, 190, 194–195, 200, 201–202, 204
   vs. diversity-with intersectionality 195–196
   representation 123–126, 189
intersectional positionality 14
'intersectional praxis' 194
'intersectional recognition' 185, 186, 188
intersectional solidarity 29, 49–50, 185, 186
intersectionality 10–11, 28
   definitions and conceptualizations of 1, 17, 25–26, 50–51, 81
   in equality policy documents 16, 57–58, 65–70, 76, 77–78
   knowledge and representation 186–189
   meanings and uses of 108–110
   'mutual shaping' approach to 27, 182, 194
   ontological project of 42, 44, 48, 52
   policy and practice implications 177, 200–203
   politics of 177, 190–200
   politics of knowledge 52–53
   representational 28
   resistance to 14, 30, 191
   structural 28
   see also applied concepts of intersectionality; operationalization of intersectionality
intersectionality theory 25–26, **82–84**, 177, 178–179, 187, 193, **206–210**
   additive vs mutually constitutive 23, 26–27, 65, 95, 106–107, 182, 183, 187
   appropriations and co-optations 29–32
   levels of analysis 27–28, 106–107
   privilege, relationality and disadvantage 23, 28–29, 106–107

intersectionality wars 191
intersectionality-based policy analysis (IBPA) 34
intersectionally marginalized groups 8, 11, 17, 36, 43, 45–47, 51, 58, 187, 189–190, 203–204
   diversity-within intersectionality 101–102
   generic intersectionality 91–92
   impact of austerity on 70
   intersections of equality strands 105
   multi-strand intersectionality 97
   pan equality intersectionality 94–95
   US 41
   see also representation
'intersections of equality strands' 17, 80, **84**, 97–98, 102–105, 107, 108, 109, 110, 184–185, 186, 187–188, 190, 192, 193, 194, 197, 199, 200, 201, 203, 204, **210**
   coalition 147, 155, 156, 157, 159–160, 161, 165, 166, 169, 173, 174, 175
   representation 114, 115, 126, 131, 134–135, 142, **144**
Ishkanian, Armine 39

J

Jesudason, Sujatha 47
Jordan-Zachery, Julia S. 34

K

knowledge, politics of 52–53

L

La Barbera, MariaCaterina 35
Labour government 4–5, 6, 59, 197
Larasi, Marai 71
Lawrence, Stephen 5
'left behind, the' 60
Left politics 59, 60
Lennon, Erica 164
Lépinard, Éléonore 185–186, 188
LGBTI sector 2–3, 4, 8, 103, 105–107, 186
   disabled LGBTI groups 103–104
   networks of organizations 12
   representation 45
   self-organization 116
   siloed thinking 151, 152–153
   and trans rights 164, 168–169, 171, 173
local equality strategies, equality networks 149, 155–160
local governments, generic intersectionality 89–90
London LGBTQ Learning Network 2–3
Luft, Rachel E. 109, 177

M

Macpherson inquiry 5
mainstreaming 7, 33, 63, 64, 70, 90, 104
   'multi-strand mainstreaming model' 36–37

May, Theresa 89
May, Vivian M. 29–30, 35
McConkey, Jane 136
medical model of disability 99
Mehrotra, Gita 167
migrants' rights sector 8, 38–39, 186
  self-organization 116
Minister for Women and Equalities 6
Mistler, Brian J. 164
Mügge, Liza 32
'multiculturalism' 86
'multiple identities' 65, 66, 107
multi-strand intersectionality 17, 80, **83**, 95–97, 106–107, 107–108, 109–110, 178, 182–183, 185, 187, 190, 192, 193, 194, 198–199, 200, 201, 203, 204, **208**
  coalition 147, 149, 153, 155–156, 157–158, 160, 162, 163, 164, 166, 173, 174–175
  representation 114, 132–133, 136, 137, 138, 142, **144**
'multi-strand mainstreaming model' 36–37
'mutual shaping' approach to intersectionality 27, 182, 194

N

Nash, Jennifer 31, 190–191
National Equality Partnership 8
nationality 1, 6, 26
Native American/Indigenous, Chicana and Asian American movements 24
neoliberalism 30, 35, 197, 200, 202
networks *see* equality networks
new public managerialism 197
NGO sector 8, 9
  neoliberalization of 197, 200
  see also equality NGO sector
non-binary identity 163, 172–173, 199, 203

O

ontological project of intersectionality 42, 44, 48, 52
operationalization of intersectionality 11–12, 16, 23–25, 32, 39–50, 51, 52, 177, 179, 182, 190, 193, 197–198, 204
  impact of austerity on 71–73
  public policy 16, 32–37, 51, 52
  social movements 16, 32, 37–39, 51, 52
  see also coalition; representation; solidarity

P

pan equality intersectionality 17, 80, **82**, 93–95, 106, 107, 109, 178, 180–182, 185, 190, 192, 193, 197, 198, 199, **207**
  coalition 147, 155, 157, 159–160, 165, 166, 174
  representation 133, **144**
Parken, Alison 36–37
participation 201
  and representation 115, 127, 142

Peña Saavedra, Anita 39
people of colour
  disabled people of colour 99–100
  see also women of colour
Phillips, Anne 44
political intersectionality 28
'political lobbying,' restrictions on 74
political solidarity 49
politics
  definition of 11
  of intersectionality 177, 190–200
  of knowledge 52–53
positionality
  of author 2
  intersectional 14
postcolonial theory 44, 45–46
poststructuralist theory 44, 45–46
power relationships, equality NGO sector and the state 73–76
practice, definition of 2
privilege 28–29, 45, 48–49, 50, **82–84**, 106, 107, 114, 119, 120, 149, 161–162, 163, 164, 165, 166–167, 170, 172, 173, 183, 187, 193, 194, 196, 198–199, **206–210**
procedural approach to intersectionality 37
'protected characteristics' 5, 7, 59, 61–62, 62–63, 64, 66, 70–71, 73, 75, 81, 90, 92, 93, 96, 108, 139, 140, 157–158, 167
PSED (public sector equality duty) 5–6, 7, 59, 61, 62, 63

R

race 1, 26, 31, 99, 190, 191, 192
  current government policy 6
  Department for Levelling Up, Housing and Communities responsibility for 5
  England 87, 89
  generic intersectionality 86–89
  as a 'protected characteristic' 5
  Scotland 7, 64, 67–68, 69, 77, 87, 89, 95
  see also Black women; racial justice sector; racism
Race Disparity Unit 62
race equality councils 137
Race Equality Framework for Scotland 2016–2030 (CRER) 68, 89
race/gender 107–108, 190, 191, 192
racial justice sector 8, 88–89, 180, 186, 191, 192–193
  generic intersectionality 91–92, 138–141
  multi-strand intersectionality 95
  networks of organizations 12
  self-organization 116
  siloed thinking 151
racialized sexism 1
racism 1, 2, 25, 99
  institutional racism 5, 88
  and white feminism 24

reactive approach to intersectionality 37
'Red Tape Challenge' 61
refugee sector
  exclusion from Equality Act 2010 5
  siloed thinking 151
relationality 28–29
religion 1.5, 5
representation 11, 16, 113–116, 141–143, **144**, 145, 186–189, 193, 200, 202, 204, **206–210**
  acting on behalf of 129–132
  descriptive 43–45, 113, 114, 143, 188
  developing others as representatives 128–129
  diversity-within intersectionality 114, 126, 131, 133–134, **144**
  enabling others to act for themselves 126–127
  equality organizations and intersectionality 120–126
  intersectional organizations 123–126
  representation in practice 126–132
  representational conflicts 132–141
  and equality organizing 116–120
  generic intersectionality 114, 115, 133, 135–139, 140, 142–143, **144**
  group representation 44, 188
  'inclusion without representation' 133, 134
  intersectional organizations 123–126
  'intersections of equality strands' 114, 115, 126, 131, 134–135, 142, **144**
  multi-strand intersectionality 114, 132–133, 136, 137, 138, 142, **144**
  operationalization of intersectionality 11, 16, 23, 43–47, 52
  opposing understandings of intersectionality 139–141
  pan equality intersectionality 133, **144**
  and participation 115, 127, 142
  and self-organization 115, 116–117, 123–124, 131, 141, 142, 143
  single-strand equality organizations 115, 118–119, 121–122, 123, 124, 129, 136, 138, 143, 188–189
  substantive 43, 44–45, 113, 143, 188
  symbolic 43
  women of colour 124, 126, 136, 138–139, 140–141, 142
representational intersectionality 28
research
  research design 12–13
  ethnography 15–16
  networks 12–14
  participation 14–15
  research methodology 217–221
  research participants 211–216
  research objectives 11

Roberts, Dorothy 47
Rodriguez, Jenny K. 47

S

Saward, Michael 45, 189
Scholz, Sally J. 49
Scotland 192
  diversity-within intersectionality 101
  equality networks 12
  equality NGO sector 2, 8–11
  equality policy 5, 7–8, 51
  generic intersectionality 90–91
  impact of austerity on 70–71
  PSED (public sector equality duty) 5, 7
  trans rights 171–172
  see also UK
Scottish Government 66, 67, 68, 69
  see also Scotland, equality policy
Scottish Labour Party 7
Scottish National Improvement Project 63
Scottish National Party 7
self-organization 10, 17, 47, 59, 60, 103–104, 198, 202, 203
  and representation 115, 116–117, 123–124, 131, 141, 142, 143
service delivery, individualization in 197, 200
sex see gender
sexism 1, 25, 163
  and trans rights 161, 162, 173
  see also gender; women's sector
sexual orientation 1, 5, 26
  see also LGBTI sector
siloed thinking 18, 34, 89, 97, 136, 149, 150–155, 165, 171, 174, 194
single-strand equality organizations 12, 13, 17, 37, 42, 173, 178, 183–184, 190, 194, 200, 201, 202, 203–204
  applied concepts of intersectionality 88, 94, 96, 97–98, 99, 100–102, 103, 105
  representation 115, 118–119, 121–122, 123, 124, 129, 136, 138, 143, 188–189
Sisters Uncut 39
Social Mobility Commission 62
social solidarity 49
Socialist Feminist Network 163
socioeconomic disadvantage, and inequality/inequalities discourse 59–60
solidarity see coalition and solidarity
Southall Black Sisters 86
standpoint theory 114, 187
Strolovitch, Dara Z. 41, 43, 195
structural intersectionality 28
substantive representation 43, 44–45, 113, 143, 188
  see also representation
symbolic representation 43
  see also representation

INDEX

T
Tarrow, Sidney G. 147
Tilly, Charles 147
Tormos, Fernando 49
Townsend-Bell, Erica 33, 182
trans sector 6, 198, 203
  trans inclusive feminisms 161
  transfeminisms 161–162, 164
  and women's sector 160–165, 166, 168–169, 170, 171–173, 175, 192
Truth, Sojourner 23
Tungohan, Ethel 39
typology of intersectionality *see* applied concepts of intersectionality

U
UK
  equality NGO sector 2, 3–4, 42, 52
  equality policy 4–6, 36, 39, 40, 51
  exit from European Union 6, 70
  generic intersectionality 86–89
  intersectionality 24
  see also England; Scotland; Wales
UN CEDAW Committee 61

V
Verloo, Mieke 37
violence against women 53
  violence against disabled women 133–134

W
Walby, Sylvia 12, 26–27, 36, 62, 182
Wales 5
  'multi-strand mainstreaming model' 36–37
  see also UK
Ward, Jane 41, 109, 177
Wells, Ida B. 23
white led/predominantly white organizations 98–99, 190, 191–192
white supremacy 1, 25, 30, 31, 99, 163, 192
'white working class' 60
women
  Black women 1, 9, 10, 23, 24, 26, 30–31, 51, 108, 180, 188, 190–191, 194
    representation 136, 140–141
  gender/woman 149, 161, 196
  Indigenous women 1, 23
  violence against 53, 133–134
  see also gender; women of colour; women's sector
women of colour 1, 36, 72, 107–108, 180, 188, 191
  generic intersectionality 91–92
  and intersectionality 23, 24, 30–31, 51
  representation 124, 126, 136, 138–139, 140–141, 142
  Scotland 64, 66–67, 68, 69, 77, 101
  trans women of colour 162
  violence against 53
  violence against disabled women 133–134
  see also Black women; women's sector
Women's Budget Group 10
Women's Place Uk 163
women's sector 48, 183, 196, 199, 200
  England 63
  Scotland 63
  siloed thinking 151
  and trans rights 160–165, 166, 168–169, 170, 171–173, 175, 192
  see also feminist sector

Y
Young, Hannah 36–37
Young, Iris Marion 44
Yuval-Davis, Nira 26, 31

Z
Zajicek, Anna 34

www.ingramcontent.com/pod-product-compliance
Lightning Source LLC
Chambersburg PA
CBHW051534020426
42333CB00016B/1923